The Social Construction of Lesbianism

D1289648

The Social Construction of
Lesbianism

Celia Kitzinger

Inquiries in
Social Construction Series

⑤SAGE Publications
London · Newbury Park · Beverly Hills · New Delhi

First published 1987
Reprinted 1989 (twice), 1990, 1993

Inquiries in Social Construction Series
Editors: Kenneth Gergen and John Shotter

SAGE Publications Ltd
28 Banner Street
London EC1Y 8QE

SAGE Publications Inc
2111 West Hillcrest Street
Newbury Park, California 91320

SAGE Publications India Pvt Ltd
C-236 Defence Colony
New Delhi 110 024

SAGE Publications Inc
275 South Beverly Drive
Beverly Hills, California 90212

British Library Cataloguing in Publication Data

Kitzinger, Celia
  The social construction of lesbianism.
  1. Lesbianism
  I. Title
  306.7'663   HQ75.5

  ISBN 0–8039–8116–3
  ISBN 0–8039–8117–1 Pbk

Library of Congress catalog card number 87–062029

Printed in Great Britain by J. W. Arrowsmith Ltd, Bristol

HQ
15.5
.K58
1987

Contents

For my parents
With love

Preface

The old model of lesbianism as pathology, which dominated social scientific theorizing until the 1970s, is an easy target for criticism and has been widely challenged for its methodological inadequacies and ideological biases. But the more recent self-styled 'gay affirmative' research has generally been acclaimed by feminists and lesbians within and outside social science. In 'gay affirmative' research, lesbianism is constructed in liberal humanistic terms as an alternative lifestyle, a way of loving, a sexual preference, a route to personal fulfilment or a form of self-actualization. It is this more recent and apparently 'pro-lesbian' research, and the ordinary everyday social constructions of lesbianism which it draws upon and helps to construct, that is the target of my critique in this book.

The central argument of this book is that so-called 'gay affirmative' research, far from being a liberating force, represents a new development in the oppression of lesbians. Drawing on my own research, as well as an extensive review of the literature, I argue that the shift from 'pathological' to 'gay affirmative' models merely substitutes one depoliticized construction of the lesbian with another, while continuing to undermine systematically radical feminist theories of lesbianism. Gay affirmative researchers have tried to 'add lesbians in' to existing psychological theories. But these theories have not just left lesbians out. They have been constructed in accordance with liberal humanistic ideology so that it is impossible to put lesbians back in, except in individualistic terms as persons making private sexual choices and enjoying particular kinds of personal relationships. These constructions are incompatible with radical feminist and lesbian separatist constructions in which lesbianism is fundamentally a political statement representing the bonding of women against male supremacy.

Liberal humanistic constructions of lesbianism are widespread not only within psychology and its allied disciplines but within the contemporary Women's Liberation Movement: many (liberal) feminists today talk about lesbianism as no more than a choice of lifestyle, a sexual preference, the outcome of 'true love', or a route to 'true happiness'. By contrast, the *radical* feminist argument is based on the belief that the institution of compulsory heterosexuality is fundamental to the patriarchal oppression of women: lesbianism, then, represents women's refusal to collaborate in our own betrayal. It is this identification of heterosexuality as central to women's oppression that is characteristic of the radical (or revolutionary) feminist approach. So while, for example, it is possible to present the argument that all women should become lesbians either from within a liberal humanistic ideology or from a radical feminist perspective, the rationale behind these two arguments is entirely different: liberal humanism argues that lesbianism helps women to achieve liberal humanistic goals (happiness, sexual fulfilment, better personal relationships) whereas radical feminism argues that lesbianism helps to achieve radical feminist goals (the overthrow of male supremacy). In this book, I argue that liberal humanistic ideology, especially when used ostensibly in support of lesbianism, as in much recent social science research and within the contemporary feminist movement generally, prevents women from recognizing male power and identifying our oppression.

This argument is introduced in Chapter 1, which uses the literature on lesbianism and male homosexuality to illustrate the rhetorical techniques through which social science constructs the conditions for its own legitimacy. In this, as in subsequent chapters, I draw on material predominantly or exclusively concerned with male homosexuality, in addition to material concerned solely with lesbians, both because of the relative paucity of research on female as compared with male homosexuality and because of the frequent incorporation of women as an afterthought into models based on male homosexuality. Furthermore, the research on lesbianism and male homosexuality spans a range of social scientific (and other) disciplines, including social and clinical psychology, psychoanalysis, anthropology, sociology, biology, psychiatry, and sexology. My own training in psychology leads the focus to research in this area, but the boundaries between psychology and related disciplines are fuzzy, and research under other social science labels is often both salient and 'psychological'.

In Chapter 2 I begin to explore the content of scientifically legitimated constructions of lesbianism, from the early sexology at the turn of the century to contemporary gay affirmative research. After describing my methodological approaches in Chapter 3, I show, in the following three empirically based chapters, the operation of liberal humanistic ideology in the construction of lesbian identities (Chapter 4), lesbian politics (Chapter 5) and in heterosexual attitudes to lesbians (Chapter 6).

In the last chapter (Chapter 7) I suggest that if future research on lesbianism is to avoid complicity in the silencing of lesbianism as a political reality it must reject the traditional model of science as an objective search for truths or facts about the world; instead researchers must examine their own rhetoric, and evaluate their political commitments. Above all, we must begin to recognize and to deconstruct the liberal humanistic ideology pervasive throughout research in this field.

The research reported here has appeared in different forms elsewhere as follows:

'Psychology Constructs the Lesbian: The Politics and Science of Lesbianism', paper presented at the Social Psychology Section of the British Psychological Society, University of Sheffield, September 1983 (abstract appears in Bulletin of BPS, 36, A106).

'Researching Lesbianism — Discovering Q', *Studies in Sexual Politics* 2: 35–47.

(With Rex Stainton Rogers), 'A Q Methodological Study of Lesbian Identities', *European Journal of Social Psychology* 15: 167–87.

'Introducing and Developing Q as a Feminist Methodology', in S. Wilkinson (ed.) *Feminist Social Psychology*. Milton Keynes: Open University Press.

'Liberal Humanism as an Ideology of Social Control: The Regulation of Lesbian Identities', paper presented at International Interdisciplinary Conference on Self and Identity, Cardiff, July 1984 (abstract in Bulletin of BPS, 37: A114; also to appear as a chapter in K. Gergen and J. Shotter [1987] *Texts of Identity*, Sage Publications, of whose symposium it formed a part).

Acknowledgements

Many people have listened to what I am trying to say in this book, and have helped me to say it better. I am very grateful to Rex Stainton Rogers who was generous with his time and thoughtful with his criticism in supervising the Ph.D thesis from which this book is drawn. I would like to thank Sheila Kitzinger for listening to my various drafts through many long telephone conversations, and for providing a liberal humanistic foil for my arguments. I am also indebted to the other Q methodologists and social constructionists whose work provided helpful stimulus to my thinking, especially Alison Thomas, Jenny Kitzinger, and Wendy Stainton Rogers, and to Halla Beloff, Steven Brown and William Stephenson, who provided much needed encouragement. Farrell Burnett has been a careful and enthusiastic editor. My thanks go also to Martha Hatch whose love and support sustained me throughout the writing of this book.

The research reported here was funded for the first three years by the Social Science Research Council (now the Economic and Social Research Council), and for the last six months by a Demonstrator- ship at the University of Reading.

Finally, my greatest thanks must go to all the lesbian women who participated in this research and who taught me the myriad of different ways in which women cope with oppression, accommodate to it in our everyday lives, and fight back.

1
Rhetoric in Research on Lesbianism and Male Homosexuality

> Every group in power tells its story as it would like to have it believed, in the way it thinks will promote its interests. (Becker and Horowitz, 1972)

The established approach to a literature review, reflected in numerous introductory sections of research papers and first chapters of books on homosexuality, is based on the implicit question 'What does previous research tell us about homosexuality?' This standard approach presents as its aim the advancement of scientific knowledge: its authors use the conventional language and concepts of the social sciences to describe and assess the research findings they review, cataloguing their merits and demerits, attempting to resolve competing theories and results, or summarizing and defining the parameters of the 'known' as a springboard for their own empirical or theoretical leap into the unknown. The overwhelming majority of literature reviews on homosexuality and lesbianism share this ostensible aim of advancing knowledge about homosexuality within the standard rules of scientific endeavour.

The first two chapters of this book offer alternative approaches to the standard literature reviews of this kind. Instead of addressing the question 'What does the literature tell us about homosexuality?', I ask first, in this chapter, 'What can we learn from the literature about the construction of social scientific accounts?' and then, in Chapter 2, 'What can we learn from the literature about attempts to manage and control homosexuality?'

Within the sociology of science, a variety of techniques of analysis of scientific writing have been employed. Some authors have compared scientists' formal accounts of scientific activity with what the researcher observed in the laboratory (Knorr-Cetina, 1983) or with informal (Gilbert and Mulkay, 1980) or media (Barber and Fox, 1958) presentation of the same material. Others discuss the problems of reading back from the accounts to what 'actually happened' (Woolgar, 1976) or compare reported results with their own re-analysis of raw data (Wolins, 1962). From a Marxist perspective, scientific papers can be conceptualized as commodities, like pieces of plastic or carburettors, with a known exchange value for money, degrees, or reputation (e.g. Pickvance, 1976); from the perspective of games theory research papers result from competitive activity and are analogous to scoring a goal (Smith, 1984); from a psychoanalytic or 'psychocritical' (Coward, 1977: 12) perspective, scientific accounts are traced back to the personality problems and unconscious psychological mechanisms of the account provider (e.g. Fisher and Fisher, 1955; Kurtz and Maiolo, 1968; Riebel, 1982).

The approach I adopt in this chapter deliberately avoids comparison of the scientific account with any presumed 'reality', whether external or internal to its authors. Instead of demonstrating the discrepancy between different accounts of the same research (formal, informal, re-analysed, media-produced) or illustrating the dependence of accounts on their social context or psychological origins, such discrepancies and dependencies are assumed and the chapter explores the rhetorical features of scientific writing which act to conceal these elements and to reinforce and perpetuate the received image of scientific objectivity.

Despite calls for a sociology of psychological knowledge (Buss, 1975), the majority of research into the rhetorical features of science has been concerned with reports from within the natural sciences — work on the discovery of the optical pulsar (Garfinkle et al., 1982), on the structure of deoxyribose nucleic acid (Bazerman, 1981), gravitational radiation (Collins, 1982) and oxidative phosphorylation (Gilbert and Mulkay, 1982), for example. Gusfield's (1976) study of the literary rhetoric of drinking-driver research is a rare exception. Nonetheless, social psychology has been described as an 'outstanding example' of the inherently rhetorical nature of science, appealing to subjectively shared, rather than indubitably true premises, and containing extrafactual, extralogical arguments designed to persuade and seduce (cf. Simons, 1980: 120). Weigert (1970) characterizes social scientists generally as engaging in wilful self-serving forms of selling and displaying indoctrination and ingratiation no different from the practices of advertisers or politicians: according to Weigert, journal editors and readers are courted by means of various impression-management techniques, and weaknesses in theory or research are concealed or rationalized.

Social scientific writing on homosexuality serves as a particularly interesting case study for research into scientific accounting procedures for five reasons.

Firstly, unlike the physical sciences, normally seen as offering the template of science upon which other disciplines have traditionally modelled themselves, the social sciences confront a certain reluctance on the part of the public to accord them the prestige attached to inclusion within the charmed circle of 'science' (Gellner, 1985:

112). This credibility problem leads to the incorporation into psychological and sociological accounts of comparatively more overt and conscientious efforts to depict themselves as 'truly scientific'. One analysis of the opening chapters of introductory sociology textbooks found, for example, that:

> Sociology stands out in its lengthy attempt to defend its place in the world of science. Psychologists and economists come closest to the sociological pattern. . . . Political scientists, chemists and physicists seem to accept their place in the knowledge structure without such a defense and, in most cases, proceed directly to their subject matter. (Kurtz and Maiolo, 1968: 40)

Furthermore, because many academics view research on homosexuality and lesbianism with a considerable degree of suspicion and hostility (sufficient that researchers are often warned that they are risking their academic careers by studying this topic — my own experience and that of Crew and Norton, 1974; Katz, 1976: 8; and McDaniel, 1982, amongst others), the emphasis on 'scientific' presentation is often compounded in an attempt to forestall criticism and counteract ridicule: this makes research on homosexuality a particularly rich source of scientific accounting procedures.

Secondly, the social sciences in general deal with topics debated and commented on beyond the specialized scientific circles devoted to their study. Unlike oxidative phosphorylation, for example, homosexuality is widely discussed in terms of religion (the moral fervour generated by the Kinsey reports in the 1950s is matched today by the religious appropriation of AIDS as God's answer to a new Sodom and Gomorrah), and, more recently, politics. Both religion and politics are defined not just as extrinsic to but as incompatible with the pursuit of 'pure' scientific knowledge, and research on homosexuality has, therefore, to deal with the problem of defining its own claims to knowledge as distinct from, and superior to, the claims made from within these competing 'lay' perspectives. The rhetorical ploy labelled here (following Halmos, 1978) as 'mythologizing of expertise' is an attempt to deal with this problem by fiat, asserting the cognitive supremacy of accurate scientific conceptualizations over common 'stereotypes', 'myths' and 'prejudices'.

Thirdly, following the recent shift from predominantly pathology-based (pre-1970s) to predominantly (though not exclusively) life-style-based models of homosexuality — a shift sufficiently marked for some adherents of the new model to characterize it as a paradigm shift in the Kuhnian sense (Gonsiorek, 1982a) — adherents of this new approach are generally dissatisfied with the vast bulk of past research on homosexuality and are highly sceptical about its scientific credibility (e.g. Birke, 1980; Shavelson et al., 1980; Suppe, 1981). This scepticism leads them to engage in a variety of accounting procedures to explain the apparent existence of pervasive and long-standing 'error' in the scientific research of their field. As Mulkay and Gilbert (1982) point out, 'most practising scientists regard the existence of error as a threat to the enterprise of science', and an elaborate repertoire of interpretative resources is employed to account for such 'mistakes' while never questioning the traditional conception of scientific rationality itself. Representation of scientific progress based on the 'up the mountain' story (Rorty, 1980), whereby all previous research is seen as a steady progression towards recognition of the truths now attained, is one important way of accounting for past error.

Fourthly, the degree of dissensus and controversy within recent psychological theorizing about homosexuality is potentially sufficient to pose a severe threat to the traditional conceptualization of psychology as a science. Researchers working within variants of the long-established 'pathological' model (e.g. Kronemeyer, 1980; Moberly, 1983) confront proponents of the more recent 'lifestyle' model (most notably those publishing in the *Journal of Homosexuality*) across a conceptual chasm unbridgeable by scientific experiment or empirical advance. Controversy is not, of course, always a threat to science, and scientists rarely, if ever, present an entirely consensual account of the phenomena they investigate — indeed, it has been suggested that controversy within science is a means whereby the academic community as a whole 'hedges its bets': with a diversity of opinion on any given topic, they can't *all* be wrong. Nonetheless, the bulk of work in a given area typically shares certain unquestioned first principles or indubitable propositions which determine the research questions considered appropriate. Given a different set of first principles, different questions would be asked, and when this situation arises, the adherents of each set of first principles see the answers generated in response to the questions derived from the other set not as wrong, and to be subjected to detailed criticism, but as simply irrelevant (Gouldner, 1970: 7). For example, Garfinkle (1981) points out that the shift from medieval to Newtonian theories of motion involved the rejection of the old question 'Why does an object in motion keep moving?'; Newton argued that the question itself was misguided, and as the answer gave the trivial 'it just does'. Similarly, Darwinian biology fails to answer Aristotle's question as to why, out of all the species that could possibly exist, only some in fact do (i.e. Why porcupines but not unicorns?).

The scientific advance that Darwin made can partly be seen as a rejection of that question and the substitution of a different question, namely: given that a species comes to exist (however it does), why does it continue to exist or cease to exist? (Garfinkle, 1981)

Similarly, the research questions generated by the 'pathological' model of homosexuality (as much as 70 percent of pre-1974 psychological research on homosexuality was devoted to the three questions 'Are homosexuals sick?', 'How can it be diagnosed?' and 'What causes it?' [Morin, 1977]) are rejected as irrelevant by the 'lifestyle' researchers, whose alternative questions (concerning, for example, the pathology of the homophobe or the enhancement of intimate gay relationships) are in turn dismissed by the 'pathologists'.

Dissent and controversy of this fundamental nature may come to be subsequently viewed as, Garfinkle (1981) suggests, constituting a major epoch in the development of a science, but it also poses a potentially severe threat to the traditional conceptualization of science itself by exposing the uncertain nature of knowledge claims and their reliance on a bedrock of a priori assumptions. Merton (1971) argues that dissensus causes social scientists to feel insecure about their professional roles, and Ezrahi (1971: quoted in Barnes and Edge, 1982: 239) cites peer consensus as a major modulator of scientific credibility. As Barnes and Edge (1982: 239) point out, 'where experts publicly disagree, their authority and influence are reduced'.

Consequently, contemporary researchers on homosexuality engage in rhetorical devices which have the dual function of both explaining the errors of their opponents and, simultaneously, reinforcing the institution of science. The rhetoric of 'scientific method' is the prime example of discourse of this type, whereby rival researchers are excommunicated from the scientific fold and their findings dismissed as 'not proper science'.

Finally, both historical 'error' and contemporary controversy lead to a generally greater awareness among scientists of the contribution of extrascientific and psychosocial components to scientific research. Woolgar (1983) shows how scientists tend to see their theories as 'reflective' of reality during periods of scientific consensus, whereas during the (relatively short-lived) periods of controversy, science is more likely to be represented as 'mediative' or 'constitutive' of reality. Controversy, claims Collins (1983a: 95) acts as an 'auto-garfinkle' for scientific knowledge in that the taken-for-granted rules of science are thrown into question by the fact that they no longer produce unproblematic outcomes.

References to extrascientific contributions to scientific theories (e.g. social mores or personal prejudice) are commonplace in research on homosexuality in accounting for error. However, whereas in traditional scientific accounts such allusions function as explanations of past failings and exhortations to better practice, the same observations are used by antiscientists, both within and outside the scientific professions, to challenge the epistemological basis of the social sciences per se. Deconstructing the traditional claims of science to represent a dispassionate search for objective truths, antiscientists like Szasz (1971) use research on homosexuality as a paradigmatic example of the thesis that social science reflects social norms, functions to reinforce and legitimate the ideological hegemony of the powerful (in this case, heterosexuals) and defines as 'sick' those who refuse to conform to the dominant definition of reality. According to this argument, social science is expressly intended to fulfil this controlling and manipulative function: is not something that happens 'by mistake' when researchers stray from the path of methodological purity, but is the very raison d'être of social science. Homosexuality joins the nineteenth-century disease of 'masturbatory insanity', the soviet diagnostic category 'reformist delusions', and the eighteenth-century disease of slaves, 'drapeto- mania' (manifested by their tendency to run away from the plantations) as diseases constructed to reinforce and legitimate the status quo (Stone and Faberman, 1981).

Useful as this thesis is for discrediting 'pathology' based research on homosexuality (and both 'lifestyle' researchers and Gay Libera- tionists generally have used it in this way), its representation of social science as *inherently* ideological and manipulative means that it also embodies an implicit critique of contemporary 'lifestyle' based social scientific research. (An explicit, feminist-informed rendering of this critique is presented in Chapter 2.) Because its critique is potentially directed against their own scientific practices as much as against those of their opponents, 'lifestyle' researchers are generally careful to differentiate their own condemnation of previous research from that of the scientific deconstructionists (cf. Gonsiorek, 1982c and Hencken, 1982, for overt attempts at such differentiation). All three of the techniques already mentioned (the 'up the mountain' story, the rhetoric of scientific method, and the mythologizing of expertise) serve this purpose, but utility accounting is an important additional rhetorical technique. Using utility accounting, the 'lifestyle' researchers offer themselves and their work to be of service to the gay community: unlike researchers of the past, who admittedly exploited, oppressed and degraded homosexuals, contemporary lifestyle theorists offer techniques of positive gay-identity acquisition, methods of dealing with internal- ized homophobia, research supporting the right of the lesbian mother to child custody, and the need for gay-affirmative education in schools.

The rest of this chapter is devoted to a discussion and exploration of the construction of formal social scientific accounts of homosexuality and lesbianism. Despite my own clear theoretical allegiances (discussed in Chapter 2), I attempt, in this chapter, to bracket the question of the scientific validity of the theoretical models or empirical research under investigation, maintaining 'an attitude of rigid abstinence from epistemological judgements' (Berger, 1965). The aim here is not to serve as an arbiter among these competing psychologies but to examine how each selectively portrays itself and its location within the scientific domain in such a way as to reinforce the image of psychology and its allied disciplines as the sole purveyors of legitimate knowledge about the social world. They are discussed in relation to five themes (inevitably neither mutually exclusive nor exhaustive) each of which contributes, in its own way, to the image of science as 'valid knowledge': the 'up the mountain' saga, the rhetoric of scientific method, the mythologizing of expertise, the utility account, and, finally, the stylistic features of scientific writing as they might be approached from the perspective of literary criticism.

The 'up the mountain' saga

The literature reviews which typically introduce research papers on homosexuality and lesbianism display, to varying degrees, a certain optimism about the role of social science research on this topic: while lamenting the poor quality of much of the past research, they are confident that future work (by themselves or their colleagues) will be a significant improvement. This optimism represents one aspect of what Tyler (1973) describes as a 'hopeful psychology'.

> Modern scientific psychology is rooted in hope. It was initiated at a time when the idea of progress had taken a powerful hold on men's [*sic*] imaginations. Theories that man had degenerated since his beginnings in some far past golden age and theories that man's history is nothing but an endless series of cycles from perfection to decadence to dissolution had by the middle of the nineteenth century given way to the theory that steady progress had occurred since the dawn of human history and would continue to occur. It was science that had made such progress possible, and the establishment of a science of man's own mental life was seen as an important step in the triumphant advance that was to lead to a golden age in the future rather than the past. (Tyler, 1973: 1021)

The story that scientists tell about this arduous and uphill journey towards the golden age (described by Medawar [1963] as a technique in which 'you concede, more or less graciously, that others have dimly groped towards the fundamental truths that you are now about to expound') is what Rorty (1980) has called the 'up the mountain story'. Its function is to illustrate the superiority of contemporary over past research findings: in its less gracious version, all previous researchers are presented as fundamentally inadequate scientific investigators, who perpetrated elementary methodological or theoretical crimes; in its most gracious form, present-day scientists may be dwarfs standing on the shoulders of giants, but can see further for all that. The story of scientific progress as ever onward and upward is exemplified in accounts of research on homosexuality.

Once upon a time, the story goes, researchers thought that homosexuals were sick and perverted. This was because they were blinded by religious prejudice and trapped by the social conventions of their time: their research lacked present-day sophistication and objectivity. Now, in our sexually liberated age, with the benefit of scientific rigour and clear vision, objective up-to-date research demonstrates that lesbians and gay men are just as normal, just as healthy, and just as valuable members of a pluralistic society as are heterosexual people. Other researchers have noted this same story, and, according to Krieger (1982), 'all contemporary research discussions [of homosexuality] reiterate some version of it.'

Professional research on homosexuality (male and female) first started to appear during the late nineteenth and early twentieth centuries (Krafft-Ebing, 1882; Forel, 1908; Ellis, 1934), but writings prior to the 1950s or 1960s seem to the modern reader more like religious tracts than scientific papers, and contemporary psychologists generally dismiss the work of earlier generations as hopelessly unscientific. Freedman (1971: 56) comments that 'prior to the last ten years, the psychological research on homosexuality was limited and of dubious value', and Wirt (1981) says that 'almost all serious scholarly work on the subject of homosexuality has been done in the past ten years . . . credible theory and empirical studies of merit did not exist before about 1970.'

Just as in the marketing of any product, 'old' is bad and 'new' is better. Earlier research is dismissed as embodying 'antiquated viewpoints' (Sang, 1978), 'outdated references' (Marson, 1982), 'archaic practice' (Marmor, 1972), 'ossified doctrines' (De Cecco, 1981), 'outmoded notions [and] outworn societal standards' (Kameny, 1971a) or 'old ways of thinking' (Browning, 1984). 'The scientific community', says Socarides (1972), 'deserves up-to-date information', and this same emphasis on the new improved product is reflected in many titles ('New Light on Homosexuality' [Marano, 1979]; *The Mendola Report: A New Look at Gay Couples*

[Mendola, 1980]). Old research is presented as inevitably disadvantaged by its lack of access to these new ways of thinking: 'early medical researchers were hindered in their work by a scarcity of knowledge about hormones' (Browning, 1984), and 'Thomson did not have the benefit of later research exposing the myth of the vaginal orgasm' (Sang, 1978).

The 'up the mountain' research saga is familiar from the histories of research in other areas, which, like the story of research on homosexuality, depict this same apparent progress of social science from the dark ages of conformity to the dictates of social convention, forward into the brave new world of scientific rigour and objectivity. The history of the notion of 'masturbatory insanity' is often described in this way: Hare (1962), for example, describes the emergence and consolidation of the idea that 'self-abuse' causes 'all disorders incident to the brain, melancholy, catalepsy, imbecility, loss of sensation, weakness of the nervous system and a variety of similar disorders' (Tissot, 1766, quoted in Hare, 1962) as the result of fallacies of reasoning — the biased sample, false analogy, causal nomenclature and the therapeutic fallacy — all of which were gradually overcome through 'progress in the application of the scientific method'. The histories of research on blacks and on women are often told as similarly indicative of psychology's slow progress towards 'truly scientific' understandings — from the early depiction of blacks and women as inferior beings, through a focus on them as the innocent victims of prejudice, to the now common portrayal of racism and sexism as part of a pathological personality pattern.

The allegorical meanings of these histories is clear: past research findings symbolize human error, ignorance and taboo, while current research findings represent the application of reason, logic and rationality, and contemporary psychology symbolizes the triumphant conquest of scientific objectivity over bias and prejudice. Science shows us the way up the 'inevitable escalator to enlightenment' (Williamson, 1983), and the 'up the mountain' account functions as a 'theodicy justifying the ways of homo sociologus [or psychologus] to students, and showing the fabled routes by which we have reached our present pinnacle' (Douglas, 1971: 44).

Ironically, then, social science's admittedly bad track record of research on homosexuality is used to justify the need for yet more social scientific research. Lengthy reviews of past research, describing the 'sorry state of the literature' and 'extraordinary inadequacy of the research findings' end with a plea for 'solid empirical research on homosexuality', which is considered 'neither impossible nor improbable' (Suppe, 1981). 'It is only with the rubble of bad theories that we shall be able to build better ones' argue Bentler and Abramson (1981). Given that one could argue, with equal logic, that a method that has demonstrably failed to add anything to the sum total of human knowledge about homosexuality should be abandoned forthwith, the 'up the mountain' saga can be seen as a selective and partial account of scientific development, designed expressly to enhance the image of science. Instead of undermining the faith of the consumers, the 'built-in obsolescence' implicit in the saga serves to ensure the long-term survival of psychology by continuously renewing its market.

Mythologizing of expertise
Scientific expertise brings with it the power to define reality. As Goode (1969) says, 'Nothing has greater discrediting power today than the demonstration that a given assertion has been "scientific-ally disproven". Our contemporary pawnbrokers of reality are scientists.' One way in which science has achieved this power is through the mythologizing of expertise, which credits scientists with access to knowledge denied to ordinary mortals.

A pervasive feature of professional accounts is their explicit contrast between 'scientific' and 'lay' conceptualizations. 'Common-sense' or 'folk' notions of homosexuality and lesbianism are stigmatized as based on 'taboo', 'myth', 'stereotype', 'fallacy' or 'ideology', and contrasted with the scientific version, represented as 'truth', 'fact' or 'reality'. Throughout social scientific writing on homosexuality there is this juxtaposition of stereotype against reality, myth against fact, 'popular thought' against 'truth' (Bieber, 1971: 430), 'schoolroom smut' against 'rational scrutiny' (West, 1968: 11), 'old wives' tales' against 'reputable data' (Bell and Weinberg, 1978: 6), and 'Gay Lib militancy' against 'scientific objectivity' (Pattison, 1974). 'Stereotypes often depict . . . but current research shows . . .' (Peplau and Gordon, 1983: 227); 'It is a popular myth that . . . but the data indicate . . .' (Hedblom, 1973); 'Most people see their heterosexual responses as . . . but trained observers understand that . . .' (Tripp, 1975: 36); 'Common sense suggests . . . However, the reality is quite different' (Hess, 1983); and 'There is a widespread belief that . . . whereas in fact this is far from the case' (Chesser, 1958: 30). One researcher dismisses the theories of another with the statement 'One might expect that sort of uninformed flap from Germaine Greer, but not from a scientist' (Karlen, 1972).

This careful and recurrent differentiation between what ordinary people 'think' (or accept 'unthinkingly') and what scientists 'know' serves to reinforce the image of science as the only legitimate purveyor of valid knowledge: 'all other versions of reality must be seen as whimsical and arbitrary and, above all, in error' (Goode, 1969). The attempt to discredit alternative 'popular' versions is clearly evident in the following two extracts:

> What passes for an informed and enlightened view of sex among educated laymen [*sic*] is twenty to fifty years out of date. The sexological truisms of intellectual cocktail parties are just a few cuts above phlogiston theory in accuracy and relevance. (Karlen, 1971: vii)

> Only in popular thinking are homosexuality and inversion synonymous. For several decades biologists and experimental psychologists have recognized that these are distinctly different phenomena. (Tripp, 1975: 22)

In discrediting popular understandings of homosexuality in this way, the social scientist engages in irony: 'to do irony is to say of something that appears one way that it is in fact something other than it appears' (Woolgar, 1983: 249). Irony in scientific writing carries with it the implication that science can tell what something is 'really' like, thus constructing the known as external to the particular subjectivities of the knowers. This is, as Smith (1974) argues, 'a view of knowledge which holds that to be properly a knowledge it must somehow transcend the social contexts to which the knower is necessarily bound.' Thus social scientists are supposed to be able to distance themselves from the moral biases, political ideologies and unconscious fantasies of ordinary social participants. Exhortations to this effect are not uncommon in the literature:

> In order to come to a balanced judgement of the matter of the correct attitude to homosexuals, one has to try to cast personal feeling to one side, and to discount the particular prejudices of our society, which has so long unthinkingly stigmatized all such persons as 'perverse', 'heretical', or 'criminal'. The task calls for a high degree of intellectual honesty. (West, 1968: 257)

Many researchers use this image to 'sell' their own version of homosexuality, playing off their role as ordinary social participant against their role as social scientist:

> Initially, I became aware of my own biases, established them and looked beyond them for the facts. (Ettorre, 1980: 13)

> As a zoologist, I cannot discuss sexual 'peculiarities' in the usual moralistic way. (Morris, 1967: 87)

> The present authors have attempted as far as possible to free their theoretical ideas and their clinical interpretations from the unconscious fantasies which distort scientific objectivity. (Chassegut-Smirgel, 1964: 3)

Science declares war on myths, ideologies and moralizing. In the scientific literature myths are continually being 'challenged' (Peplau, 1983), 'demolished' (Harry, 1984), 'strangled' (McCaffrey, 1972b: 1), 'smashed' and 'shattered' (Levine, 1980). Ideologies are 'defeated', 'exposed', or 'overcome', and we are exhorted to 'clear away some of the ideological debris that must be swept aside before scientific results can be accumulated' (Bowman, 1949). Ideology is, for these scientists, as Gouldner (1976: 3) points out, 'a pathological object . . . irrational cognition . . . defensive discourse . . . false consciousness'. Implicit in this rejection of ideology is an image of 'true', authentic, non-ideological science towards which we should aspire.

'Good' social science is, almost by definition, that which contradicts common social beliefs about homosexuality, and most researchers are concerned to present their own work in this way. Bieber (1971) starts an article by stating his concern to 'dispel some widespread misconceptions' and articles are given titles such as 'Homosexuality: The Stereotype and the Real' (McCaffrey, 1972b) or 'The Ageing Male Homosexual: Myth and Reality' (Kelly, 1977). Bell and Weinberg (1978) describe the 'stereotypes' of homosexuality as causing people to feel 'outraged, fearful or despairing' and then work through each stereotype in turn, concluding that 'the present investigation . . . amply demonstrates that relatively few homosexual men and women conform to the hideous stereotype most people have of them' (p. 230).

Research by other scientists cited favourably by an author is also typically presented as countering popular myths and ideologies. Goode and Haber (1977), for example, comment that 'one of the most important contributions of the pioneering "Kinsey Reports" was to break down sexual stereotypes.' Wirt (1981) comments favourably on a volume which, he claims, 'does not offend by taking a militant stance on important issues, though it does correct many widely held misperceptions with convincing data.' Similarly, Ruse (1984) celebrates the fact that 'scholarly thinking about homosexuality has progressed well beyond strident declarations of unreasoned ideology.'

The demonstration that scientific findings *contradict* stereotypes and ideologies serves to assert the independence of science from ordinary ways of thinking about homosexuality and hence to reinforce the image of science as a privileged way of knowing. Conversely, it is this same image of science as having privileged access to objective truths that leads to the demonstration of scientific reliance on stereotypes, ideology and cultural mores as part of a critique of the professional literature. The complaint that science merely reproduces social stereotypes relies implicitly on this same image of science as privileged knowledge which, despite its alleged deficiencies in this particular instance, *can* be divorced from ordinary, everyday conceptualizations of the social world. Contemporary feminist writers, for example, often comment on the extent to which scientists have approached lesbians 'not with the objective eye of ideal science, but more with assumptions based on centuries-old prejudice' (Birke, 1980: 108), or demonstrate how 'traditional theories of lesbianism have contributed to the creation and maintenance of stereotypes about lesbianism' (Browning, 1984: 12). Similarly, De Cecco and Shively (1984) condemn the 'uncritical use of popular concepts' in research on homosexuality, Gonsiorek (1981) accuses Masters and Johnson of 'mimicking the latest shift in public opinion' and complains that they 'subscribe to a number of myths', and Glickman (1980), in an unfavourable review of Wolf (1979) says that the book 'enforces a number of stereotypes'.

Just as the 'discovery' of experimenter effects stands as testimony to the potency of positivist science (because only within the positivistic paradigm can they be a 'discovery' rather than a given, cf. Sampson, 1978), in the same way the use of the demonstrable reliance of social science on social norms as part of a critique of scientific studies indicates the potency of the idealized norm of universality. The criticism demonstrates adherence to the belief, expressed by Richter (1972: 39) that social science is (or should be) 'free to move ahead of the culture of the society as a whole, and sometimes in directions quite incompatible with the prevailing emphasis of societal culture'.

Overall, social scientists are quite willing to admit that they or, preferably, their colleagues have failed, on particular occasions, adequately to transcend the 'folk knowledge' or 'lay understandings' to which they as ordinary social participants are privy. What they are *not* usually prepared to do is to accept the characterization of social science itself as ultimately based on and derived from these folk or lay versions of reality (cf. Gergen, 1982: 136).

Whether the origin of this divorce between 'scientific' and 'lay' knowledge is traced to the capitalist creation of a gulf between professional expertise and popular culture (Gorz, 1974), or to the patriarchal discrediting of women's alternative versions of reality (e.g. Smith, 1974), most sociologists of science recognize it as political in its implications. Pollner, writing about reality disjunctures in general, says:

> The very nature of reality disjunctures, the fact that the other has looked at the world and experienced it in contrary ways, assures that the choice

of a particular version as definitive of 'what really happened' receives less than universal support. The decision to nevertheless act upon a particular version as the grounds of further inference and action (over and against competing possibilities) comprises the politics. Because the decision to act upon a disputed version of the world typically includes as one of its consequences the discrediting of another's ability to properly perceive reality, the politics of which we speak is often 'a politics of experience'. (Pollner, 1975: 427)

Tracing the development of the disjuncture between professional and lay knowledge in the physical sciences, Romanowski (1973) locates the origin of the split with the shift from scholastic science (which incorporated the geocentric concept of the universe) to the Copernican–Galilean view. She says:

> The Aristotelian geocentric view of the universe had the characteristic of corresponding to a commonsensical, intuitive view that any man [*sic*] has of his physical environment: for example, the sun does in fact seem to rise in the East and set in the West, revolving around a perceptibly immobile Earth. [The geocentric view] did not disturb commonsensical perspectives . . . whereas Galilean and Copernican views go counter to every perception we have of our world. . . . Scholastic science allowed a continuous contact between perception and conception of the universe. The Copernican and Galilean view instituted a radical break between perception and conception of the world. (Romanowski, 1973: 98)

Because the new scientific theory was divorced from usual common-sensical perceptions, scientists distrusted ordinary language and increasingly used the language of mathematics. The initial public resistance to this radically disturbing change was overcome through the use of rhetorical persuasion (cf. Romanowski, 1973) to the extent that a demonstrable gulf between professional and lay conceptualizations of phenomena now verges upon being a necessary feature of scientific discourse, and is apparently essential to the evaluation of theories as 'great' (Davis, 1971).

Commenting on the development of hypothetico-deductive and quantitative approaches in psychology, Levine (1974) describes the hundred-year-old collective decision about what psychology's method was to be as 'at heart a political and social decision designed to give the newly emerging field of psychology independence from philosophy, and a standing with the earlier developed physical sciences'. Psychology's insistence on the 'lay-professional' gulf can also be seen as part of a wider attempt to ally itself with the prestigious physical sciences, thus increasing its own power and prestige.

Scientific method

Basic to the contrast between 'scientific' and 'lay' theories of homosexuality is a faith in the superior efficacy of the scientific method. 'Psychologists,' says Hudson (1972: 164), 'have deemed themselves categorically different from plain men [*sic*], being possessed of a higher magic known as the Scientific Method.' Furfey inadvertently illustrates Hudson's point in extolling the merits of scientific method in sociology:

> As trained sociologists we assume that we command a deep and realistic knowledge of society which is denied to ordinary persons. Fortunately there is some reason to believe that this is more than an idle boast: for we are in possession of a certain methodology, a certain well-tried scientific technique for distinguishing between truth and falsehood in the studies we make of our society. This method is characterized by *objectivity* — a term which implies that our results do not depend on our subjective prejudices but on objective reality. Those untrained in this method are, to that extent, handicapped. (Furfey, 1971: 202)

The scientific psychologist, says Hudson (1972: 106) 'defends the scientific method with just the clarity of purpose that the business-man defends private enterprise: both are faiths that their owners cannot afford to have shaken'.

It is this conceptualization of scientific method that enables the presentation of science according to the 'received view' (Gergen, 1982) or 'storybook version' (Mitroff, 1974) as a neutral, apolitical domain of technical expertise, advancing inexorably and dispassionately towards objective and empirically verifiable truths about the nature of reality. The detached and impersonal social scientist is engaged in a logical and ordered method of formulating and testing hypotheses and theories and, through strict adherence to Mertonian norms, arrives at accurate observations of social phenomena. As Douglas (1971: 46) says, 'since the 1930s the hypothetical-statistical method has increasingly been presented as *the* valid paradigm for research methods in any area of specialization.' The use of mathematical formulae to lend a spurious objectivity to banal and debatable pronouncements has, since then, become commonplace. Meyer and Freeman (1977) furnish an especially blatant example in documenting their claim that 'the elements of a sexual episode can be identified and presented in mathematical form suitable for experimental testing' with the following formula, said to represent a male homosexual episode:

$$B = f(CSM_x + CSM_y \ldots + US) \times A$$

where:
B = consummatory behavior
CS = conditioned stimulation

M = stimuli socially sex typed as predominately associately with males
US = unconditioned stimulus (genital tactomotor stimulation)
A = preparatory behaviors + arousal = f(CSM1 + CSM2 . . .)
× = amplifier

The meaning of this is simply that sex between men occurs when apparently 'innate' sexual responses ('unconditioned stimuli') combine with so-called 'learned' sexual responses to increase sexual arousal. By concealing a number of unexamined assumptions about sexual response, the wilful obscurity of their paper serves to contribute more to the mystification of science than to the development of scientific precision.

Hypothetico-deductive statistical research methodologies fulfil certain important social needs for the scientific community. As is the magic wand to the magician, or the sceptre to the monarch, scientific methodologies function as a vital prop and symbol of scientists' power. Compared with more open-ended or qualitative methodologies, they provide more easily inspected criteria of accomplishment (useful in assessing promotion prospects etc.), and permit replication by different investigators, hence providing a basis for the development of standards of professional competence and facilitating the bureaucratic management and regulation of scientific research (Collins, 1968; Jennings, 1983). These scientific methodologies also make room for scientists of low or medium ability (the 'plodding technicians') who, while unlikely to generate important theoretical advances, are able to contribute modest empirical studies, and thus take part in scientific activity:

> Scientific discovery and the formulation of revolutionary new theories may require persons of extraordinary intelligence, but the more mundane tasks of experimentation, testing and controlled observation can be carried out by reasonably intelligent persons capable of mastering the standardized training techniques made possible by a determinate methodological framework. (Jennings, 1983: 20)

Few social scientists, however, would want to cite research on homosexuality as an exemplar of 'good' scientific method. On the contrary, social scientists across all disciplines and from a wide variety of theoretical frameworks typically conclude their literature reviews with statements reflecting profound dissatisfaction with the scientific status of work in this field. Suppe's analysis represents a fairly common view of the literature:

> Judged by any reasonable standard for scientific research, much of the sex-research literature is highly defective and its claimed results therefore suspect. This is especially true of reports of homosexuality and other forms of deviant sexual behavior. Experimental bias is rampant: Generalizations are frequently based on inadequate samples . . .

samples are often highly distorted . . . Data frequently are highly subjective . . . Control groups are not always used . . . When standard research instruments are used, their known deficiencies often are ignored. General claims that cannot be squared with or substantiated by the available data are asserted confidently. . . . One finds throughout the literature quantitative claims unsupported by experimental studies. . . . Conceptual inadequacy is not uncommon. (Suppe, 1981)

All of these criticisms recur frequently throughout the literature, generally directed at the methodology of those researchers whose results contradict the author's own theories. The rival's conclusions are not warranted by the data: 'conclusions are reported without data to back them up' (Jenkins, 1984); 'Wolff often strays too far from the data she has obtained' (Sang, 1978); '[their] statements . . . lack any support from data' (Hoffman, 1976). And the opponent's data is invalid or unreliable because it was collected from too few people (the charge of the small sample, Sang, 1978; Jenkins, 1984), or from the wrong people (the biased sample, Butler, 1979; Krieger, 1982; Weinberg, 1970), or it was collected using faulty instruments (the biased test, the biased theoretical model, observer bias; Money, 1979), all representing 'flagrant violations of basic scientific method' (Kameny, 1971a). The charge of making 'a priori' statements (Browning, 1984; Davison, 1976) suggests that the rival researcher has abandoned the scientific method altogether.

There is now a substantial body of social scientific writing on homosexuality in which professionals castigate each other for failing to live up to the norms of ideal scientific practice. Both sides in this scientific debate seek to discredit the work of their opponents by invoking evidence that they have strayed from the path of methodological purity. Throughout this ritualistic combat, there is a uniform acceptance of certain underlying principles of scientific inquiry, and a considerable degree of consensus on how to evaluate other people's scientific contributions. This means that the underlying assumptions comprising the notion of good scientific methodology are implicitly accepted and therefore reinforced. For example, one researcher first complains — in a rash of alliteration — that the 'sickness theory of homosexuality is shabby, shoddy, slipshod, slovenly, sleazy, and just-plain-bad science' and then goes on to exalt the scientific method, claiming that

the person who could give a good course in science, scientific method and logic and could persuade large numbers of psychiatrists and psychoanalysts to take it in order that they could learn to recognize bad science and practice good science would be a major benefactor of mankind. (Kameny, 1971a)

As Mulkay and Gilbert (1982) point out in their discussion of 'asymmetrical accounting for error', the elaborate accounts scientists generate to explain the perceived failings of science treat 'correct belief' as the normal and relatively unproblematic result of following correct scientific method, while error is portrayed as due to the intrusion into research of non-scientific influences (biased samples, deficient research instruments, prejudiced researchers) which distort scientists' understandings. 'Asymmetrical accounting for error is a device by means of which scientists make their actions appear to exemplify the traditional conception of scientific rationality and, thereby, foster the commonly accepted image of science' (Mulkay and Gilbert, 1982). Like the Azandi, who 'explain away' apparent incongruities or failings in the predictions of their magic oracles by saying that a taboo must have been breached, or that sorcerers, witches, ghosts or gods must have intervened (Evans-Pritchard, 1950), social scientists explain away the perceived failings of research in their field by saying that standards of objectivity must have been breached, or that statistical inadequacies, sampling errors, procedural failings or logical mistakes must have intervened. The failings of science, like the failings of magic are used reflexively to prove once more the faith that generated the failures.

But there is another way in which a large body of admittedly 'bad' research can be of positive benefit to the scientific community. Compared with the physical sciences, the social sciences have little in the way of concrete achievements or social applications with which to justify themselves (see following section on Utility Accounting). In an area where there is little evidence that following *accepted* scientific practice will result in legitimate knowledge, it is particularly important to provide evidence that *failing* to follow such procedures results in *illegitimate* knowledge. If you cannot show virtue rewarded, you can at least demonstrate how those who stray from the path of methodological purity perish in ignorance. Sindermann (1982: 198) has commented on 'the relish with which the scientific community exposes phonies', and deliberately fraudulent science (Burt's fabrication of his data on IQ, the Piltdown man fraud, and W.T. Summerlin's black painted mouse, cf. Hardley, 1984) is particularly useful to the scientific community in so far as it enables the presentation of such activities 'not as intrinsic to science but as alien contaminations' (Gouldner, 1970). In this way fraudulent scientists are scapegoated to ensure the purity of the scientific community of chosen people, presenting them as a society of dedicated searchers after the truth, harbouring only the occasional 'false prophet' (Kohn, 1986) or 'betrayer of truth' (Broad and Wade, 1983).

The label of 'pseudoscience' serves a similar purpose. It functions as a convenient label with which to discredit your rivals (and, unlike the charge of 'fraudulent science', has the added advantage of not attracting a libel suit), by defining their competing theoretical formulations as outside the realm of serious consideration, mere imitations of the 'real thing'. More than that, it also enables the social scientist to show off his or her product, 'real science' to best advantage, specifying just what it is about 'real science' that deserves our respect. Introducing a volume of research reports on homosexuality, Gonsiorek (1982c) writes:

> One of the more important purposes [of this volume] is to train the reader to be a skeptical and discerning consumer of the past, current and future literature on mental health and homosexuality. To this end, a number of otherwise seriously flawed studies may be put to use as illustrations of poor technique or methodological problems.

Researchers on lesbianism and male homosexuality commonly accuse their rivals of being 'pseudoscientific' (Gundlach and Riess, 1968; Karlen, 1972), 'unscientific' (Suppe, 1984b) or 'ethnoscientific' (Ross and Rapp, 1983), which accusation affords them the opportunity to restate and reinforce the norms of scientific methodology (so flagrantly breeched by the pseudoscientists), the implication being that if only the correct scientific procedures were followed, truth (or at least, knowledge increasingly isomorphic with the structure of reality) will be revealed. The uniformly bad reviews social scientists wrote in response to Masters and Johnson's (1979) book on homosexuality, *Homosexuality in Perspective*, enabled them to restate the normative principles of scientific method. Amongst widespread complaints about definitional problems, the dangers of observer bias, the problem of reliability and the need for replication in Masters and Johnson's work (see comments by Money, Saghir, and Rundle, all interviewed in Marano, 1979), the following two extracts most vividly illustrate the use that can be made of 'bad' science to reinforce scientific norms:

> With *Homosexuality in Perspective* Masters and Johnson leave scientific objectivity and methodology behind and plunge headlong into a world of pop psychology, glib and facile theorizing, pseudoscientific mimicking of the latest shift in public opinion, and propaganda . . . A number of criteria must be met before the name 'scientific' may be applied to any research. Foremost among these, in all scientific disciplines, is that the techniques and procedures used be replicable . . . Judged on the basis of the criteria for replicability, the data they have presented cannot be called either scientific or objective. (Gonsiorek, 1981: 81)

> The book purports to be a scientific study. Here we can only assume that Masters and Johnson have either given up any interest in convincing a

scientific audience, or they have been so enraptured by their own
activities that they no longer feel themselves subject to ordinary
scientific rules. For example, in table after table we are told that data are
significant, but none of the data is treated to statistical analysis. There
are many pages about the development of the population sample for the
study, but we are never told exactly how the sample was recruited, what
were the precise criteria for admission to the study, what proportion of a
homosexual population the study group represents, or how it differs
from other segments of the homosexual cohort. (Cooper, 1980: 288–9)

The first author goes on to query the representativeness and
appropriateness of the sample, to accuse Masters and Johnson of
operating in an intellectual vacuum, and says that they manifest 'a
secretiveness that violates the scientific canons described earlier';
and the second author concludes that they demonstrate 'an airy and
smugly self-satisfied dismissal of ordinary demands for scientific
credibility or methodology'. Thus 'pseudoscience' serves a useful
didactic function: it allows — even demands — that the 'correct'
procedures be restated and their unquestioned virtues held up in
contrast with the miserable offering on which the critics pour their
opprobrium. In this way research on homosexuality, because rather
than in spite of the poor regard in which much of it is held, has been
used to reinforce the status of psychology as a scientific discipline.

Utility accounting
Social scientists of every theoretical persuasion claim that their
research on homosexuality or lesbianism has important social
implications. Representation of research as 'useful' to society is
commonplace throughout social scientific research generally. Introductory textbooks in sociology often organize their material of
instruction around social problems or with an eye to the beneficial
applications of social scientific principles (Park, 1967), and many
researchers incorporate the image of 'useful science' into their
work, writing as though 'the results and methods of science are
applied directly to technical and practical problems and those
external tasks provide the stimuli, goals and partial justification for
scientific work' (Ravetz, 1973). In sociology, Loewen (1970) calls
this the 'Enlightenment proposition', and noting the frequency of
this same argument among social psychologists, Potter and Mulkay
(1982) have dubbed it the Standard Utility Account (SUA).

In research on homosexuality, utility accounting typically relies
on the statement of humanitarian ideals about helping to cure the
sick, solve the problems of discrimination and work towards making
the world a better place. Offering to 'cure' the homosexual, Bieber
(1971) points out that 'science today can give guidance to help

relieve much human misery'. In much recent research, science is credited with helping to solve the problems of oppression, and it is now the 'gay affirmative' or 'lifestyle' researchers who hold out the most powerful image of science in the service of suffering humanity. Bell (1975) hopes that his work will have 'a practical impact on the oppressive situation homosexuals face, and on public attitudes toward homosexuality', and Henley and Pincus (1978) say that their findings 'suggest new directions for attacking prejudice from the basis of broader understanding of its roots'. Many researchers offer their scientific endeavours to the gay community, claiming that their work aims to 'enhance the life experience of gay men and lesbians' (Gonsiorek, 1982b), 'help homosexuals through the difficult developmental tasks which lead to greater adjustment, satisfaction, acceptance and happiness' (Coleman, 1982), 'improve the quality of their interpersonal relationships' (Davison, 1976), and 'maximize the growth potential of the individuals being studied' (Sang, 1978). 'We have got to learn what we can about sexual orientation — and about related issues like homophobia,' writes Ruse (1984), ' — so we can build a better world.'

More generally, utility accounting includes references to the presumed usefulness of the research to the legal and/or helping professions in terms of enabling them to make 'informed decisions' about homosexuals (Rand et al., 1982; Pagelow, 1980) and the need for studies to provide 'sound information for social policy decisions' (Levine, 1980). The overall image is, as Williamson (1983) describes, one of 'science and society marching forward into the future hand in hand like the children in the Start-Rite ad.'

However, considerable scepticism has been expressed as to just what, precisely, the social sciences have offered in the way of social application. A number of researchers have argued that 'attempts to justify psychological research in terms of its social utility lead inexorably to bathos' (Hudson, 1972: 111; see also Park, 1967, on sociology's lack of utility). This conclusion was rendered inescapable when a recent request in the Bulletin of the British Psychological Society for examples of achievements in psychology was met with a discussion of psychology's success in developing the advertising for and design of the 'Black Magic' box of chocolates (Duncan, 1986).

Despite the strong arguments that have been advanced against conceptualizing social science in terms of social utility (e.g. McKee, 1970; Caplan and Nelson, 1973), utility accounting is commonplace; as Bellah (1983) says, 'the issue of the "usefulness" of social science might be less salient at the moment did it not bear so directly on decisions about funding.' 'Lack of financial support', Eysenck (1953: 306) wrote, back in the relatively affluent 1950s, 'is a very serious impediment to the development of the social sciences.' In the 1980s it is more serious still, and psychologists are increasingly using the language of the marketplace in attempting to peddle their wares, arguing that good marketing or advertising strategies are essential if psychology is not to 'suffer the fate of the Pogo stick, Hula hoop, and skateboard' (Hayes, 1986; see also Canter and Breakwell, 1986).

> Utility accounting offers a powerful source of justification: In our society it is difficult to discredit any action which can be successfully depicted as facilitating control over the physical or social worlds. By characterizing research in terms of the Standard Utility Account scientists fashion a potent legitimation for the acquisition of funds and other scarce resources. (Potter and Mulkay, 1982)

Similarly, Barnes points out:

> It is a brave social scientist who will be prepared to say firmly, as Rutherford did of his research on atomic fission, that his [*sic*] proposed inquiries have no practical application at all. It is a brave bureaucrat who will provide funds for such 'useless' topics, particularly if they can easily be identified by their titles by hostile politicians. 'Lesbianism in Lesotho' is said to be a recent example. (Barnes, 1979: 82)

Given the importance of justifying social scientific investigations in terms of their usefulness, researchers on homosexuality have focused on the practical benefits their work provides for homosexuals and for society generally. Some authors have suggested that it was the perceived need to provide a convincing utility account that led to the removal of homosexuality as a disease from the APA's *Diagnostic and Statistical Manual* in 1973. The long history of psychology's attempts to 'cure' homosexuals was remarkably unsuccessful (Acosta, 1975). Better, from the perspective of the utility account, to redefine homosexuality as non-pathological than to admit the uselessness of one's therapeutic intervention (Silverstein, 1984). (Similar suggestions have been made about the diagnosis of 'psychopathic' and 'sociopathic' personalities, which also resisted attempts at 'cure', leading to the substitution of imprisonment for hospitalization [Young, 1971].)

Regardless of individual social scientists' views about the desirability or likelihood of their research having important social implications, the standard utility account is routinely used to justify the continued financial support of social science.

Textual persuasion and literary effects
Textual persuasion in an academic paper (or book) begins with its title, which, like a newspaper headline, is designed as 'a brief and

áttractive manner of presenting the reader with a sample of the paper's offerings' (Tannenbaum, 1953). Law and Williams (1982) record a discussion between biochemists planning a joint publication in which the need for a 'snappy' title is explicitly discussed; the title these scientists come up with, which summarizes their results, represents a technique of catching the reader's attention also used by researchers on homosexuality, as in titles such as 'Homosexuals may be Healthier than Straights' (Freedman, 1975) or 'Avoidance Latencies reliably reflect Sexual Attitude Change during Aversion Therapy for Homosexuality' (MacCulloch et al., 1978). Other titles simply offer us 'truths', 'realities' and 'facts' to replace the stereotypes and myths of prescientific thinking: *Queer People: The Truth about Homosexuals* (Plummer, 1963), 'The Facts about Homosexuality' (chapter title in Chesser, 1958), 'The Realities of Lesbianism' (Martin and Lyon, 1976) or 'Realities of Gay and Lesbian Aging' (Berger, 1984). Many titles are phrased as questions to which the subsequent text claims to provide the answer: 'Are Homosexuals Sick?' (Ruse, 1981); 'Is Homosexuality a Cause for Concern?' (Berry, 1980); 'What is a Lesbian?' (Chapman, 1965); 'Do Lesbians make Good Parents?' (Richardson, 1978); 'Is there a Relationship between Homosexuality and Creativity?' (Williams, 1972); 'Is Homosexuality Hormonally Determined?' (Birke, 1981) and 'Who should be doing What about the Gay Alcoholic?' (Zigrany, 1982). Some of these pseudoquestions come with their own multiple-choice response format, thus restricting the range of possible answers. Marmor (1972), for example, offers his readers a choice between the following two conceptualizations, 'Homosexuality — Mental Illness or Moral Dilemma?' Similarly we are offered 'Sickness or Sin?' (Bancroft and Myerscough, 1983: 165), *Homosexuality: Disease or Way of Life?* (Bergler, 1956) and, from a different theoretical perspective, 'Attitudes toward Homosexuality: Preservation of Sex Morality or the Double Standard?' (MacDonald et al., 1972). Both the posing of questions and the stating of facts in academic titles serve to lure the reader into believing that the text which follows is able, by virtue of the application of the scientific method, to present factual information and to adjudicate between competing answers to questions.

Another widely noted feature of scientific writing is the use of passive sentence constructions. One study of the syntax of scientific English found that 26 percent of all declarative sentences were in the passive tense (Cheong, 1978): novels and plays use about 8.2 passives per 1000 words, whereas scientific writing uses on average 23.8 passives per 1000 words (Svartvik, 1966). Horton describes the disappearance of the researcher as one of the mysteries of contemporary social science:

> His [sic] respondents speak, the social system functions loudly, but he who gave respondents language and the social system life is obscured beneath a fog of editorial 'we', 'they' or 'it'. (Horton, 1964)

In research on homosexuality, as in scientific writing generally, 'the findings indicate', 'the study reveals', 'the data suggest' and 'research demonstrates'. This reliance on passive sentence constructions serves at least two purposes. It contributes to the aura of objectivity, and it permits the use of language as camouflage. A spurious sense of objectivity is achieved in scientific reporting because the passive construction edits out the voice of the individual researcher, with the implication that the voice is that of Nature, or that the facts are literally speaking for themselves, and that anyone who followed the same experimental procedures would arrive at these conclusions.

> By reducing explicit references to human agency to a minimum, authors construct texts in which the physical world often seems literally to speak and act for itself. When the author is allowed to appear in the text, he [sic] is presented as being forced to undertake experiments, to reach theoretical conclusions, and so on, by the unequivocal demands of the natural phenomena which he is studying, or as being rigidly constrained by rules of experimental procedure. (Mulkay, Potter and Yearley, 1983: 197)

In addition to fostering an illusion of objectivity, the passive sentence construction joins terminological oversophistication (or Big Words, Kemeny, 1959) and 'jargomania' (Kirk, 1961) in divorcing scientific from everyday language and camouflaging the dependence of social science on the normal language conventions and categories of the culture. According to linguists, the use of the passive voice 'results in the excessive use of dangling participles, multiple modifiers, and tortuous and vague statements' all of which 'foster circumlocution' (Cheong, 1978: 4). The use of big words and complicated sentence structure, combined on occasion with extra-ordinary prolixity (compressing the most words into the smallest idea, Kupferberg, 1978), can create a scientific style that is unintelligibly dense and wilfully obscure. According to Adams (1980: 591), its effect is the creation of a privileged elite of the initiated:

> To write such contorted jargon that any critic can promptly be told he [sic] has absolutely misunderstood one is to achieve a sort of facile safety, if not total authenticity: such a gambit may be made to carry with it the implication of a thought so subtle and intricate that the coarse web

of language altogether fails to catch it. When half a dozen people get together and agree they understand one another, [even] though nobody else can, the privileged position becomes even more privileged. (Adams, 1980: 591)

Other social scientists have made a similar analysis of the obscurity of the prose favoured in the professional writing of their disciplines. 'The arcane vocabulary and syntax of stereotypical academic prose,' says Becker (1986: 30) 'clearly distinguishes lay people from professional intellectuals, just as the ability of professional ballet dancers to stand on their toes distinguishes them from ordinary folks.' Similarly, Meerloo (1967) points out that 'Not being understood often gives the feeling of magic power': it also enhances the real power of science by concealing triviality under jargon, confusion beneath circumlocution and through the phony representation of personal action in terms of the remorseless and impersonal operation of scientific method.

Finally, objectivity in scientific reporting is constructed through a central metaphor which runs throughout research reports on homosexuality and lesbianism — a visual metaphor. Social science is presented as making visible the invisible, exposing the hidden and concealed, shedding light on those dark corners that have been shrouded in ignorance, and exposing the reality for all to see.

Visual imagery is incorporated into much of the standard language of the social sciences generally, in which 'surveys' from particular theoretical 'perspectives' serve to 'highlight' or 'reveal' facts or 'observations' hitherto 'overlooked', in consequence of which certain 'revisions' or 'insights' are achieved, which 'illustrate' or 'throw light on' the need to 'review' one's analytic 'focus'. In research on homosexuality this visual imagery becomes a central motif.

Adapting the language of the gay subculture to its own purposes, social science presents homosexuals and lesbians as invisible people, hidden in dark closets, inhabiting a shady twilight world, shrouded in cloaks of prejudice, clouds of ignorance, fogs of taboo and mists of obscurity. We are 'invisible women' (Guth, 1978) — 'the invisible minority' (Lee, 1977; Potter and Darty, 1981; Almvig, 1982; Pillard, 1982) or 'almost invisible' (Pagelow, 1980). If not invisible at least concealed: 'the hidden segment' (Toder, 1978), the 'hidden minority' (Antony, 1982), the 'hidden population' (Cochran, 1984). Into the obscurity, the social scientist brings the light of reason to dispel the darkness; light is continually being shed, candles lit, dark cupboards opened, and blankets or cloaks of ignorance removed to reveal homosexuals as they really are. We are offered 'new light on homosexuality' (Marano, 1979) and 'illuminated by a few candles of factual knowledge' (Cappon, 1965: vii). As Berg (1958: 9) points out, 'even a little light is better than none where all is darkness.' Although homosexuality is 'shamefacedly clouded' (Bergler, 1954), and 'shrouded in mystery and taboo' (Rorhbaugh, 1981) science dispels the 'clouds of ignorance' (Chesser, 1958: 29), and 'rips away the distorting cloak of stereotype' (Pattison, 1974). Icebergs also make an occasional appearance, their tips representing knowledge, their submerged and hidden bulk symbolizing the great unknown: female homosexuality is described as an 'iceberg phenomenon, indicating that most of the community lies below the surface of society' (Hooker, 1962, quoted in Hedblom, 1972: 35), or research on homosexuality is said to resemble 'a science of icebergs that is based exclusively upon above surface observations' (Simon, 1973: 80). The images scientists use to describe what they find in the murky depths, behind the cloaks and in the cupboards, varies with theoretical perspective. West (1968: 11), for example, claims that 'the cupboard has been opened and the skeleton glimpsed', whereas Silverstein (1984) finds something more pleasant, describing homo-sexuality as having been 'a plant kept in a dark closet that blooms only when brought into the well-lit office of the psychologist or psychiatrist'. A less popular , but still common variant of this visual imagery relies on an implicit contrast between those of the researcher's own theoretical persuasion, who pierce the darkness and illuminate the facts, and whose visual acuity is in no doubt, and adherents of alternative theoretical positions who are accorded a variety of visual deficits, including 'myopia' (Ellis, 1971: 223), 'wearing blinders' (Riess and Safer, 1979: 258), looking 'through a glass darkly' (Fluckiger, 1966) and blindness (Riess and Safer, 1979: 258).

This pervasive visual imagery fulfils a number of useful functions for social scientific research generally. The rhetoric of making visible the invisible can be identified as part of what Woolgar (1983: 246) has characterized as the 'discovery account', in which the act of discovery is represented as 'an occasion when an independently existing reality (or aspect of reality) is revealed for what it always has been.' The discovery account thus avoids any suggestion that social scientists manufacture or construct reality: instead they are represented as devising research which enables them to remove intervening factors (such as social biases) which have obscured what was there all along. 'Discovery' enables the researcher to detect what before was concealed, but which has an existence independent of the act of perception. The visual imagery transmits an implicit epistemology, which acts to enhance scientific credibility.

The apparent objectivity of science, and the superiority of its method of knowing about the world, is thus created through a series of purely literary devices which construct the image social scientists choose to convey.

In the preceding sections I presented five techniques used in scientific writing on homosexuality which function to reinforce the status of social science. Collectively, research reports on homosexuality and lesbianism, from both sides of the pathological-lifestyle divide, constitute, as I have shown, an impressively coherent public-relations job on behalf of social science.

Many readers will recognize these rhetorical techniques as amongst those they use in their own scientific writing — combined, perhaps, with additional techniques such as the use of references as persuasion (Gilbert, 1977) or the ritualistic and magical use of statistics employed 'as a drunk uses a lamppost — more for support than for illumination' (Shepherd, 1984). There is, at one level, a widespread acknowledgement of the way in which the official discourse of science serves to mystify, conceal, and misrepresent scientific research, and much scientific humour derives, as Gilbert and Mulkay (1984: 176) have shown, from precisely this awareness of the discrepancy between actual scientific practice and our rhetorical presentation of it. The scientific 'proto-joke', which appears in a variety of guises, typically consists of two lists of phrases, one referring to formulations which can be used in the formal research literature and the other supplying their informal equivalents. These examples are quoted from those collected by Gilbert and Mulkay (1984: 176–7):

What we write	*What we mean*
While it has not been possible to provide definite answers to these questions . . .	The experiment didn't work out, but I figured I could at least get a publication out of it.
Three of the samples were chosen for detailed study . . .	The results on the others didn't make sense and were ignored.
Of great theoretical and practical importance . . .	Interesting to me.
It is suggested that . . . it is believed that . . . it appears that . . .	I think.
Fascinating work . . .	Work by a member of our group.
Of doubtful significance . . .	Work by someone else.

As Gilbert and Mulkay (1984: 178) point out, 'the proto-joke comes close to being a satire directed at the official discourse of science.' The wide circulation of humour of this kind in scientific circles is indicative of the extent to which scientists themselves recognize their use of rhetorical and persuasive techniques in formal scientific writing, and the acknowledged discrepancy between formal and informal accounts of the same research (see also Mitroff, 1974, and Gilbert and Mulkay, 1984, for analysis of this discrepancy). When asked to explain their use of rhetoric, the accounting procedures offered typically include reference to 'winning the games scientists play' (Sinderman, 1982). Some social scientists present a purely self-serving and individualistic account in which they depict themselves as conforming to the traditional language of scientific writing as part of their effort to 'scale the ivory tower' (Lewis, 1975): 'in order to get my PhD', 'to get publications', 'to make my work sound impressive'.

Some social scientists have suggested to me that their use of scientific rhetoric is mere convention which oils the wheels of science much as conformity with the rules of etiquette ensures the smooth management of social relationships: other scientists, they say, automatically translate what is written back from the formal rhetorical mode into the informal discourse that both reader and writer 'know' lies behind it. Other social scientists present an account which relies on the argument that they are playing the white/heterosexual/male scientist's game better than he plays it himself, and carrying out research of such manifest scientific superiority that he will be forced to accept their results proving that blacks/gays/women are okay people. In this account scientists present themselves as playing the scientific game not (just) for personal benefit, but to advance the cause of their people, and it is this account that is sometimes responsible for the rigid conventionality of much contemporary research on homosexuality and lesbianism. Accepting that science is a powerful form of legitimation, many 'lifestyle' researchers have been lured by their interest in achieving gay rights into correcting the research errors of the 'pathologists' with their own superior endeavours. Irrespective of its impact for the gay and lesbian movements (discussed in Chapter 2), their work serves a useful function for social science by upholding and reinforcing its institutionalized norms.

In this chapter I have argued that regardless of the motives underlying researchers' continued use of traditional scientific rhetoric, their collusion with such practices serves to reinforce the institutionalized power base of social science and perpetuate its claim to be the only legitimate purveyor of valid knowledge about the social world.

But I am not arguing for the purging of rhetoric from the language of science. The alternative to traditional scientific rhetoric is not terminological purity or linguistic hygiene: there is no 'neutral', 'objective' or hygienic language we can use. There are, however, persuasive and convincing rhetorical styles that do not rely for their effect on the reiteration and reinforcement of the power of science.

There have been, in recent years, some changes in the rhetoric used in scientific writing about homosexuality, representing, to some extent, a move away from the image of science as the only legitimate form of knowledge. Foremost among these is a marked shift from what Byrne (1977) calls the rhetoric of 'distanciation', a persuasive device whereby ' "we" could look at "them" while uttering a discrete tsk tsk from time to time' (Byrne, 1977), to the rhetoric of 'experiential authority' (Clifford, 1983). Distanciation is one element in what I have referred to as the 'mythologizing of scientific expertise': the researcher is presented as a detached and objective outsider, arriving at impartial conclusions through the operation of the scientific method. In traditional research on homosexuality, as Gusfield (1976) noted in scientific writing on drinking drivers, neither researcher nor audience are considered to be members of the researched group, and the scientist avoids the cardinal sin of 'going native'. In contrast, the classic anthropological persona (as embodied most notably in the writing of Malinowski) is based on its author's claims to experiential authority — squatting by the camp-fire, tent pitched among the tribal dwellings: 'experiential authority is based on a "feel" for the foreign context, a kind of accumulated savvy and sense of the style of a people or place' (Clifford, 1983). Claims to experiential authority are typically legitimated through 'fables of rapport' which narrate the attainment of full participant-observer status in a manner paralleling the 'up the mountain' account discussed earlier. As Clifford says,

> They normally portray the ethnographer's early ignorance, misunderstandings, lack of contact, frequently a sort of childlike status within the culture. In the Bildungsgeschichte of the ethnography these states of innocence or confusion are replaced by adult, confident, disabused knowledge (Clifford, 1983)

Taking the concept of experiential authority to its logical conclusion, gay researchers have increasingly proclaimed, like Lee (1977) 'No longer will we allow the heterosexual scientists to tell us who and what we are. We are the experts on our own identity.' These authors announce their own membership of the researched group, and lay claim to special research abilities or insights on that basis: Krieger (1982), for example, claims that 'as an insider, the lesbian has an important sensitivity to offer', Porter (1984) describes himself as 'able to draw upon fifteen years experience of the gay world' and Anthony (1982) says 'my particular lifestyle gives me an advantage in understanding and establishing rapport with my lesbian clients.' I have used this technique myself: 'the lesbian researcher . . . possessed nine years' participation in the lesbian, gay and feminist subcultures; hence problems such as "getting individuals to give information to the outsider" or "passing as deviant" were minimal' (Kitzinger and Stainton Rogers, 1985).

The persuasive impact of 'insider' rhetoric is quite different from the rhetoric of distanciation. The latter imparts the traditional image of the detached and objective researcher: its claim to credibility is that anyone using the same specialized skills and scientific methods could arrive at the same conclusions. By contrast, 'insider' rhetoric brings with it the implication of special sensitivities, unusual skills, and privileged access to exclusive groups or elusive information. Its claim to credibility rests on the personal experiences of the investigator who has acquired the intimate knowledge divulged.

Both distanciation and 'insider' rhetoric are designed to persuade the reader to accept the information offered as valuable contributions to the literature. Both present an image or persona of the researcher as separate from (at least some of) the audience, either by virtue of the scientific method, or by virtue of her or his experiential authority. Some authors attempt to combine the two — assuring us of their insider status, but also insisting on their 'objectivity' (e.g. Ettorre, 1980: 13), presumably hoping thereby to convince both the gay/lesbian movements (by whom, increasingly, only 'insider' research is viewed as legitimate) and the scientific community (which, on the whole, retains its traditional preference for 'objectivity'). But it is also possible for a scientist to attempt to persuade by invoking an image of the scientist as just an ordinary person: Becker describes his favoured persona like this:

> We [social scientists] are just plain folks who emphasize our similarity to ordinary people, rather than differences. We may know a few things others don't, but it's nothing special. 'Shucks, you'd of thought the same as me if you'd been there to see what I seen. It's just that I had the time or took the trouble to be there and you didn't or couldn't, but let me tell you about it'. (Becker, 1986: 36–7)

As Becker (1986: 37) points out, 'Such writers want to use their similarity to others, their ordinariness, to persuade the reader that what they are saying is right.' The impact of 'insider' or 'ordinary person' rhetoric does not rely on or perpetuate the power of social science.

All scientific writing is necessarily rhetorical. In the absence of linguistic hygiene, our choice is only in the type of rhetoric to use — a selection of soapboxes to stand on. There is a potential infinity of ways of conveying the 'same' information — each subtly affecting the reading of that information. The selection of one of this infinity constitutes rhetoric.

> Even if any given terminology is a *reflection* of reality, by its very nature as a terminology it must be a *selection* of reality; and to this extent it must function also as a *deflection* of reality. (Burke, 1968, quoted in Campbell, 1975: 393)

The question is not *whether* to use rhetoric in scientific writing, but *how* to use it, in whose interests, and how to recognize and analyse its use.

2

Social Scientific Accounts

> The true goal of the community psychologist seems to be to replace a clear political vocabulary with an obscure psychiatric semantic. (Szasz, 1966: 99)

Psychology's use of disease terminology to characterize socially and politically deviant behaviour functions, as many researchers have pointed out, as a powerful form of social control. Members of oppressed and socially marginalized groups are, generally, disproportionately diagnosed as suffering from mental illnesses and are overrepresented on the wards of psychiatric hospitals (Cochrane, 1977; Chesler, 1972; Al-Issa, 1980). Antipsychiatrists have seen this as the deliberate use of diagnosis as a tool of oppression to punish and control those who fail to conform to the dominant group's expectations of them — ethnic minorities whose behaviour departs from that of the majority culture (Mercer, 1986), or women who reject the stereotypical 'feminine' role (Chesler, 1972). This latter position is supported with references to the construction of 'diseases' peculiar to the oppressed group, such as 'West Indian psychosis' (Mercer, 1986: 121) and the invention of the menopause as a deficiency disease (McCrea, 1983). Two often quoted prototypical examples of such diseases are 'drapetomania' and 'dysaethesia aethiopis', diagnosed by the nineteenth-century physician Cartwright (reprinted, 1981): both diseases are peculiar to slaves, the former manifested by their tendency to run away from the plantations, the latter (also known as 'rascality') caused by idleness and cured by whipping and hard physical labour. A partial list of similar 'diseases' would include: 'masturbatory insanity', discussed in the context of Victorian morality by Szasz (1980); 'reformist delusions', a Soviet diagnostic category whose political relevance is discussed by Stone and Faberman (1981); 'state benefit neurosis', an illness characterized by refusing to take poorly paid employment when more money is available through state benefits, diagnosed by Price (1972) and discussed by Pearson (1975) in terms of social inequalities; and 'hyperkinesis', described in 1975 as 'the most common child psychiatric problem' characterized by fidgetiness, impulsivity, clumsiness, and a refusal to sit still or comply with school rules (Conrad, 1975), and discussed in terms of children's oppression in the magazine of young people's liberation, *FPS* (1975: 9). The 'disease' of homosexuality has also been widely criticized in these terms (e.g. Szasz, 1971).

Through the diagnosis of mental illness in those who pose a potential threat to the dominant social order, competing conceptualizations of reality are neutralized by assigning them an inferior ontological status. The perpetrators of these alternative world views are 'conceptually liquidated' through being represented as 'congenitally befuddled about the right order of things, dwellers in a hopeless cognitive darkness' (Berger and Luckmann, 1967: 132). The label of mental illness serves, then, to invalidate and depoliticize incipient challenges to the dominant version of reality, explaining them in terms of individual weaknesses and personal pathology. As Pearson says:

> Conformity — rather than being viewed as a *social* accomplishment — is elevated to the status of 'health'. Nonconformity is disqualified as 'sickness' . . . A view of conformity and deviance as a social accomplishment, which is what any critique of the medical model entails, raises the uncomfortable questions of how men [*sic*] construct and maintain social order and how they might reconstruct it. And these are political questions. (Pearson, 1975: 48, his emphasis)

In the next section I will explore how the invention of 'lesbianism', and the construction of lesbian pathology, served to depoliticize the threat posed to male-defined versions of reality, explaining away women's heretical rejection of heterosexual intercourse and 'feminine' behaviour in terms of disease, and obscuring its political dimensions.

My main critique in this chapter is directed, however, not against the conceptualization of lesbianism as pathology but against the 'lifestyle' and so-called 'gay affirmative' research which is widely applauded by the gay and parts of the feminist movements. The 'pathological' model of lesbianism has already been widely criticized in the professional literature for its methodological and theoretical inadequacies and its ideological biases, and it no longer represents the dominant psychological approach to lesbianism. In its place is a model of lesbianism (and male homosexuality) as a normal, natural and healthy sexual preference or lifestyle, and the issue of pathology has shifted to the diagnosis and cure of the new disease of 'homophobia' (fear of homosexuals). Such research is cited enthusiastically by many gay people and, especially in the anti-gay climate encouraged by the AIDS scare, liberal humanistic beliefs about homosexual normality and mental health are often experienced as reinforcing and affirming gay and lesbian culture.

For many women whose first understanding of their own lesbianism took place in the context of the pathological model, the 'lifestyle' alternative has offered an important means of self-identification, and the label 'homophobia' has offered both an explanation of and a weapon against hostility towards lesbianism. The critique I develop in this chapter is based on the argument that the 'lifestyle' interpretation of lesbianism individualizes and de-politicizes the lesbian threat, just as effectively as did the (now largely discredited) 'pathological' model. In developing this critique, I want to start by arguing that an exclusive focus on the role of diagnosis as an instrument of social control avoids consideration of other fundamental mechanisms within psychology which, in less blatant but equally effective ways, serve the same function of obscuring the political and of reinforcing status quo ideologies.

The pathologization of incipient or explicit challenge to the dominant social order is just one of a number of ways in which action is removed from the political sphere and located instead in a 'private' domain, personal to the individual. Personalization of the political is achieved in a variety of ways across a wide range of psychological research topics through psychologists' 'individuo-centricity' (Pepitone, 1981) — their insistent focus on the individual and internal as opposed to the institutional and sociopolitical. Psychological analyses of conflict offer, as Billig (1976) shows, particularly good examples of this personalizing tendency, showing as they do a strong bias towards the representation of conflicts as 'misunderstandings', 'misperceptions' or as derived from psycho-logical features within individuals (as in, for example, theories of the instinctual origin of aggression which conceal the extent to which anxiety and the urge to compete are carefully fostered in a capitalist society [Ingleby, 1974: 325]). Conflict resolution is thus reduced to re-establishing understanding and improving communi-cation skills, obscuring its political context. Applied to the field of industry, this personalized type of analysis has done much to smooth over the political rift between employer and employee using the rhetoric of interpersonal relations (Elliott, 1953/4), and, similarly, the concept of 'unemployability' serves to obscure political features by locating the causes of unemployment inside the unemployed, who are described as lacking the appropriate inter-personal skills (Hollway, 1984: 26).

Citing the case of a woman who, on complaining to a psychiatrist about violence from her husband, is asked to consider her own complicity in this, Garfinkle (1981) describes this 'argumentum ad Valium' (p. 142) as 'a striking and tragic example of how an indivi-dualistic problematic allows the scientist to blame the individual and absolve the institution' (p. 155). Person-blame interpretations of social problems not only free the government and other primary social institutions from responsibility for the problem; they also provide and legitimate the right to initiate person change rather than system change programmes, thus reinforcing the status quo.

> Why should we even consider fundamental social changes or massive income redistribution if the entire problem can be solved by having scientists teach the criminal class — like a group of laboratory rats — to march successfully through the maze of our society? . . . I think you would do well to consider how much less expensive it is to hire a thousand psychologists than to make even a miniscule change in the social and economic structure. (D. Bazelon, 1972, quoted in Caplan and Nelson, 1973)

Psychological explanations thus act to conceal political divisions and to perpetuate the status quo through an insistent emphasis on individual responsibility, internal causation and individual solutions to problems. As Caplan and Nelson say:

> One searches in vain for serious treatment — whether as dependent, independent or merely correlated variables — of social *system* variables as they may relate to those psychological variables with which psychologists ordinarily concern themselves. Examples of social system variables that one might expect to play a role of some consequence are the following: the concentration of wealth and power, unequal educational or occupational opportunity, particularistic dispensation of justice at the hands of the police and the judicial system, national budgetary priorities for destructive as compared to social welfare purposes, and the militarization of the economy. (Caplan and Nelson, 1973, their emphasis)

This emphasis on individualism is one of the core values of liberal ideology, and it is the values of liberalism generally which pervade and are fundamental to social scientific theory and practice. Liberalism, in the sense in which I am using it here, is the specific set of ideas, developed with the bourgeois revolution, asserting the importance and autonomy of the individual as a discrete unit possessing certain rights independent of the state and anterior to its very existence.

In the early stages of its development, liberalism was a powerful radical ideology which 'attacked and dissolved the rigid world of custom and authority' and liberated in this dissolution 'a myriad of newborn individuals having for the first time a life of their own' (De Ruggiero, 1959). In the seventeenth and eighteenth centuries, liberalism, brandishing the natural, equal and inalienable rights of man, challenged prevailing injustices and ancient privilege, weakened the hold of absolute monarchy, and inspired the movement towards the abolition of slavery, and for religious freedom.

Integral to its achievements in these areas was the invocation of a separation between the 'public' or 'political' domain (in which the state has a legitimate interest) and the 'private' or 'personal' area of an individual's life, in which the state should have no power to intervene (except in certain unusual and heavily circumscribed situations). The 'self' became a newly valued object of moral, political and social concern (Trilling, 1972; Lyons, 1978), and society was conceptualized as the voluntary association of discrete persons, coming together so as to maximize the achievement of 'self fulfilment', 'individual potential' and 'personal development'.

> Almost all liberals retain a belief in the ontological primacy of 'the individual', together with a concomitant tendency to regard society and its institutions and all collectives as less 'real' than the individuals of which they are either in whole or in large part composed. . . . From this conception of 'the individual' and of his [sic] relations to the world and to other individuals flows much of the liberal system of political values. (Arblaster, 1972: 90)

Although, as Schultz (1972: viii) says, the term 'liberal' suffers from 'a serious case of intellectual incoherence', the bundle of prescriptions that constitute liberal political and moral values also generally includes an avoidance of extremes (a 'middle of the road' policy) and an emphasis on rationality: indeed, the whole notion that human nature is amenable to scientific enquiry and can be rationally studied in the form of 'psychology' is itself part of liberalism's commitment to a rational world view. (Rossides, 1978: xvii). Moreover, the subject of psychology (and of much of the rest of social science) is precisely this liberal construction of the discrete self-contained individual. In this sense, psychology embodies and reflects liberal ideology both in its (purportedly) rational methodological approach to the study of the individual, and through its very topic of discourse, or subject of investigation.

The incorporation of liberal ideology into social scientific theory and practice is unsurprising given the widespread acceptance of liberalism in the Western world generally. As critics of liberalism have frequently pointed out, liberalism is not just one creed among many in a supposedly pluralistic society, but is the ideology of pluralism itself. Liberalism is 'all-pervading, the ideological air we breathe, not a doctrine or a set of ideas only, but a whole climate of opinion' (Arblaster, 1972): it is 'an intellectual compromise so extensive that it includes most of the guiding beliefs of modern western opinion' (Minogue, 1963: vii): and, according to Rossides (1978: 535), 'though intellectually diverse, the vast bulk of

American sociologies are unified by their acceptance of liberal society.' Because the liberal values asserting the importance and autonomy of the individual and his or her rights to equality of opportunity, privacy, and self-fulfilment are the predominant and accepted values of Western society, they have lost their particular identity and history for most members of liberal society and they are accepted as the norm, rather than recognized as constituting a specific ideology (Eisenstein, 1981). As Koerner (1985: 1) points out, the enthusiastic proclamation of 'the end of ideology' was actually a byproduct of the widespread acceptance and institutional-ization of liberal ideology in the West. 'Many liberal opinions seem so obvious as to be unquestionable', says Minogue (1963: 17); 'its ideological roots are buried very deep, in an understanding of the world of whose bias we are hardly aware.'

Viewed from this perspective, the differences between so-called 'positivistic' or 'behaviourist' psychologies, and those labelled 'humanistic' or 'antipositivistic' are rapidly diminished, in that both share the liberal construction of the individual subject. Where the former place atomized individuals in laboratories and subject them to experimental conditions, or inflict on them the mechanical emptiness of psychometric testing procedures — ignoring or denying their sociocultural context — the latter typically celebrate the uniqueness of the individual person and his or her personal growth and self-actualization either in opposition to an oppressive society from which she or he could potentially achieve liberation, or, sometimes, with little mention of sociocultural context at all. Humanistic psychologies are, in fact, often welcomed precisely because of their focus on the individual and on the maximization of individual potential. Both sides in the 'humanism'–'antihumanism' debate share the common liberal conceptualization of the individual as a discrete entity — whether to be moulded to fit society or liberated from it. Describing individualism as 'the theoretical Achilles' heel of humanist psychology', Henriques et al. argue that

> The humanist commitment of radical psychology has become part of the liberal intransigence of psychological practice inside a great variety of social institutions. Individualism has become the norm . . . And in the face of the new right's attacks on the welfare state in the name of individual freedom, humanist social science can only assert the moral superiority of its own version of individualism. The force of humanist psychology (and social science) is increasingly tied to an insecure claim about who can best defend the interests of the individual. (Henriques et al., 1984: 11)

And it is through the individualistic focus of contemporary liberal psychology, that the personalization of the political is achieved.

In their exclusive focus on the oppressive role of diagnosis and 'cure', the early antipsychiatry lobby (Szasz, Laing, Chesler, Goffman, etc.) failed to mount a critique against the personalization of the political inherent throughout psychology more generally. The limitations of their critique, with its emphasis on madness, medicalization and the custodial and segregative function of the asylum left the way open for — even encouraged — the reorganization of psychology and psychiatry and its proliferation into new sites through the development of what Rose (1986: 80) calls the 'therapies of normality'. The florid madmen and lunatics who so liberally illustrated nineteenth-century textbooks have been replaced, as the major recipients of psychological attention, with ordinary people: the stressed and depressed, the nervous and neurotic, the maritally dissatisfied and sexually inhibited. As Rose (1986) argues, psychology is not, in the majority of cases, imposed coercively upon unwilling subjects, but is actively sought out by people who have come to identify their own distress in psychological terms, believe that psychology can help them, and are grateful for the attention they receive. Psychology ministers to those who want to stop smoking, improve their memories, lose weight, think creatively, gain self-confidence, be more assertive, control their drinking, rear happier children, discover their 'inner selves' and fulfil their full potentials. As Rose says:

> These therapies of normality transpose the difficulties inherent in living on to a psychological register; they become not intractable features of desire and frustration but malfunctions of the psychological apparatus that are remediable through the operation of particular techniques. The self is thus opened up, a new continent for exploitation by the entrepreneurs of the psyche, who both offer us an image of a life of maximized intellectual, commercial, sexual or personal fulfilment and assure us that we can achieve it with the assistance of the technicians of subjectivity. (Rose, 1986: 82)

Contemporary psychology and psychiatry have moved out of the asylum and into the family, the school, the workplace, and the community. The terminology and interpretative schema of psychology, psychiatry and psychoanalysis has invaded everyday speech and forms part of people's commonplace, taken-for-granted understandings of the world. As a result, 'our ideas about what constitutes a person's character and how behavior is talked about have been irretrievably altered' (Lakoff, 1980: 442). Psychology has helped to constitute the very form of modern individuality:

> Psychology is productive: it does not simply bias or distort or incarcerate helpless individuals in oppressive institutions. It regulates, classifies and administers; it produces those regulative devices which form us as

objects of child development, schooling, welfare agencies, medicine, multicultural education, personnel practices and so forth. Further, psychology's implication in our modern form of individuality means that it constitutes subjectivities as well as objects. (Henriques et al., 1984: 1)

The subjectivities constituted by contemporary psychology reflect its own insistent emphasis on the 'personal' as opposed to the political, and it is these depoliticized subjectivities that are promoted in contemporary liberal-humanistic (so-called 'gay affirmative') research. Much of this research fosters absorption in the 'essential self' of the lesbian, located in a 'private' sphere only tangentially related to the public and political. Through a focus on the privatized 'true self' of the lesbian, in which her 'real' identity is located, psychologists promote such 'human' goals as self-actualization, self-fulfilment, and personal happiness for lesbians, thus emphasizing person-change rather than system-change, and distracting attention from the sociopolitical and institutional aspects of lesbian oppression and the lesbian threat.

The argument I present in this chapter is that psychology has (on the whole) shifted from pathologizing lesbianism, with the associated attempts to prevent and eradicate it, to an alternative strategy which relies on constituting and regulating subjectivities about lesbianism which, while not preventing or eradicating it, render it politically innocuous. Abandoning an old and increasingly unworkable method of personalizing the political (pathologization), psychology has adopted new methods which locate 'personalized' subjectivities on the positive end of attitude continua and at the top of hierarchical models of gay identity development. The depoliticization of lesbianism is achieved in today's psychology in a form adapted to the new social context of today: its effectiveness as a form of social control is undiminished.

The sick lesbian
Professional research on lesbianism first started to appear in the late nineteenth and early twentieth centuries, with the work of men like Krafft-Ebing (1882), Forel (1908) and Bloch (1909). From then until the early 1970s the vast bulk of this research supported the view that lesbians were sick in one way or another — the products of disturbed upbringings or the perverted results of genetic mishaps. The supposed 'causes', the specifics of the morbidity concerned, and the appropriate techniques of 'cure' varied from one author to another, but this general consensus of lesbianism as pathological was commonplace throughout the psychological disciplines. (Reviews and critiques of this older 'pathological' literature can be found in Klaich, 1974; Hart and Richardson, 1981; Browning, 1984.)

The conceptualization of lesbianism as pathology still has its adherents amongst the professionals. In a recent report, one psychoanalyst describes lesbians as 'psychological orphans' (Moberly, 1983: 86) suffering from 'a state of incompletion' (p. 66) which 'does imply pathology' (p. 86), adding that 'we find much evidence of childishness; marked dependency needs; jealousy and possessiveness; a sense of inferiority; and depression, some suicidal thoughts and attempts, and the phenomenon known as aphanisis or "fear of total extinction"' (p. 52). In *Overcoming Homosexuality* a clinical psychologist presents a similar diagnosis of homosexuality as pathological:

> Homosexuality is a symptom of neurosis and of a grievous personality disorder. It is an outgrowth of deeply rooted emotional deprivations and disturbances that had their origins in infancy. It is manifested, all too often, by compulsive and destructive behavior that is the very antithesis of fulfillment and happiness. Buried under the 'gay' exterior of the homosexual is the hurt and rage that crippled his or her capacity for true maturation, for healthy growth and love. (Kronemeyer, 1980: 7)

Many researchers (e.g. Szasz, 1971; Klaich, 1974) have argued that in constructing lesbianism as pathology scientists have taken the place of priests in condemning and rooting out socially unacceptable behaviour: 'diagnosis is but a semantic lever to justify the elimination of the (alleged) illness' (Szasz, 1971: 303). Lesbianism is then 'cut out' either symbolically, as in lobotomy or clitoridectomy, or metaphorically, as in aversion therapy, systematic desensitization, orgasmic reconditioning and psychotherapy. Such methods locate the heresy in the body, mind or biography of the patient and attempt to eradicate it. Comparatively recent attempts at 'cure' include psychosurgery on two gay men (Schmidt and Schorsch, 1981), and hynotherapy on a young lesbian (Roden, 1983).

Analysed in its historical context, the development of the 'disease' theory of lesbianism can be seen as an attempt to replace women's developing political analysis of gender and sexuality, with a personalized and pathologized alternative.

Before the rise of sexology in the late nineteenth and early twentieth centuries romantic friendships between women were commonplace and did not attract any opprobrium. Contemporary historians have documented how:

> In the eighteenth and early nineteenth centuries many middle class women had relationships with each other which included passionate declarations of love, nights spent in bed together sharing kisses and intimacies, and lifelong devotion, without exciting the least adverse comment. (Jeffreys, 1985: 102)

In America it was still possible, until as late as the first decade of the twentieth century, for passionate tales of love between women to be related in periodicals like *Ladies' Home Journal* and *Harper's* totally without self-consciousness or awareness that such relationships might be considered unhealthy or taboo (Faderman, 1980: 298). On the rare occasions when sex between women was discussed in medical textbooks it was presented as an extension of masturbation or as studious preparation for marriage (Cook, 1979).

Male indulgence of love between women ceased abruptly with the first wave of feminism, which brought a political analysis to sexual relationships. The period 1880 to 1914 witnessed a massive political campaign by women to transform male sexuality: beginning with protest against men's use of prostitutes and sexual abuse of children (the campaign for the repeal of the Contagious Diseases Acts), early feminists went on to demand male sexual abstinence ('Votes for women and chastity for men', Pankhurst, 1913, quoted in Weeks, 1981: 164) and set up men's chastity leagues, such as the White Cross Army. Many pre-First World War feminists also argued for spinsterhood and celibacy for women — partly because this freed women from servicing men and enabled them to dedicate themselves to political activity, partly as a political response to inequities between men and women.

In 1913, when more than 60 percent of the members of the Women's Social and Political Union were unmarried (Jeffreys, 1982), Christabel Pankhurst stated categorically that spinsterhood was a deliberate political choice in response to the conditions of sex slavery:

> There can be no mating between the spiritually developed women of this new day and men who, in thought and conduct with regard to sex matters are their inferiors. (Pankhurst, 1913, quoted in Jeffreys, 1982)

As feminists increasingly challenged male dominance in all areas, and as new social and economic forces (e.g. the expansion of clerical opportunities providing female employment, Weeks, 1981: 165) presented middle-class women with the possibility of choosing not to marry and be financially dependent on men, women's friendships with other women became a real alternative to marriage (rather than an adjunct to it), and as such came to be seen by men as a threat. The early sexologists (Krafft-Ebing, 1882; Havelock Ellis, 1934; Forel, 1908; Bloch, 1909) responded in two ways: firstly through the 'discovery' of women as sexual beings and the glorification of heterosexuality, attempting thereby to achieve the 'coertion or conscription of women into heterosexuality through the orchestration of female sexual pleasure by improved male sexual

technique' (Jackson, 1981); and secondly through the morbidifica-
tion of lesbianism. This latter strategy relied on the construction of
'the lesbian' as someone defined by a specific and potentially
describable 'essence' which set her apart from normal women. Love
between women was then metamorphosed into an abnormality, and
it was claimed that only those who were perverted in this way would
want to change their subordinate status. The psychoanalyst Karl
Abraham wrote, for example:

> In some cases [women's] homosexuality does not break through to
> consciousness; the repressed wish to be male is here found in a
> sublimated form in the shape of masculine pursuits of an intellectual and
> professional character and other allied interests. Such women do not,
> however, consciously deny their femininity, but usually proclaim that
> these interests are just as much feminine as masculine ones. They
> consider that the sex of a person has nothing to do with his or her
> capacities, especially in the mental field. This type of woman is well
> represented in the women's movement of today. (Abraham, 1907)

Similarly, Krafft-Ebing described the lesbian in terms that left no
doubt about the link between lesbianism and the burgeoning
feminist movement of his day. Feminists attempting to avoid
stereotypical 'feminine' behaviours, or struggling for women's right
to education, were slotted into his picture of pathology.

> For female employments there is manifested not merely a lack of taste,
> but often unskillfulness in them. The toilette is neglected and pleasure
> found in a course boyish life. Instead of an inclination for the arts, there
> is manifested an inclination and taste for the sciences. Occasionally there
> may be attempts to drink and smoke. Perfumes and cosmetics are
> abhorred. The consciousness of being born a woman, and, therefore, of
> being compelled to renounce the University, with its gay life, and the
> army, induces painful reflections. (Krafft-Ebing, 1882: 34)

The effect of the new science of sexology was to scare women
back into marriage and conformity with fears of abnormality. One
reason historians (e.g. Faderman, 1980) have cited for the demise of
the first wave of feminism was the success of the sexologists'
diagnosis of feminists as suffering from the newly invented disease
entity of lesbianism. As the following extract from a talk given by a
lesbian feminist in 1904 at the Annual Meeting of the Scientific
Humanitarian Committee suggests, the feminists of the time failed
to mount a coherent counterattack to the charge of lesbianism
amongst their numbers:

> When we consider all the gains that homosexual women have for
> decades achieved for the Women's Movement, it can only be regarded
> as astounding that the big and influential organizations of this movement

have up to now not raised one finger to secure for their not insignificant number of Uranian [lesbian] members their just rights as far as the state and society are concerned, that they have done nothing — and I mean not a thing — to protect so many of their best known and most devoted pioneers from ridicule and scorn as they enlightened the broader public about the true nature of uranianism. (A. Ruhling, 1904, quoted in Lauritsen and Thorstad, 1974)

The second wave of feminism, starting in the late 1960s and early 1970s benefited, from the start, from the lessons of the past. In a frequently reprinted and widely circulated article, Radicalesbians deal explicitly with the threat posed by the 'lesbian' label:

Lesbianism is the word, the label, the condition that holds women in line. When a woman hears this word tossed her way, she knows she is stepping out of line . . . . Lesbian is a label invented by the Man to throw at any woman who dares to be his equal, who dares to challenge his prerogatives (including that of all women as part of the exchange medium among men), who dares to assert the primacy of her own needs. . . . To have the label applied to people active in women's liberation is just the most recent instance of a long history; older women will recall that not so long ago, any woman who was successful, independent, not orienting her whole life around a man, would hear this word. (Radicalesbians, 1969)

In another early and frequently quoted statement, the author says:

The accusation of being a movement of lesbians will always be powerful if we cannot say 'Being a lesbian is good.' Nothing short of that will suffice as an answer. (Mary, 1970)

There is still less than total agreement within the contemporary Women's Liberation Movement as to the desirability — and political implications — of widespread lesbianism: even in recent times this issue has caused deep rifts within the Movement (e.g. the 'political lesbian' debate, Onlywomen Press, 1981). But the combined efforts of second-wave feminism and Gay Liberation have been sufficiently effective that the old conceptualization of lesbianism as pathology no longer carries the credibility it commanded from the early until the middle years of this century. In 1973 the American Psychiatric Association conceded (after continual disruption of its meetings by gay activists) that homosexuality per se does not constitute pathology, and removed it as such from its *Diagnostic and Statistical Manual*. Well before that year, increasing numbers of psychologists and sexologists were advancing alternative non-pathological explanations for and accounts of lesbianism, and it is formulations of this liberal humanistic type which represent the 'respectable' scientific interpretations of lesbianism in contemporary psychology.

Liberal humanistic research on lesbianism

Since the mid-1970s research on lesbianism has, increasingly, moved away from the earlier pathological models towards conceptualizations which represent lesbianism in terms of individual choices and lifestyles or private quests for self-fulfilment and loving interpersonal relationships: the lesbian and gay man are no longer a species apart, but human beings of equal worth and dignity to heterosexuals, contributing to the rich diversity of humankind. Chesebro summarizes the potential implications of this research, and captures its flavour:

> It is no longer clear . . . if a distinction now exists between homosexuals and heterosexuals, if anyone can be humanistic and also reject a particular mode of self-actualization selected by a persecuted minority, if moral injunctions can ever be made of any relationship involving human love, or if the legal system can ever intervene morally in the private, consenting relationships of adults. (Chesebro, 1981: x)

In labelling research of this type 'liberal humanistic' I am using a term which many of its authors would happily accept for themselves, and also locating this research in the context of both the liberal philosophical tradition discussed earlier, with its emphasis on the inherent dignity and worth of the individual, and the similar focus of humanistic psychology on individual growth and self-actualization. This focus on the individual is, as Brummett points out, central to liberal humanistic psychologies:

> They seek to develop the potential of the 'whole' person. They urge acceptance of the individual on his/her own terms and reject changing the person radically to what he/she is not. (Brummett, 1981: 296)

Rejecting deterministic models of human development, humanism 'considers the complete realisation of human personality to be the end of man's [sic] life and seeks its development and fulfilment in the here and now' (Lamont, 1965: 287).

Szasz (1962) has characterized humanism as meaning that 'personal autonomy, dignity, liberty and responsibility are considered positive values' and Berger et al. (1973) also describe the concept of 'individual dignity' as occupying a central place in contemporary psychological explanations. In the industrialized Western world, they argue, the psychologically constructed individual no longer finds support, sustenance and meaning from the public symbols of institutional roles, but retreats instead into private worlds for life-enhancing meanings. They link this shift with the demise of the concept of 'honour' as a central moral principle, and its replacement with 'dignity':

The concept of honour implies that identity is essentially, or at least importantly, linked to institutional roles. The modern concept of dignity, by contrast, implies that identity is essentially independent of institutional roles. To return to Falstaff's image, in a world of honour the individual *is* the social symbols emblazoned on his escutcheon. The true self of the knight is revealed as he rides out to do battle in the full regalia of his role; by comparison, the naked man in bed with a woman represents a lesser reality of the self. In a world of dignity, in the modern sense, the social symbolism governing the interaction of men [*sic*] is a disguise. The escutcheons *hide* the true self. It is precisely the naked man, and even more specifically the naked man expressing his sexuality, who represents himself more truthfully. (Berger et al., 1973: 84)

Similarly, in the psychologized liberal humanistic world of 'individual dignity', the lesbian is rarely allowed to define herself in terms of her role, her sociopolitical location, her representation of herself as a challenge to the patriarchy. The political slogans that describe her in purely institutional, or counterinstitutional, terms ('lesbianism is a blow against the patriarchy'), like the symbols of her identification with women as a group, or the emblems of her rejection of the institution of compulsory heterosexuality (inscribed upon her badges and emblazoned on her banners) — all are described as mere outward regalia which conceal the real human being underneath. The very role of 'lesbian' itself, which locates the individual in terms of her group membership, is described as an artificial and dehumanizing category; people are to be seen as individuals with their own separate and distinctive selves, not pigeon-holed into labelled boxes. The 'real' identity of the lesbian is represented not in her overtly and explicitly political activities, or in her identification of herself as a lesbian, but in the private sanctum of her inner self, her unique human identity, which transcends this one limited aspect of her total being.

Liberal humanism thus functions to remove lesbianism from the political domain. Retaining the privatized concept of lesbianism introduced by the pathologists, liberal humanism replaces 'lesbianism as personal pathology' with 'lesbianism as personal choice of lifestyle' or 'source of sexual/emotional/personal fulfilment' — a private and depoliticized identity.

Four overlapping themes run throughout liberal humanistic research on lesbianism (and male homosexuality): 1) a belief in the basic underlying similarity of homosexual and heterosexual people; 2) a rejection of the concept of homosexuality as a central organizing principle of the personality; 3) an assertion that homosexuality is as natural, normal and healthy as heterosexuality; and 4) denial of the notion that lesbianism or male homosexuality pose any threat to the nuclear family and society as we know it.

The most pervasive of these themes is the characterization of lesbians as basically just the same as heterosexual women. The denial of any differences between subcultural or countercultural groups and the dominant society is common throughout liberal humanistic social science, and has been labelled 'assimilationism' (Adam, 1978: 119), 'the melting pot ideology' (Babad, et al., 1983), and 'liquidation by merger' (Berger and Luckmann, 1967: 139). Identifying this technique as a major recurring theme in social scientific writing on homosexuality, Chesebro (1981) describes it as 'mainstreaming' and he adds that 'a massive body of published social scientific research is unified by this mainstreaming perspective' (p. 182).

It was Kinsey's famous invention of the 'heterosexual–homosexual continuum' (borrowed, in part, from Freud's theories of innate bisexuality and polymorphous perversity) that set the stage for the widespread professional dissolution of any specific differences between lesbian and heterosexual women. The key notion of the earlier (largely psychiatric and psychodynamic) tradition of research on homosexuality was that homosexuality was a powerful character trait; that to do homosexual things required a certain kind of psychological history, and that this history, combined with homosexual experience, was powerfully influential on the whole range of a person's non-sexual activities. In this model homosexuality is constituted as a 'master status trait' (Hughes, 1945) and all of a person's acts are interpreted through the framework of her or his homosexuality: a homosexual orientation is seen as having profound consequences for the entire life pattern of the individual (cf. Gagnon, 1977: 235). The research by Kinsey and his colleagues began the shift towards the depathologization of lesbianism and male homosexuality. Instead of being a 'condition', lesbianism was reconstructed as a sexual experience that any woman could enjoy.

Kinsey demonstrated that a large percentage of women had, at one time or another, engaged in lesbian sexual activities (28 percent of the American women he interviewed), and he argued that the sheer frequency of sex between women made implausible the concept of the 'lesbian' as a type of person defined by her 'sexual orientation'. The core of this argument is that there are no 'homosexual' or 'lesbian' people, only homosexual or lesbian acts that anyone can (and many do) enjoy:

> Only the human mind invents categories and tries to force facts into separated pigeon holes. The living world is a continuum in each and every one of its aspects. The sooner we learn this concerning human sexual behavior, the sooner we shall reach a sounder understanding of the realities of sex. (Kinsey et al., 1948: 639)

Kinsey's expansion of the original bipolar conceptualization into a six-point continuum (ranging from exclusively heterosexual to exclusively homosexual sexual experience) is now widely accepted in the professional literature, and the subjects of psychological research on homosexuality are often asked to rank themselves along it. The Kinsey continuum has been celebrated for its presentation of sexuality as a multifaceted phenomenon, neither dichotomous nor permanent. According to De Cecco (1981), Kinsey demonstrates that 'sexual orientation fluctuates over a lifetime, and for some people, as often as the weather.'

Through a focus on sexual expression as the 'meaning' of homosexuality (i.e. homosexuality as an act rather than the homosexual as a type of person), differences between the lesbian and the heterosexual are dissolved. Lesbianism is not a distinctive, unitary, frozen state; sexuality is innately plastic, and every human being has the physiological capacity to respond both heterosexually and homosexually.

> Homosexuality, as sexual conduct and desire, therefore, is not limited to a small proportion of individuals but seems to be an integral aspect of human sexuality. (De Cecco, 1981)

All the major and influential research projects since Kinsey have tended towards this same liberal approach of dissolving any specific differences between lesbian and heterosexual women. Gagnon and Simon (1973: 176) head their chapter on lesbianism 'A Conformity Greater than Deviance' and emphasize that 'in most cases the female homosexual follows conventional feminine patterns in developing her commitment to sexuality and in conducting a sexual career' (Simon and Gagnon, 1967). Bell and Weinberg (1978) — whose research was reported in the media under the headline 'Not So Different' (*Sunday Telegraph*, 15 October 1978) — have argued that there are more differences *amongst* lesbians than between lesbian and heterosexual women, and coined the word 'homosexualities' (plural) to emphasize our heterogeneity. And Masters and Johnson (1979) take this line of reasoning to its logical conclusion by demonstrating, through exhaustive laboratory research, that there are no differences in physiological response between lesbian and heterosexual women, or between homosexual and heterosexual men: they have the same genital apparatus, which functions according to the same physiological rules, and their sexual activities constitute overlapping, rather than discrete, sets. This theme of the basic similarity of gay and straight people is reiterated throughout a great deal of contemporary research, and MacDonald (1981) recommends to textbook writers that 'outdated investigations that attempt to probe the causes of homosexuality should no longer be given precedence over more recent studies that indicate the diversity of homosexual expression and the similarities among heterosexual and gay lifestyles.' He recommends the *Journal of Homosexuality* as 'an excellent resource'.

Liberal humanistic social science, then, shows a strong tendency to deny or minimize the differences between lesbians (or gay men) and heterosexuals: 'a homosexual is a *person*, more like than unlike thee and me' (Calderone, 1976). Lesbians are portrayed as being just like normal people ('just folks', cf. Cooper, 1980), and there is a refusal to acknowledge or discuss lesbian differences. Our behaviour and beliefs are reduced to those forms congruent with the dominant order.

Compatible with this focus on sex as the defining characteristic of lesbianism, it is argued that homosexuality constitutes a relatively small and insignificant part of the 'whole person', and is not a central organizing component of the self. The second theme that runs throughout liberal humanistic research is the argument that, while acknowledgement of one's homosexuality (both to self and to significant others) is important, ultimately, the identification of the self solely or mainly in terms of one's homosexuality relies on a limited and inaccurate definition: personhood is more than this one aspect of the self. Karlen (1971) estimates that, on average, the exclusive homosexual engages in overt sexual relations with someone of the same sex only 1 hour and 45 minutes per week. Any definition or description of the self, it is implied, must take account of the person's activities during not only this short period, but during the other 166 hours and 15 minutes too. 'Where,' ask Simon and Gagnon (1967), 'is the research literature that reports on the attributes and activities of the lesbian when she is not acting out her deviant commitment?' As Nuehring, et al. argue:

> Gay life is but a part of the homosexual individual's whole social, intellectual and emotional life — even when special relationships among gays are being considered. Two or more homosexuals, in an ongoing acquaintanceship, friendship, or love affair devote but a portion of their interaction to pursuits that could be described as homosexual or homosexual related. (Nuehring et al., 1975: 41–2)

The labels 'homosexual', 'lesbian' and 'gay' are thus seen as dehumanizing categorizations which are erroneously assumed to 'reflect or even summarize the homosexual's place and purpose in the world' (Bell and Weinberg, 1978: 112–13). Insistence on defining the self primarily in these terms destroys individual identity (Pattison, 1974): such individuals have overidentified themselves with a category and need to develop 'a sense of personal and individual integrity' and an understanding that 'self-worth is a matter of personal merit' (Fein and Nuehring, 1974, quoted in Nuehring et al., 1975).

Thirdly, the liberal humanistic framework presents homosexuality in and of itself either as bearing no necessary relationship to mental health (the conclusion of the literature review completed by Gonsiorek, 1982b), or, alternatively, suggests that lesbians and gay men are healthier than heterosexuals (Freedman, 1971), more intelligent than heterosexuals (Weinrich, 1976, quoted in Ruse, 1981: 707), and have more honest (McCandlish, 1982), and sexually satisfying (Masters and Johnson, 1979) relationships than have heterosexuals. The role of the mental health practitioner is not, then, to convert the lesbian to heterosexuality, but to 'offer support and affirmation to [the lesbian] in her pursuit of self-actualization' (Steinhorn, 1982). As Anthony puts it, summarizing the traditional goals of humanistic therapy:

> In reviewing my experiences with lesbian clients, I see them struggling with the same issues as other people: that is, how to live self-actualizing lives through gaining a strong sense of self-esteem, establishing and maintaining meaningful relationships, and pursuing satisfying work. There is no particular psychotherapy for lesbians, but, rather, psychotherapy for women who happen to be lesbians. (Anthony, 1982: 53)

Lesbianism is, in this analysis, a normal, natural and healthy aspect of the self: 'Homosexuality appears to be natural for a statistical minority of the population and when practised between willing partners is a harmless mode of sexual expression' (Wilson and Nias, 1976).

The fourth, and final, theme central to liberal humanistic research on homosexuality is the notion that lesbians (and gay men) pose no threat to either heterosexuality or the social system, but can be integrated into society and contribute to its rich variety. This belief is in sharp contrast to the arguments of the 'pathologists' who present lesbianism as a threat to the nuclear family and society as we know it, and make cautionary references to the collapse of the Roman empire (Feuer, 1975: 179; Hendin, 1978). This (mostly) older research tends to claim that lesbianism is pathological because it is 'capable of influencing the stability of our social structure' (Caprio, 1954, quoted in Ponse, 1978), because lesbians are 'unwilling to make any contribution to society' (Hauser, 1962: 28), and are 'rotting the fabric of the arts as well as the more solid principles of family life' (Simpson, 1979: 231). Socarides describes how even 'latent' lesbianism can undermine the dominant patriarchal order in his complaint that:

Women with unrecognized homosexual tendencies may produce profound effects on their husbands' creative, productive, and functional
abilities — economically, socially and sexually. Consumed by love for
their homosexual partners, they shunt aside all other considerations.
(Socarides, 1965: 468)

Both Socarides and Romm, amongst others, have argued for
therapy for lesbians (meaning conversion into heterosexuality) on
the grounds that only thus will lesbians become 'worthwhile
members of society' (Romm, 1965) and be 'restored to a productive
and socially valuable personal and community life' (Socarides, 1965:
469).

Liberal humanistic researchers, for whom lesbianism is an
alternative lifestyle rather than a pathological manifestation, argue
overwhelmingly that homosexuals and lesbians 'are on the whole
successful and valuable members of society' (Freedman, 1971) and
'productive citizens' (Saghir et al., 1970) who can 'enrich the
majority culture' (Hess, 1983). According to Jefferson (1976),
'homosexuality is no social threat', and Phillips et al. (1976) add that
'no demonstrable harm to the rest of society due to the existence of
a cadre of homosexuals within its ranks has ever been shown'.
Gonsiorek (1982a) describes the 'primary task' confronting gay men
and lesbians as 'the creation of an equal, healthy, ethical and useful
place in society' and Lessard (1972: 205) says that 'gay is good for us
all.' According to Pillard (1982), 'the freedom gay men and women
are winning for themselves in the long run will be liberating for
everyone.' 'The homosexual culture,' says Seidenberg (1973), 'is a
valuable asset to civilization'. The basic validity of the social order is
taken for granted by both sides in this dispute. The debate is centred
on the extent to which lesbians conform with or can be assimilated
into the existing social system.

In the liberal humanistic model, then, there is no sharp categorical
division between homosexual and heterosexual. Homosexuality is
conceptualized as a sexual preference or choice of lifestyles, a
completely normal or natural and relatively insignificant part of the
whole person, testifying to the rich diversity of human expression.
Lesbianism is represented as entirely compatible with mental
health, and the life goals of the lesbian are depicted as broadly
similar to those thought to be sought by the heterosexual —
personal fulfilment, self-actualization, and satisfying interpersonal
relationships. Finally, lesbians are seen as capable of participating
in and contributing to the wider society generally, and of playing a
useful role within the dominant social institutions.

When psychology's predominant conceptualization of the lesbian
was rooted in pathology, its practitioners engaged in energetic

attempts to shape the subjectivities of both lesbians and non-lesbians in accordance with this model (Jeffreys, 1985). Now that psychology's predominant model is liberal humanistic, the subjective understanding of lesbianism as pathological is itself stigmatized as 'pathological': the concept of 'homophobia' represents an overt attempt to mould subjectivities in the liberal humanistic framework. The concept and definition of the 'well-adjusted' lesbian is another such attempt. The next two sections describe the invention of the well-adjusted lesbian and the construction of homophobia as overtly political exercises through which psychologists engage in the manipulation of subjectivities to fit the privatized definitions of liberal humanistic ideology.

Lesbian identities and the well-adjusted lesbian
The very notion of the 'well-adjusted' or 'healthy' lesbian is a liberal humanistic construction. Within the pathological model the concept is a contradiction in terms; lesbianism per se is sick, and heterosexuality is defined as an essential attribute of the 'well-adjusted' person.

Definitions of 'adjustment', like definitions of pathology, carry with them a freight of implicit values. Psychologists have proposed various lists of criteria of positive mental health (Jahoda, 1958) or of the mature personality (Allport, 1961), incorporating such hallmarks as warm relating of self to others, emotional security, realistic perception, skills and assignments, self-insight, and a unifying philosophy of life. Each of these proposed criteria of maturity, adjustment or mental health represents, as Smith (1978) argues, a value claim about the nature of the good life, about the kind of personality that is desirable or preferable. These value claims typically reflect their originators' own sociopolitical backgrounds and interests.

An early analysis of the concept of 'adjustment' as employed in sociology textbooks (whose authors at that time were predominantly white, male, middle-class, and of semi-rural Protestant extraction) found that ideal adjustment was defined as conformity with middle-class morality and motives, and participation in the gradual progress of respectable institutions.

> The less abstract the traits and fulfilled 'needs' of 'the adjusted man' [*sic*] are, the more they gravitate toward the norms of independent middle-class persons verbally living out Protestant ideals in the small towns of America. (Mills, 1943)

Similarly, individual-difference research typically places the professional psychologist in a highly positive light: the more similar the subject is to the professional in terms of education, socio-economic background, religion, race, sex, and personal values, the better adjusted she or he is likely to be as assessed on psychological tests. Increased education, for example, favours such indicators of adjustment and maturity as cognitive differentiation, low scores in authoritarianism, and open-mindedness (cf. Gergen, 1973). 'When mental health professionals purvey adjustment, they may be accepted as technical experts when they are actually covert gurus of value advocacy' (Smith, 1978). The value claims implicit in pro-posed criteria of lesbian maturity and adjustment, then, represent value claims about the kind of subjectivities that are desirable or preferable in lesbians. Claims about what a 'well-adjusted' lesbian thinks, feels and believes about herself represent an overt attempt to mould lesbian subjectivities.

In so far as the pathologists conceive of differences amongst homosexuals in their degree of mental health, it is the homosexual who accepts the 'disease' model and seeks out psychiatric help to convert to heterosexuality, who represents the most adjusted (or least mentally disturbed) homosexual. As Ellis (1971: 223–4) says, 'some of the sickest people in the world are so defensive that they never admit they're disturbed . . . the homosexuals we see in therapy are often less disturbed than those who refuse to come for help,' and homosexuals in therapy with the intention of changing their sexual orientation are described as 'far less masochistic and destructive than their partners or associates, who will not even attempt any realistic effort to relieve their anguish' (Socarides, 1972). With the liberal humanistic invention of the well-adjusted homosexual, the situation is reversed: the lesbian or gay man who wants to convert to heterosexuality is now the *least* well-adjusted. Known as 'ego dystonic homosexuality', this desire features as a diagnostic category in the American Psychiatric Association's *Diagnostic and Statistical Manual* (1980). As MacDonald (1976) puts it, 'before you were sick if you liked being a homosexual; now you are sick if you do not like being a homosexual.'

The concept of the well-adjusted lesbian, however, far from absolving lesbians of the need to consult mental health practitioners, has resulted in the proliferation of new reasons why lesbian subjectivities are in need of psychological attention. The need for 'appropriate therapeutic interventions' in lesbian couple relation-ships in order to 'provide the basis for a fulfilling relationship which fosters personal growth' (McCandlish, 1982), to 'help the members of the couple achieve a more satisfying relationship with each other and with the heterosexual world in which they live' (Decker, 1983), and to 'help lesbian couples cope with jealousy' (Morris, 1982), or solve their sexual problems (Richardson and Hart, 1980) is now well-established.

But psychology's most important role is in the treatment of the new disturbance of ego dystonic homosexuality, usually referred to in the literature more colloquially as 'self-hatred' (Richardson and Hart, 1980; Pillard, 1982) or 'internalized homophobia' (Gartrell, 1984). The concept of internalized homophobia puts one more barrier between the lesbian and mental health:

> The truly gay person must root out internalized homophobia. . . . By a process of ruthless Augustinian introspection, one must examine one's soul for remnants of guilt, shame, self-hate and fear, and perform the necessary excisions. (De Cecco, 1981)

The process of freeing oneself from internalized homophobia is often marketed as a process considerably facilitated by contact with a 'gay affirmative' mental-health practitioner, and there is now a sizeable literature proposing means whereby professionals can 'help lesbians to come to terms with their sexuality' (Sang, 1977: 268), 'enhance lesbians' self-image' (Hess, 1983) and 'assist lesbian identity integration' (Masterton, 1983). According to these authors, the acknowledgement of one's homosexuality 'marks the beginning of a new adolescence — a series of stages with developmental tasks' (Coleman, 1982) and the role of the mental-health practitioner is to be 'helpful in facilitating [homosexuals] through the stages to a healthier and more mature outlook' (Coleman, 1982). A variety of models of lesbian and gay identity development have been constructed as the theoretical rationale underlying these therapeutic interventions and the image of the 'well-adjusted', healthier or more 'mature' lesbian promoted by these various models is drawn, almost exclusively, from the tenets of liberal humanistic ideology.

Criticisms of these models have been directed against their male bias (Faderman, 1985), their reification of stages (Weinberg, 1984), their lack of acknowledgement of the situational determinants of identity (Omark, 1981, quoted in Troiden, 1984) and their insistence on a single linear developmental path in the face of the 'dazzling idiosyncrasy' of sexual identity (Suppe, 1984a). With the exception of Faderman's (1985) tangential approach (she argues that radical feminist lesbians may go through Minton and McDonald's [1984] stages in reverse order), the ideological basis of these models of adjustment has not been examined.

One of the earliest and most widely cited models, subsequently used in other studies (e.g. Hess, 1983; Anthony, 1982) is Vivienne Cass's (1979) six-stage model of homosexual identity formation, intended to be applied to both gay men and lesbians. 'Identity', she says, 'refers to organized sets of self-perceptions and attached feelings that an individual holds about the self with regard to some social category.'

In this model the gay person is conceptualized as moving from an initial stage of 'identity confusion' marked by uncertainty about his or her sexual identity, through a second stage of 'identity comparison', marked by a sense of alienation from heterosexual society, to a third stage of 'identity tolerance', in which the person admits to his or her own homosexuality and seeks out the gay community. With the support and validation of other homosexuals, the person progresses to the fourth stage of 'identity acceptance' and from there to 'identity pride', the fifth stage, marked by gay activism and 'purposeful confrontation with the establishment'. But the sixth and final developmental stage for homosexuals is 'identity synthesis'. In this stage, 'the "them and us" philosophy espoused previously, in which all heterosexuals were viewed negatively and all homosexuals positively, no longer holds true', supportive heterosexuals are trusted and 'viewed with greater favor' and the person 'comes to see no clear dichotomy between the heterosexual and homosexual worlds.' In Cass's words ('P' denotes her hypothetical gay person):

> P accepts the possibility of considerable similarity between self and heterosexuals, as well as dissimilarity between self and homosexuals. . . . With this developmental process completed, P is now able to integrate P's homosexual identity with all other aspects of self. Instead of being seen as *the* identity, it is now given the status of being merely one aspect of self. This awareness completes the homosexual identity formation process. (Cass, 1979: 234–5)

At the highest developmental level, then, the individual lesbian represents herself exactly in accordance with the personalized ideology of the liberal humanistic psychologists. She believes herself to be essentially the same as heterosexuals, sees her lesbianism as a normal aspect of her 'whole self', and is integrated into society, trusting and feeling comfortable in the heterosexual world. This model draws on liberal humanistic themes, incorporates them into its stages and reifies them as the natural fruits of developmental maturity.

Amongst other researchers concerned with the creation of well-adjusted lesbians, many have used Cass's model (e.g. Hess, 1983; Anthony, 1982). Its major alternative is the more recent model by Minton and McDonald (1984), which is in fact very similar to Cass's and draws explicitly on her model. Their version delineates three stages in the maturational process leading to well-adjusted homosexual identity.

In the egocentric stage, which typically occurs during childhood or early adolescence, the person engages in genital sex, emotional attachments, fantasies or daydreams with or about members of his or her own gender. In the next stage, the 'sociocentric', conventional assumptions about homosexuality are internalized, leading to secrecy, guilt, shame and isolation. The person in this stage may refuse to acknowledge his or her homosexuality, and this is detrimental to the self because 'mechanisms of avoidance and denial bind large amounts of psychic energy that could be channelled into more productive and rewarding activities.' In the final 'universalistic' stage the person achieves an 'integrated sense of self' and 'the identity of the individual will be transformed from role identity to ego identity.' 'To achieve fully the homosexual identity', they say, 'it must be integrated with all other aspects of the self.'

In a backhanded acknowledgement of the effects of the socio-political oppression of homosexuals, the authors are pessimistic about the attainment of this last stage for most homosexuals: 'the question arises as to whether identity synthesis can ever be achieved for all but a few as long as prejudice and discrimination prevail.'

This model, then, like Cass's arises out of and reinforces liberal humanistic ideology, and this same view of the 'fully mature', 'well-adjusted' lesbian as a living embodiment of liberal humanistic virtues is reiterated throughout the literature. The well-adjusted lesbian sees her lesbianism as a natural and healthy aspect of her 'whole self'. She 'considers her sexual orientation [*sic*] to be but a component of her identity' (Adelman, 1977) and says to herself, 'My homosexual identity is one very important aspect of myself but not my total identity. I feel comfortable in both the homosexual and heterosexual worlds' (Anthony, 1982). 'Identity synthesis,' says Suppe (1984a), 'involves not only accepting but also getting past one's homosexuality.' Similarly, according to Porter (1984), the well-adjusted male homosexual sees himself as someone who 'among the many aspects of his personality happens to be attracted emotionally and sexually towards certain others of the same sex.' Homosexual-identity development is geared towards the acquisition of 'a positive self-concept which enhances self worth and facilitates personal growth' (Hess, 1983).

This insistent focus on the internal psychological workings of the lesbian, her need for personal growth and self-actualization, serves a number of functions. Most obviously, perhaps, it serves to reassert her need for mental-health practitioners; the lesbian may no longer be sick by virtue of her lesbianism, and hence in need of cure, but she continues to require psychological services to assist her in gaining developmental maturity as a lesbian. In directing the lesbian's attention away from the outer world of oppression and offering her a satisfying inner world as a substitute, psychology offers salvation through individual change rather than system change. The individual is responsible for the amelioration of her situation, and she is urged to find individual solutions to her problems.

Furthermore, research of this type overtly discourages explicit political action and, particularly, the explicit rendering of a lesbian identity in political terms. In hierarchical models of gay identity development such as Cass's (as in many of those purporting to describe black identity development, e.g. Hall et al., 1975), the radical political identity is represented as the penultimate step on the ladder to maturity. The ultimate and highest level of development, and that most clearly demonstrative of adjustment, is represented as a liberal humanistic identity. Many lesbians (and gay men), says Coleman (1982), introducing his developmental model — which also culminates in a stage labelled 'integration' — 'become locked into one stage or another and never experience integration'. The gay movement, which 'generally is not known for its tendencies towards maturity' (Porter, 1984), can inhibit personal growth by encouraging the person to become angry and desire social change: 'it is relatively easy to escape from the burdens of the growth process by remaining in the rebellious and heretical stage, accepting a life pattern which rests on hatred and anger at the conventional world' (Rosenfels, 1971: 136). Politicization is often represented by liberal humanists as a passing, if necessary, stage in identity development; this is true of politicization not only as a lesbian or gay man but also in the politicization of other oppressed groups. As one commentator puts it:

> Those who retain the qualities of stridency and humorlessness are those . . . [who] have not yet been able to overcome the sense of their own racial or sexual unworthiness. And so this behavior appears to be a kind of therapy, a necessary stage, like a neurotic in psychoanalysis acting out his [*sic*] neurosis in the extreme before he is cured. (Lessard, 1972: 216)

The individual following the proper developmental pattern (perhaps with the aid of a mental-health professional) works through the early stage of 'internalized homophobia', through subsequent intermediary stages, to achieve the dizzy heights of liberal humanistic self-conception, in which the alleged deviance ceases to be of any great importance in the person's life, and she or he becomes a creative, self-actualizing, loving human being integrated into and contributing to the wider society generally. The concept and definition of the well-adjusted lesbian thus represents an overt attempt to shape lesbian subjectivities in accordance with the individualized and depoliticized ideological stance of contemporary liberal humanistic psychology.

The sick homophobe
Like the concept of the well-adjusted lesbian, the notion of 'homophobia' ('an irrational, persistent fear or dread of homosexuals', MacDonald, 1976) is an invention of liberal humanistic psychology. In the contemporary study of attitudes towards homosexuals, attitudes that depart from liberal humanistic ideology are labelled 'homophobic', and homophobia is described as a 'severe disturbance', (Freedman, 1978: 320) and 'a mental health issue of the first magnitude' (Marmor, 1980). In this way, liberal humanistic psychology replaces the sick homosexual with the sick homophobe: 'I would never consider a patient healthy unless he [*sic*] had overcome his prejudice against homosexuality' (Weinberg, 1973: 1).

The shift from classifying homosexuals as sick to classifying homophobes as sick is only one of a number of such diagnostic reversals in the history of psychology. Other instances include the change from the nineteenth-century diagnosis of 'masturbatory insanity' (which equates masturbation with pathology) to the twentieth-century diagnosis of 'masturbatory orgasmic inadequacy' (in which failure to masturbate is equated with pathology, cf. Szasz, 1980), and the shift from the psychological discoveries of black inferiority (still the dominant model of the 1920s), to psychological diagnosis of the pathology of the racist (cf. Samelson, 1978).

Since the early 1970s a large number of scales have been devised to diagnose the condition of homophobia (e.g. Smith, 1971; MacDonald et al., 1972; Dunbar et al., 1973; May, 1974; Larsen et al., 1980; Cuenot and Fugita, 1982) and there is unanimous agreement in the literature that subjects with high levels of homophobia, as assessed on one or other of these scales, are also personally defective in other ways.

Experimental investigation has led to the characterization of homophobes as authoritarian (MacDonald and Games, 1974), dogmatic (Hood, 1973), and cognitively rigid individuals (MacDonald and Games, 1974), who have low levels of ego development (Weis and Dain, 1979), a low tolerance for ambiguity (MacDonald and Games, 1974) and feel a need to support a double standard between the sexes (Glassner and Owen, 1976; MacDonald and Moore, 1978). They 'hold traditional, stereotyped attitudes about women and define narrowly the terms of acceptable sexual behavior for themselves' (Minnigerode, 1976), are 'intolerant of specific heterosexual practices and feel greater guilt concerning their own sexual impulses' (Dunbar et al., 1973), are 'sexually rigid' (Smith, 1971) or 'erotophobic', and are 'more susceptible to a variety of personal problems and difficulties with interpersonal relationships' (Hudson and Ricketts, 1980). Despite diversity of professional opinion as to which of these negative characteristics is the most typically associated with homophobia, no research has ever produced findings to contradict this sorry picture of the homophobe.

And just as mental health practitioners offer their services to help lesbians attain liberal humanistic self-conceptions (marketed as 'developmental maturity'), so too, intensive psychoanalysis (Weinberg, 1973) and special educational programmes (Morin, 1974; Morin and Garfinkel, 1981; Serdahely and Ziemba, 1985) have been proposed as means whereby the rigid and guilt-ridden homophobe might be 'cured'.

Although research on homophobia has been criticized on a number of counts, especially for its male bias (Faraday, 1981) and its scapegoating of individual 'homophobes' at the cost of ignoring the institutionalized oppression of lesbians and gay men (Plummer, 1981), few researchers have criticized the ideology in which the operational definitions of homophobia are rooted (except as part of an argument that homophobia scales should eschew ideology and present a totally 'objective' definition of homophobia [Plasek and Allard, 1985]).

Research on attitudes to homosexuality before the invention of homophobia generally relied on survey methodology, and the strong ideological biases of the early survey researchers are, with the benefit of hindsight and a changed sociopolitical climate, patently obvious. One researcher, for example, labels as 'tolerant' or 'neutral' in attitude people who say such things as: 'it is a little bit unnatural, due to some hormone imbalance; they are unhealthy people who need treatment' (Gorer, 1971), and another investigator finds the view that homosexuality is 'only natural for them' and that (male) homosexuals include 'some of our most sensitive, refined and valuable people' so unaccountably favourable that he labels people holding these views as 'extremists' — balanced by the 'extremists' at the other end of his attitudinal spectrum who want homosexuals 'eradicated', 'hanged publicly' or 'castrated' (Hauser, 1962: 154–5). The values incorporated into this older research on homosexuality are what many would now describe as 'conservative' or even 'homophobic' (Kessler, 1981).

The values incorporated into homophobia research, by contrast, are the values of liberal humanism. Analysis of the operational definitions incorporated into homophobia scales reveals that they share a common emphasis on the four overlapping themes I have described as characteristic of the liberal humanistic approach to

homosexuality: that homosexuals are no different from heterosexuals, that like heterosexuals they differ among themselves and
have the same need for self-actualization, that homosexuality is as
natural, normal and healthy as heterosexuality; and, finally, that
homosexuals can be integrated into and contribute to society as a
whole.

Homophobia scales typically consist of between about ten and
thirty or so Likert-type items, with a two-, three- or five-point
response format, ranging from 'strongly disagree' to 'strongly
agree'. The person's homophobia score is calculated by assigning
them a homophobia point for each 'pro-gay' item to which they
have responded with disagreement, and each 'anti-gay' item to
which the person has responded 'agree'. The diagnosis of homophobia thus depends upon the investigators' decision as to which
items count as 'pro' and which as 'anti' gay. This decision is made
uniformly, throughout the homophobia literature, in accordance
with the dictates of liberal humanistic ideology.

Firstly, homophobia research equates lack of prejudice with a
failure to differentiate between heterosexuals and homosexuals.
The 'unprejudiced' person must say that there is no difference
between homosexual and heterosexual — that homosexuality is
merely a sexual preference or choice of lifestyles, a totally neutral
sexual orientation.

Disagreement with each of the following statements, for example,
is penalized by a 'homophobia' point:

> Homosexuals are just like everyone else, they simply chose an
> alternative lifestyle. (Hansen, 1982)

> The basic difference between homosexuals and other people is only in
> their sexual behaviour. (cf. Dannecker, 1981)

> Other than their sex lives, there is very little difference between
> homosexuals and everybody else. (Price, 1982)

> A person's sexual orientation is a totally neutral point upon which to
> judge his or her ability to function in any situation. (Thompson and
> Fishburn, 1977)

> There are no physical, emotional or spiritual differences between
> homosexuals and heterosexuals. (Hansen, 1982)

Belief in the notion that homosexuals cannot be distinguished from
heterosexuals on the basis of any presumed differences in attitudes,
appearance, or behaviour, is one of the most common dimensions
of homophobia scales (cf. Plasek and Allard, 1985: 25), and the
mentally healthy, non-homophobic person is defined as one who
adheres to this liberal humanistic belief.

The second component of liberal humanistic ideology incorporated into homophobia scales is the rejection of the concept of homosexuality as a central organizing principle of the personality. Homosexuality does not define or summarize the whole person, and homosexuals differ among themselves just as heterosexuals do. The non-homophobe must *disagree* with items such as:

> Homosexuals are pretty much all alike. (MacDonald and Games, 1974)

> There may be a few exceptions, but most homosexuals are pretty much alike. (Price, 1982)

Homosexuals, like heterosexuals, are capable of, and should strive for, happy, loving, productive and self-actualizing lives:

> Homosexuals can lead productive, happy lives. (Hansen, 1982)

> It is important for homosexuals to express themselves and their true identities. (Hansen, 1982)

Thirdly, the non-homophobic person adheres to the liberal humanistic belief that homosexuality is 'natural', 'normal' and 'healthy'. Lack of prejudice is demonstrated by disagreeing with items such as:

> Homosexuality is unnatural. (Price, 1982)

> Homosexual activities are abnormal. (Hansen, 1982)

> Homosexuals are sick. (Black and Stevenson, 1984)

> Two boys having sex is something I would consider abnormal or unnatural. (Sobel, 1976)

And the non-homophobic person must accept that homosexuality is a natural inclination for (some) people, agreeing with statements such as:

> Just as in other species, homosexuality is a natural expression of sexuality in humans. (Millham et al., 1976)

> Homosexuality is just as natural as heterosexuality. (Millham et al., 1976)

Finally, lack of prejudice in homophobia scales is equated with failure to perceive homosexuality as posing any threat to the nuclear family and society as we know it. On the contrary, homosexuals are seen as able to play a useful and productive role in society and contribute to the progress of civilization. Non-homophobes must disagree with items such as:

> If homosexuality is allowed to increase it will destroy our society. (Price, 1982)

and must agree that

> It would be beneficial to society to recognize homosexuality as normal. (Larsen et al., 1980)

In particular, homosexuals must be seen as posing no threat to heterosexuality, and the non-homophobe must disagree with items such as:

> Most homosexuals will attempt to seduce 'straights' if given the opportunity. (Thompson and Fishburn, 1977)

while agreeing that

> If laws against homosexuality were eliminated, the proportion of homosexuals in the population would probably remain about the same. (Smith, 1971)

The belief that gay people can contribute to society, and should be 'allowed' to participate in major social institutions is incorporated into the following items with their stress on 'giving' homosexuals equality with heterosexuals. (The last two items are scored in the opposite direction).

> Homosexuals should be given social equality. (Larsen et al., 1980)

> Government should give clearance to homosexuals. (Glassner and Owen, 1976)

> A homosexual could make as good a president as a heterosexual. (Lumby, 1976)

> Homosexuals should not be allowed to vote. (Aguero et al., 1984)

> Homosexuals should not hold high government office. (Hansen, 1982)

In conclusion, the concept and operationalized definition of homophobia advances the cause of liberal humanism by appealing to individuocentric explanations of a sociopolitical phenomenon (blaming individuals who supposedly deviate from the rest of society in being prejudiced against homosexuals), and through its explicit promotion of liberal humanistic ideology as the only 'unprejudiced' attitude to homosexuality. The term derives from a psychology which has always reserved for itself the right to decide who is and who is not sick, and for which a shift from classifying homosexuals as sick to classifying homophobics as sick is far less threatening than any attempt to look at the issue in political terms. Psychology's achievement in popularizing the concept of homophobia, not only among its middle-class public generally but also in the gay, feminist and lesbian movements, represents a considerable success for liberal humanistic ideology.

Homophobia serves to depoliticize oppression against homosexuals and lesbians, and legitimates with the name of science, a
particularistic set of liberal humanistic principles as the appropriate
components of subjectivities about homosexuality. Just as the
invention of the 'well-adjusted' homosexual is based on a set of
value judgements about what the homosexual should think about
his or her homosexuality, so the invention of 'homophobia' is based
on a set of value judgements about what the *heterosexual* person
should think about homosexuality. Both terms define what count as
acceptable (healthy) thoughts in the heads of ordinary people, and
both define acceptable (healthy) thoughts about homosexuality in
terms of liberal humanistic ideology.

The radical feminist alternative

In this chapter I have argued that the psychology of lesbianism and
male homosexuality acts as an instrument of social control not just
in so far as it pathologizes homosexuality and coercively incarcerates
gay people in custodial institutions for 'cure', but also in its construction of subjectivities about lesbianism and male homosexuality in
accordance with the depoliticized individualism of liberal-humanistic
ideology. Central to this argument is the assumption that our 'inner
selves' — the way we think and feel about and how we define
ourselves — are connected in an active and reciprocal way with the
larger social and political structures and processes in the context of
which they are constructed. It is for this reason that, as many radical
and revolutionary movements of oppressed peoples have argued,
'the personal is political' (cf. Halmos, 1978). By contrast, liberal
humanistic theory postulates the existence of a private atomized
'inner self' rooted in infantile-libidinal conflicts or unconscious
motivational features, and, in its clinical conceptions, perpetuates
the salvationist notion of the person saving herself regardless of
society.

Although psychology has used the same personalizing techniques
against male homosexuality as against lesbianism, gay men have
produced relatively little in the way of political challenge, and such
challenges as have emerged fail to command widespread support
within the male gay movement, much of which, as Brake (1982)
says, is modelled on the image of the swinging self-confident
affluent homosexual male, courted by industry for the 'pink pound',
and flaunting its privileged masculinity. Despite assumptions of
solidarity between lesbians and gay men held by heterosexuals,
there is in fact, as Frye (1983) points out, little reciprocal
involvement between the male gay and lesbian communities.

Gay political and cultural organizations which ostensibly welcome and act on behalf of both gay men and lesbians generally have few if any lesbian members, and lesbian and feminist political and cultural organizations, whether or not they seek or accept male membership, have little if any gay male support. Many lesbians have left the 'mixed' gay movement in protest at gay men's sexism, obsessive sexual activity, phallocentrism, and lack of political awareness (Stanley, 1982).

Male homosexuality has been described as a form of male bonding against women (Hanisch, 1975: 75), and it is argued that the male gay movement is based on a politics of assimilation into the male-dominated culture from which they, as men, can benefit. Conforming to the liberal humanistic mould, 'the male gay rights movement attempts to educate and encourage straight men to an appreciation of the normalcy and harmlessness of gay men. It does not challenge the principles of male-supremist culture' (Frye, 1983: 144). The important differences that exist between male gay and lesbian political and ideological developments mean that my discussion of subjectivities (in Chapters 4 and 5) is centred almost exclusively on lesbianism. Gay male identities and ideologies have been discussed in some depth and from a variety of theoretical perspectives by other authors (e.g. Troiden, 1979; Cohen and Dyer, 1980; Watney, 1980; Marshall, 1981; Blachford, 1981; Weinberg, 1983).

Although some gay men have drawn on the writings of Foucault (1979) and Marcuse (1955) to present homosexuality in political terms as a challenge to capitalism arguing that there is a functional fit between the needs of capitalism and the organization of sexuality, such that the 'private' sphere of sexuality is related to historical forms of the mode and relations of production (cf. Weeks, 1980), socialist feminism, despite its established following, offers little in the way of a theoretical analysis of lesbianism; Beatrix Campbell, feminist member of *Marxism Today*'s editorial board, recently announced that 'feminism is about trying to put the pleasure back into heterosexuality for women' (Campbell, 1986).

By contrast, radical feminism offers a theory central to which is an analysis of lesbianism and heterosexuality as political institutions and a rejection of personalized interpretations. As such, it is the evolving mosaic of radical feminist and political lesbian formula-tions, which constitutes the main theoretical alternative to liberal humanistic ideology. The ideological underpinnings of liberal humanistic theories of lesbianism can, then, be highlighted by an examination of the opposing ideological framework offered by radical feminism.

Radical feminism (like liberal humanism) is not a static unitary creed or body of doctrinal beliefs, and there is ongoing debate amongst radical feminists as various possible theoretical and empirical avenues are explored and developed; fundamental to radical feminism, however, is a rejection of personalized and individualized interpretations of lesbianism. Central to radical feminism is the belief that the patriarchy (not capitalism or sex roles or socialization or individual sexist men) is the root of all forms of oppression; that all men benefit from and maintain it and are, therefore, our political enemies. Within this framework, heterosexuality, far from existing as a 'natural state', 'personal choice' or 'sexual orientation', is described as a socially constructed and institutionalized structure which is instrumental in the perpetuation of male supremacy.

> Men who rule, and male leftists who seek to rule, try to depoliticize sex and the relations between men and women in order to prevent us from acting to end our oppression and challenging their power. As the question of homosexuality has become public, reformists define it as a private question of who you sleep with in order to sidetrack our understanding of the politics of sex. For the Lesbian-Feminist, it is not private; it is a political matter of oppression, domination and power. (Bunch, 1978: 136–7)

In this analysis, neither heterosexuality nor lesbianism are 'natural': both are political constructions, the former a 'compulsory institution' (Rich, 1980) into which women are coerced, and which is 'no more "natural" than high rise flats or the neutron bomb' (Onlywomen Press, 1981: 56), the latter a political challenge to the patriarchy. The liberal conviction that lesbianism poses no threat to society, that lesbians can be integrated into and contribute to the social order, is, of course, in fundamental contradiction with radical feminist theory. 'Lesbianism,' says Brown (1976: 109), 'is the greatest threat that exists to male supremacy.' Adrienne Rich (1978) describes lesbians as 'disloyal to civilization' and adds that 'a militant and pluralistic lesbian/feminist movement is potentially the greatest force in the world for a complete transformation of society.' As such, lesbians are *not* 'just like heterosexual women', but are subjected to specific oppressions as lesbians that shape and mould lesbian consciousness (Penelope, 1986), so that lesbians may have greater insights into the functioning of male power (Brown, 1976: 113). The liberal belief (or hope) that lesbians do not try to convert heterosexual women to join their ranks is contradicted in the writings of many radical lesbians advocating political lesbianism (Johnston, 1973; Monique, 1980; Leeds Revolutionary Feminists, 1981).

Radical feminism thus contradicts each of the tenets of liberal humanistic theorizing about lesbianism. (A small group of my radical lesbian feminist friends scored a mean of 8 out of a possible 24 'homophobia' points when asked to respond 'Agree' or 'Disagree' to the items presented on pages 59–61.) Many radical feminist lesbians identify liberal humanism as their major ideological rival. Kathie Sarachild describes liberalism as a form of 'psychological terrorism' and says:

> Liberal leadership emerges whenever an oppressed group begins to move against the oppressor. It works to preserve the oppressor's power by avoiding and preventing exposure and confrontation. The oppressed is always resisting the oppressor in some way, but when rebellion begins to be public knowledge and the movement becomes a powerful force, liberalism becomes necessary for the oppressor to stop the radical upsurge. (Sarachild, 1975: 57)

The major impact of the radical feminist approach to lesbianism is in reasserting the political implications of lesbianism and replacing the so-called 'personal' back into the realm of the public and political. In this context, subjectivities about lesbianism held both by lesbians (lesbian identities and ideologies) and non-lesbians (heterosexual attitudes to lesbianism) take on meanings very different from those promoted by liberal humanistic psychology.

3

Eliciting and Assessing Lesbian Accounts

In the preceding chapters, I argued that social scientific accounts of lesbianism serve two major functions: the glorification of science as the only legitimate form of knowledge, and the depoliticization of potential social disruption through its relocation in a private and personal domain. The scientific reports cited to illustrate this thesis depend for their data, however, on accounts provided by lesbians, responding to the scientists' requests to describe themselves, their biographies, their sexual experience, their beliefs, hopes, fears and ambitions. Underlying the authoritative pronouncements of the experts are lesbian self-reports: such accounts constitute the raw material from which the research reports, exhalting the status of science and upholding status quo ideologies, are manufactured. In this chapter I first examine how social scientists have appropriated and used lesbian accounts in this way (this section), and then discuss alternative possibilities for the elicitation and reporting of accounts through interviewing (next section) and Q methodology (subsequent section) with lesbians (participant details are given in the final section of this chapter). This chapter thus serves as an introduction to the methodologies used in the studies reported in Chapters 4, 5 and 6.

The elicitation of accounts from lesbians, through interviews or questionnaires, is a common method of data collection amongst researchers in the area. A recent survey of post-1969 research on sexual orientations found that a quarter of these studies relied exclusively on face-to-face interviews, and almost 75 percent used interviews and/or questionnaires as their major data source (Shively et al., 1984). Although such 'qualitative' methodologies are often recommended as those most likely to respect the meanings of the research participants, their widespread use in research on homosexuality illustrates that they are no guarantors of such respect, and some of the most virulently anti-gay and anti-women investigators have never sullied their work with a de-humanizing statistic, or contaminated their intuitions with a controlled experiment.

In both 'pathological' and 'lifestyle' research, lesbians' accounts are subjected to a severe process of selection: strict definitions control a woman's eligibility as an account provider, so that only a select subset of accounts are elicited, and subsequent decisions as to the validity and reliability of the accounts that are elicited further restrict the range of data acceptable to the researcher. The definitions and decisions that govern the elicitation and selection of accounts are such that both the status of social science and the privatization of lesbianism are perpetuated.

The expertise of the professional is initially demonstrated in the first phase of the research — the identification and selection of subjects from whom accounts or other self-report measures are to be elicited. Although a few researchers have eliminated lesbians as informants on lesbianism and asked the analysts of lesbians to fill in questionnaires about the women instead (on the grounds that 'a well-trained and insightful psychoanalyst can do a better job of describing the life history and functioning of his [*sic*] patient than that patient might do herself' [Kaye, 1967]), most researchers have felt it necessary to obtain data directly from lesbians. This perceived need raises what is usually described as a definitional problem: Who, for the purposes of the study, is to count as a 'real' lesbian? The definition used to determine the eligibility of account providers is an important determinant of the nature of the accounts elicited and, overwhelmingly, researchers have defined lesbianism in privatized terms as a sexual orientation or type of sexual activity.

Both sociological (Faraday, 1981) and psychological (Shively et al., 1984) studies typically define the lesbian on the basis of sexual activity with another woman. (Only in 11 percent of studies is self-identification cited as a criterion [Shively, et al., 1984], and these authors are castigated for 'credulous acceptance of the respondents' self-identification' [De Cecco and Shively, 1984].) To qualify as a 'real' ('true', 'fixed', 'obligatory') lesbian, a woman must be able to demonstrate that her 'sexual orientation' is a stable part of her adult personality. The 'real' lesbian is required to be over a certain age (e.g. Saghir and Robins, 1969; Kaye, 1967), *not* sexually attracted to men (Ellis, 1969), sexually attracted to women (Gagnon and Simon, 1973; Poole, 1972) and to have 'repetitive' or 'regular' genital sexual activity with women (Bieber, 1969; Saghir and Robins, 1969; Kaye, 1967) under conditions in which male sexual partners are seen to be accessible to her (Ward and Kassebaum, 1964) and in which ideological reasons for being lesbian are absent (Defries, 1976).

Labels used to invalidate a woman's lesbianism by indicating that she is not a 'real' lesbian include 'going through a phase' (cf. Moses, 1978: 18), meaning that adolescence or the menopause is to blame; 'bisexual' (e.g. Bieber, 1969) or 'amphigenic invert' (Freud, 1977), meaning that she is also sexually attracted to men; 'facultative homosexual' (West, 1968: 13), 'jailhouse turnout' (Ward and Kassebaum, 1964) or 'contingent invert' (Freud, 1977), meaning that researchers consider that the only reason for her not having sex with men is that they are, usually temporarily, inaccessible to her; and 'pseudohomosexual' (Defries, 1976), meaning that she presents her lesbianism in political terms. These invalidatory labels are also often used to discredit the results of rival researchers by suggesting that their sample was not composed of 'real' lesbians: criticizing Masters and Johnson's research, Money (1979) says their subjects were 'really' bisexual, while Saghir (1979) claims that they were 'maladjusted heterosexuals'.

This collection of invalidatory labels has the effect of severely reducing the number of 'real' lesbians in existence: as Bergler (1954) says (in an article called 'Spurious Homosexuality'), 'there are enough homosexuals around; there is no need to augment their number by lumping pseudo-homosexuals with them.' By defining large numbers of women as outside the category of lesbianism, social scientists are then left with a relatively narrow, limited and homogenous group of 'real' lesbians from whom accounts can be elicited.

The elicitation of accounts from the sample of lesbians so defined is usually conducted with the intention of discovering 'the truth' about lesbians' lifestyles, sexual behaviours, family backgrounds, childhood experiences and so on (e.g. Kenyon, 1968; Krema and Rifkin, 1969; Poole, 1972; Gundlach and Riess, 1973; Bell and Weinberg, 1978). If lesbians already knew 'the truth' about themselves, social scientists would be relegated to the role of mere anthologists, collecting lesbians' accounts and passing them on unchanged. Rejecting this relatively humble role, researchers instead claim that a good deal of the self-report material they collect is untruthful (either deliberately or inadvertently) and that only they, the experts, can distinguish truth from falsehood. Discrepancies between 'objective' measures and subjective reports have been well-documented (e.g. between the number of beer cans in dustbins and interviewee reports of household beer consumption, Rathje and Hughes, 1975), and people cannot, apparently, be relied upon to report accurately even such an uncontroversial fact as their height (Cherry and Rodgers, 1979). Retrospective accounts are described as being particularly unreliable, being subject to 'conventionalisation' (Baddeley, 1979) and influenced by subsequent developments and by theories current at the time of interview (Yarrow et al., 1970). For researchers whose aim is to assess the 'real' or objective causes and concomitants of lesbianism, the use of self-reports is therefore deeply problematic. The researcher has access only to what women are able and willing to say about themselves on the basis of which to draw conclusions about what lesbians are 'really' like.

Discussing the use of retrospective data in research on homosexuality, Spanier (1976) identifies two main sources of possible error: faulty recall (unintentional false reporting due to poor memory or changing perceptions of past reality), and falsified accounts (intentional false reporting due to fear of being honest with the interviewer or through a desire to present a false image for ego enhancement). The task of the scientist is painstakingly to separate the kernels of truth from the chaff of falsehood in participants' accounts. Two sociologists describe how they approach this task as follows:

> We have dealt with this problem by using only those symbolic interview materials that are confirmed by the understanding we have of the gay communities and individuals derived from our observation of them. Most obviously, we let the members speak for themselves in their own words, only when they are telling the truth. (Warren and Ponse, 1977: 276)

Few other researchers are prepared to spell out so explicitly this equation of 'truth' with 'the understanding we [the researchers] have'. Instead, various controls and test–retest measures are employed as the equivalents of the 'lie scales' or 'social desirability' scales of psychometric testing. It is often asserted, for example, that many lesbians and gay men are familiar with the major psychological theories of homosexuality and may be biased towards offering the psychologically 'approved' accounts (West, 1977). Attempting to control for subjects' possible familiarity with particular theories, one recent study asked all interviewees whether they had read books about homosexuality or attended scientific lectures on the subject, and then tested every homosexual–heterosexual difference to see whether it was associated with such knowledge (Bell et al., 1981: 20). These same researchers, however, accepted as unproblematic their finding that significantly more lesbian than heterosexual women reconstruct their childhoods as containing an element of gender non-conformity. Ignoring the fact that the 'tomboy' theory of lesbianism is now well sedimented in popular culture, they argue that their results indicate that 'prehomosexual girls are much more likely than preheterosexual girls to display gender nonconformity in their play activities' (Bell et al., 1981: 147). In this example, a retrospective account is translated unquestioningly into literal historical truth, and even taken to have diagnostic implications for the future.

In general, interview material is likely to be accepted as 'true' when the researcher shares the attributions and constructions of the interviewee, and rejected or 'reinterpreted' in other situations. A researcher who dismisses the views of one interviewee with the comment that 'like many other lesbians she keeps up a facade, but behind it lurks the abyss of self-destructive feelings' (Wolff, 1971: 113), can nevertheless comment approvingly of her interviewees in general that 'the importance of the structure of childhood life with its particular family background for homosexuality had been grasped by all, whatever their IQ may be' (Wolff, 1971: 97). And this same author uses as support for her own theory that lesbianism is 'not a life chosen, but a destiny beyond choice' (p. 73) the following observation:

> I asked a number of my interviewees why they chose to live their lives in the way they did. They all stared at me in astonishment, if not with disapproval. Their unanimous answer was: 'I had no choice; it happened that way.' (Wolff, 1971: 63–4)

In another study, homosexuals who 'complain of their inability to form any sustained or deep sexual relationship' are believed, but when other homosexuals say that they accept and are happy with their homosexuality, the researcher 'reinterprets' their statements, commenting that 'self-acceptance usually turned out to be a code word for resignation and despair' (Hendin, 1978).

This 'reinterpretation' of subjects' reports so as to bring them into line with the theoretical approach of the researcher serves to incorporate deviant and potentially challenging versions of reality into the explanatory framework of the investigator, thus liquidating them.

> The deviant conceptions must, therefore, be translated into concepts derived from one's own universe. In this manner, the negation of one's universe is subtly changed into an affirmation of it. The presupposition is always that the negator does not really know what he [sic] is saying. His statements become meaningful only as they are translated into more 'correct' terms, that is, in terms deriving from the universe he negates . . . In a theological frame of reference, the same procedure demonstrates that the devil unwittingly glorifies God, that all unbelief is but unconscious dishonesty, even that the atheist is *really* a believer. (Berger and Luckmann, 1967: 133)

Through an insistence on the expert role of the researcher in distinguishing truth from falsehood in the accounts provided by homosexuals, researchers legitimate their own privatized construction of lesbianism as a personal pathology or individual choice of lifestyle, and also establish themselves as people with special powers of discrimination and interpretation. While the former claim enables the systematic rejection of political accounts of lesbianism (e.g. Defries, 1976) the latter claim contributes to the 'lay-professional' gulf, and the mythologizing of expertise (discussed on pages 10–14).

The research reported in the following chapters does not represent an attempt to compile accurate and reliable 'facts' about lesbians. Rather than using interviews to reveal what the interviewee does or thinks, and has done and thought in the past, the research focus is on the account she provides. The account itself constitutes the data. In focusing on biographical detail, for example, attention is shifted away from past events presently accounted for to the social construction of the past. My aim is not to reveal the 'real' histories, motives and life events of the participants, but to understand how people construct, negotiate and interpret their experience.

With this aim in mind, there was no need to impose strict definitions as to who, for the purposes of the research, should count as a 'real' lesbian, nor was there any need for a 'random' or 'representative' sample of lesbians. It was only necessary that women participating in the research should define themselves as 'lesbian', and that a sufficient diversity of women should be included as to facilitate the emergence of a diversity of accounts of lesbianism. (Participant details are given in the last section of this chapter.) Similarly, the accounts of lesbian identity and ideology offered by the research participants do not have to be vetted for their 'accuracy', 'objectivity', 'reliability' or 'validity'. Rather than attempting to match accounts against some objective standard of what lesbianism is 'really' like, I have accepted and discussed the accounts as attributions and constructions interesting as such in their own right. The use of interviewing to elicit accounts in this way is discussed in the next section, and the following section introduces Q methodology, and its value in research of this nature.

Interviews with lesbians
Interviews with lesbians can, then, within the theoretical framework of this study, be carried out without any checks for reliability or validity as these are usually understood, because the aim is not to obtain 'the truth' about lesbianism but to collect and explore the variety of accounts people construct about lesbianism.

What a person says in interview when presenting an autobiographical account is constructed in accordance with the individual and situational requirements of the account-provider. Autobiographical material is a reconstruction of the past told from the viewpoint of the present, tailored to meet current contingencies, structured, selected and edited as the person sees fit, and influenced by fallible memories, reconsidered passions, and selective vision. As Antaki and Fielding (1981: 38) point out, 'the account a person produces depends very strongly on the uses to which he [*sic*] wants to put it.' The accounts provided by the buyers and sellers of stolen goods to explain their behaviour are heavily preoccupied with minimizing culpability and providing grounds for the exoneration of their acts (Henry, 1976); habitual hitchhikers tell a rich collection of road stories to create a worldly image of themselves (Mukerji, 1977); child molesters may use explanations involving denial or the drinking of alcohol in an effort to disassociate themselves from others who molest children (McCaghy, 1968); convicted rapists can justify their action by describing their victim as a seductress, or may attempt to excuse their action by citing their use of drugs, their emotional problems, or by projecting a 'nice guy' image in which they argue that the rape would have been even worse if perpetrated by a different rapist (because, being nice guys, they were gentle while raping a woman who had just had a baby, or gave the victim money for a phone call when they left her) (Scully and Marolla, 1984). Similarly, apostates from the Unification Church (Moonies) typically construct an account which tells the tale of a metaphysical journey beginning with autonomy, rationality, balance and responsibility, travelling through dependency, irrationality, fanatacism and irresponsibility, and then returning to the starting point (Beckford, 1983: 89). From a constructionist perspective, these accounts are interesting irrespective of their literal truth value. As Beckford says:

> The fact that some apostates *do* delight in telling 'atrocity tales' about their former co-religionists can simply be accepted for what it is: evidence of their animus against a religious movement. The question of whether the atrocity tales are true or false is less important in this context than the fact and manner of their telling. . . . Questions about the 'reliability' or 'accuracy' of actors' accounts . . . are simply inappropriate; but their 'plausibility' or 'credibility' are very much part of the interpretative agenda. (Beckford, 1983: 85, 93)

For our accounts to be plausible, or credible, they must be among the socially available repertoire or 'vocabularies of motive' (Mills, 1940) which draw upon the currently legitimate ways of talking about one's experience (cf. Shotter's [1984] 'social accountability thesis'). Thus, as has been pointed out, there are an infinite number of possible answers to the question 'Why are they dancing?' but the answers 'to make rain' and 'to win the "Come Dancing Golden Sequin Tango Award"' are only credible in the contexts of very different societies. Whether or not either reply is 'true' can, in fact, be seen as irrelevant within the constructionist framework:

> Now, in both cases the accounts may be incorrect. The real motive of the actors in the first case might be to reinforce tribal mores, and in the second case the dancing couple may be trying to engage in surreptitious sexual dalliance. However . . . there is no question but that [the accounts] could only have been given in very different sorts of societies. The sociologist has learned something about the respective societies by discovering that *these are what could count as an account* in those societies. (Collins, 1983b: 72, his emphasis)

From this perspective, false accounts (even deliberately falsified accounts or 'lies') are as meaningful as correct accounts in so far as a plausible lie is (by definition) what *could* be a correct account in that society. Any account, says Cuff (1980: 38) which is '*defensible* in terms of its appropriateness, its propriety, as the description by a *competent* member of some event in the world', can be used as valuable data. An interviewee may, then, consciously lie about her or his beliefs, and yet still be considered to provide useful data. While I have no reason to believe that any of my interviewees were deliberately lying to me, it is worth noting that even if they were, the data so provided are nonetheless useful for my purposes. Thus, the traditional concern of interviewers with issues of validity and reliability are irrelevant here.

The interview schedule was developed in order to elicit accounts of lesbian identity and ideology in an open-ended and flexible way. After initial piloting, the final version of the schedule was as given in Table 3.1. This list of questions constituted an informal guide, or 'checklist', of points to be covered, and while I tried to ask all of them of all women, some were occasionally omitted, and I varied their order (and sometimes their wording) from interview to interview, as seemed appropriate in the context of each separate interaction. As has been pointed out, people prefer to be treated as individuals with minds of their own and they 'soon detect whether questions are standardized or tailored to their interests and histories. They resent being encased in the straitjacket of standardized questions' (Zuckerman, 1972). In particular, and bearing in mind Dexter's (1970) warning that we should 'guard against premature closure by supposing that we know all the questions and are just looking for answers', I encouraged participants to introduce topics of interest to them, and this sometimes meant that I followed up subjects not included in this schedule (e.g. anorexia, pregnancy and self-insemination, a child-custody court case, celibacy, and anorgasmia).

Interviews were conducted during 1982 and 1983, usually on weekday evenings in women's own homes, and lasted an average of one and a half hours. All interviews were tape-recorded and over half (all those relevant to the Q methodological studies) were subsequently transcribed by me. Additional written material was collected from each interviewee concerning age, marital status, nationality, place of birth, educational level and employment. All interviewees were aware of my lesbianism, and several made (unsolicited) comments to the effect that they would not otherwise have agreed to be interviewed.

Table 3.1 *Interview schedule*

1. Do you use the word 'lesbian' to describe yourself? (Gay? homosexual? bisexual?)

2. Do many people know that you're lesbian? (At work? any problems?)

3. What about your family? (Why or why not? how did you tell them? how do you think they feel about it?)

4. How did you learn about sex when you were growing up? (Parental attitudes? peer information?)

5. How did you first find out about lesbianism? (Feelings about it?)

6. When did you first begin to think that maybe that was what you were? (Was there something particular that happened that made you think you might be lesbian?)

7. What did you do about it? (Seek out other gay people? seek out counselling? information in books? feelings about it?)

8. Had you had sex with men before you decided you were a lesbian? (Why or why not? did you like it? sex with men now or in the future? sexual feelings for men?)

9. Have you had sex with a woman? (Why not?) Tell me about your first lover: how did you meet her; how did you become sexually involved? how did you feel about it? what happened to that relationship?

10. Are you now involved in an important relationship with a woman? How did you meet her? What are the most important things about the relationship for you? Is it monogamous? How has the relationship changed over the time you've been together? How do you see the relationship in the future? Are there things you'd prefer to be different between you?

11. (Explore any other important relationships with men and women.)

12. How, in your experience, is sex with a woman different from sex with a man (or how do you think it would be)?

13. Has anyone ever suggested to you that you're not really a lesbian? (Why?)

14. Do you ever wonder whether you're really a lesbian? In what ways do you feel different from other lesbians?

15. Are you a feminist? Why or why not? If yes, what are the important aspects of feminism for you? Does your feminism affect your thinking about lesbianism?

16. Some feminist women are saying that lesbianism is the logical conclusion of feminism and are choosing to become lesbians as a political statement. How do you feel about that?

17. Do you think women can *choose* to be lesbian? Did *you* choose? If you didn't choose to be lesbian, do you have any theories about why you are?

18. What is a lesbian? How would you define lesbianism?

19. Do you want (have you ever wanted) children? *or* Do you think being a mother affects the way you feel about your lesbianism? What have you told your children about your lesbianism?

20. If you had a daughter, how would you feel about her being lesbian? Do you think there's anything you can look for in a girl as she's growing up that might suggest she's more likely to be lesbian?

21. Is there anything you think people might have noticed about you when you were young that might have indicated that you were lesbian?

22. When you meet other women, at work or in other non-lesbian settings, you must sometimes wonder whether some of them are lesbian. Is there anything in particular you look for, any cues you pick up on? Do you think other people recognize you as a lesbian?

23. The last question! What are some of the positive things, the things you really like about being lesbian?

The importance of 'rapport' between interviewer and interviewee is often stressed, particularly when 'delicate' topics are discussed. Writing about the gathering of sexual histories, for example, Masters and Johnson (1974: 108), drawing an unfortunate parallel, emphasize the need for a 'receptive climate' and 'non-judgemental attitude' if the participant is to feel 'just as free to discuss the multiple facets of, for example, a homosexual background, as he [*sic*] might be to present the specific details of a chronic illness in a medical history.' The exploitation of interviewees by researchers has been discussed, by feminist (e.g. Oakley, 1981) and other writers who have commented on the 'vampirish' manner in which researchers suck data from subjects 'with a sense of righteousness as if every monograph partook of Galileo's divinity' (Dumont, 1969). Much research, says Reinharz, is conducted on a rape model:

> The researchers take, hit and run. They intrude into their subjects' privacy, disrupt their perceptions, utilize false pretences, manipulate the relationship and give little or nothing in return. When the needs of the researcher are satisfied, they break off contact with subject. (Reinharz, 1979)

In conformity with this image, one group of researchers has described sexual abuse perpetrated by a male interviewer on his female victims as a 'charming story' (Benny and Hughs, 1956), and another comments, with apparent lack of concern, that his interviews with gay men 'caused considerable dissention within the deviant world', and notes that 'some friendships were ruptured, and the request to grant an interview led to the dissolution of at least one homosexual "marriage"' (Leznoff, 1956).

I tried to conduct the interviews in such a way that women obtained immediate short-term benefits from being interviewed.

Although there were a few women who were uncomfortable with the research, my overall impression is that most women did enjoy the experience. Many women, especially those who did not have much social contact with other lesbians, said this explicitly:

> I must say, this is giving me intense pleasure, talking about myself. It's quite exciting. . . . It's exciting to be talking to a lesbian about these things I can't usually talk about with anyone. (Miranda, 19)

The opportunity to talk to an 'understanding stranger' (Dexter, 1970: 38) is generally felt to be a pleasurable experience, and 'by offering a program of discussion, and an assurance that information offered will not be challenged or resisted, self-expression is facilitated to an unusual degree . . . and this is inherently satisfying' (Benny and Hughs, 1956). I maintained contact with many women after completing the interviewing (several have become good friends) and two years after interviewing finished, I contacted about 25 percent of interviewees to ask if they would be willing to be interviewed by other researchers; none refused.

In comparison with the quantity of didactic material dealing with the conduct of interviews, there is relatively little instructional literature on interview analysis. Similarly, research reports of interview studies often describe in detail the social context and conduct of the interview itself, while glossing over the coding and analysis of interviews as a mere technical matter (Wolff, 1971; Ettorre, 1980; Mendola, 1980). This has the effect of giving the investigator's interpretation of the interviews an air of objectivity and inevitability, as though anyone faced with the same set of interview transcripts would produce a similar analysis. In fact, content analysis (on which the analysis of qualitative materials usually relies in some more or less formal way) of interview material involves coding data into units and establishing category-sets into which the unitized material may be classified and decisions as to what constitutes a 'unit' and how these units are to be categorized are highly dependent on the theoretical stance of the researcher (Manning, 1967; Potter, 1983). The research to be reported here relies instead on two Q methodological studies, which initially drew on, and the results of which are illustrated with reference to, the interview material.

Q methodology

Introducing Q methodology
Invented by William Stephenson in the 1930s (Stephenson, 1935, 1936a, 1936b, 1939), Q methodology was first known as 'the

inverted factor technique' (Stephenson, 1936a) — factor analysis of a data matrix by rows, rather than columns, so that persons, instead of tests, constitute the variables. Correlating items, the technique used in the vast bulk of quantitative psychology is referred to as R methodology — R being a generalized reference to Pearson's product moment correlation, r, to the study of trait relationships, and the designation 'Q' was coined to distinguish Stephenson's procedure.

When persons, rather than tests, are treated as the variables, factor analysis of the data matrix addresses the interrelationship of the scores over a variety of different tests for each person. Such an analysis is not possible if the tests whose scores constitute the data are traditional psychometric scales (e.g. IQ tests, anxiety scales), because the units of measurement for each test are dissimilar (i.e. Is a score of 120 on an IQ test higher or lower than a score of 26 on an anxiety scale?). Consequently, if a matrix is to be analysed by rows (persons), the data from which that matrix is constituted must either eschew external measuring devices as tests (Stephenson's Q methodology) or, alternatively, must resort to the questionable procedure of double standardization of data. The latter technique is the misrepresentation of Q devised by Burt (1937, 1940, 1972) and Cattell (1944, 1951), and perpetuated in many methodology and statistical textbooks (e.g. Hall and Lindzey, 1978; SPSS Inc., 1986). As its critics have pointed out, the double standardization of data (so that each score is expressed in terms of its deviation from its own test mean) results in a matrix that is simply a rather unwieldy transpose of a traditional R matrix, and it makes no difference to the results whether a factor analysis is carried out on this matrix by columns (R methodologically) or rows (so-called Q methodologically) — Burt's 'reciprocity principle'. This is not, however, what Stephenson intends by Q methodology.

Stephenson's solution to the problem of dissimilar units of measurement along data rows was to abandon external measuring devices as tests. Instead of asking, for example, whether someone is 'objectively' more or less intelligent than she is anxious, more or less anxious than she is sociable, he made the radical theoretical switch of asking 'How does she describe herself? How would she rank these attributes within herself?' It is then a relatively easy task to ask someone which of these characteristics they feel most defines them, which least, and which would come somewhere in between — a simple ranking task. Factor analysis of data from several people would then reveal clusters of people who have ranked these in similar orders. This is the principle upon which Q methodology's major tool, the Q sort is based. A Q sort is simply a collection of items which the person is asked to sort along a continuum from, for example, 'Very Like Me' to 'Very Unlike Me'. A 'personality' Q sort might consist, for example, of a set of items reading 'intelligent', 'sociable', 'anxious', 'dogmatic', 'introverted', 'neurotic' and so on which the person is asked to rank from most to least characteristic of the self, and the result is a model of that person's subjective view of herself. Q methodology, then, is fundamentally a means of eliciting subjectivities.

It is the value of Q in researching subjectivities that is most often either misunderstood or condemned. Many psychologists, Cyril Burt, perhaps not surprisingly, the foremost among them, found it hard to believe that anyone should be interested in people's subjective understandings of themselves at a time when psychology was just beginning to devise objective tests for measuring what people were 'really' like. Stephenson was accused of being 'unscientific' and of 'retreating from the scientific standards of behavioral psychology back to the era of introspection into private worlds' (Cattell, 1951). Ironically, then, given that the Q sort was developed precisely to enable the study of subjectivity, the Q sort was attacked *because* of its self-referent nature. From a Q methodological perspective, 'myself-as-seen-by-me' *is* the research topic which a personality-type Q sort is employed to investigate. But Burt and others, who wanted to measure 'the-self-as-it-really-is' rejected Stephenson's version outright, and interpreted Q as nothing more than the inverse of an R methodological matrix — Q methodology without the Q sort.

Where Burt succeeded in promulgating a version of Q methodology without the Q sort (factor-analysing data obtained from psychometric tests instead of from Q sorts) another group of researchers produced a mass of studies using the Q sort without Q methodology — that is, they collected Q sort data, but stopped short of factor-analysing it. Propounded largely by psychologists working in clinical settings (Butler and Haigh, 1954; Dymond, 1954; Lepine and Chodorkoff, 1955; Kerlinger, 1958, 1973) many of them devotees of Carl Rogers's client-centred therapy, this version of 'Q' became quite popular. Like Burt's adaptation of Q, which, by retaining normative psychometric tests, replaced the study of subjectivity with an 'objective' measure, so too this 'clinical' version presents Q as a measure of some 'objective' element of the person. Such Q sorts usually function as measures of mental health. For example, the psychologist can work out in advance how a 'mentally healthy' person *should* rank personality-type descriptors in describing the self, and then compare the way people actually do rank the items with this 'mentally healthy' version, either by calculating correlation coefficients, or by giving people mental health 'points' for each item correctly ranked (Dymond, 1954).

Another common variant is to correlate a person's description of her or his 'actual' self not with the psychologist's ideal of mental health, but with the psychologist's description of that person's 'actual' self: high correlations indicate adjustment on the grounds that 'the individual's personal adjustment is . . . inversely related to the degree to which experiences are denied to awareness' (Chodorkoff, 1954). Or, no less problematically, the 'actual' self is correlated with the person's own 'ideal' self, moderately high correlations indicating mental health and very high ones indicative of schizophrenia (Butler and Haigh, 1954). In all such cases, correlations between Q sorts are translated into supposedly 'objective' measures of mental health. Used in this way, the Q sort no longer permits people to explicate their own subjective views about themselves: it is no longer a Q methodological technique.

These two adaptations of Q methodology accounted for most of the published literature using Q until recently. Not until the mid-1970s, forty years after Stephenson's initial papers on Q, was there any concerted effort to reunite Q factor analysis and the Q sort, and then it came from a political scientist rather than a psychologist. The launching of the Q methodological newsletter (*Operant Subjectivity*) by Steven Brown (with the encouragement of William Stephenson, now living in retirement in Missouri) marked a new era for Q. Its explicit aim is to encourage and promote the use of Q methodological research in the operationalization of subjectivities. This research reports the use of Q methodology in this way, to investigate the subjectivities of lesbians about their own lesbianism and its political implications (Chapters 4 and 5) and to document non-lesbian subjectivities about lesbianism (Chapter 6). The rest of this section provides a brief description of the development of the Q sort items used, the administration of the Q sorts, and the rationale underlying the analysis and interpretation of Q data.

Developing a Q sort
A Q sort consists of a sample of items to be ranked by the research participants along a continuum the poles of which are defined by the researcher in accordance with the demands of the research topic. Most commonly, the items selected for use in a Q sort are verbal statements, such as the personality descriptors given as exemplars above, but visual (e.g. Stephenson, 1936b; Gauger and Wyckoff, 1973; Sappenfields, 1965) or even olfactory (Stephenson, 1936b) material also may be used. In the studies to be reported, the items were all verbal statements relating to lesbian identities (Chapter 4),

politics (Chapter 5) or attitudes to lesbianism (Chapter 6). For the first two studies, items were derived from the interview material provided by lesbians; in the final study, Q items were derived from both professional and popular sources relating to attitudes to homosexuality and lesbianism. A brief consideration of the way in which some of the Q sort items were generated for the first of these studies will suffice to give the reader an idea of the issues involved in developing a Q sort.

The first Q sort (on 'accounts of lesbian identity') was developed based on the transcripts of the first twenty-eight interviews. A full list of its items can be found on page 94; in this section I concentrate on the development of the six (out of a total of sixty-one) items which relate to aetiology. The aim in developing these items was not, of course, to discover the 'causes' of lesbianism, but to look at the accounting mechanisms employed by lesbians in dealing with concepts of aetiology.

One of the items contained in the Q sort (number 37) reads as follows:

37. My relationship with my father helps to explain why I am a lesbian.

In response to Question 17 of the Interview Schedule, a variety of possible influences of the father on a girl's subsequent lesbianism are raised by interviewees:

I think it has something to do with the way I related to my father. I didn't like him very much. So I think the way I felt about him coloured the way I related to men thereafter. Kate (7)

I was closer to my father than my mother and I suppose some people might think that was relevant. Betty (16)

I'm terribly irritated by these theories of castrating mothers and weak fathers. I don't see that that's got anything to do with lesbianism. Isobel (9)

Paula had a bad time with her father, who used to hit her mother, and he left when she was fourteen. And Ellen's father died when she was four. Belinda (23)

There is no one 'right' Q sort item (or items) that should be generated from such extracts; clearly the items developed depend on one's interests as a researcher and the purposes of the Q study. Had I wanted to look in detail at the reported relationship between lesbians and their fathers I could have created a set of items, based on this material, reading, for example:

I didn't have much contact with my father when I was growing up.

I always felt closer to my father than my mother.

As a child, I saw my father as weak and ineffectual.

My father was a physically violent man.

However, because I was interested only in the general belief that fathers are somehow implicated in their daughters' lesbianism, I derived the single item (No. 37) cited above. This statement was designed to be sufficiently general to cover all possible explanations of lesbianism involving the father whether by his death, absence, weakness, physical violence, closeness to the daughter (as in the above examples) or by any other imputed behaviour. Women interviewed subsequent to the development of this item made quite different links between their relationship with their father and their lesbianism — interpretations which were, however, covered by item 37 developed before they were interviewed, as can be illustrated by this example:

> The psychiatrist thought my love for my father had been completely betrayed by him, which I could see was true, I'd been sexually interfered with when I was eight by my father, and had hated him ever since. Maybe to have something like I had, a kind of personal shock or assault, maybe that pushes you one way or the other a bit. Alison (57)

In pursuing concepts of aetiology, a parallel item was created to reflect similar aetiological attributions to the mother:

> 3. My relationship with my mother helps to explain why I am a lesbian.

Women cited various other environmental influences supposedly related to lesbianism, including, for example:

> It sounds a bit clichéd, but I don't know if it was because I went to boarding school when I was nine years old. Eva (21)

> On one of the Gay Life programmes, someone said that women who become lesbians usually felt themselves in the past to be apart or outside in some way. And I can say, 'okay, if you want to look at it like that. . . .' Like my family are all much more sort of academic and academically oriented than I am, so I felt apart and outside of all that. Patricia (14)

> Apart from spending a lot of time in hospital, because that's something you might say made me a lesbian. Belinda (23)

The large number of possible environmental causes cited were covered by the umbrella item:

> 32. There was nothing in my childhood that predisposed me to be a lesbian.

Other aetiological factors cited were variations on the 'innate' theories:

Well, if I look at my mother's family I might say it's genetic. Betty (16) (With lesbian mother and gay maternal uncle)

I think that so much of our makeup is chemical and electrical . . . . So I think it's something biochemical, something innate. I do have this basic idea that people have this chemistry inside them which points them in certain directions. Joan (22)

These were covered by the item:

34. I believe I was born a lesbian.

Finally, one of these first twenty-eight lesbians (No. 5) was a political lesbian who said she had chosen to become lesbian through her commitment to feminism, a belief about which many other women expressed considerable scepticism. The following two items were designed to cover these views:

10. I came to lesbianism through feminism.
26. You cannot choose to be a lesbian; if you are, you are.

Together these six items cover the major attributions of lesbian aetiology. There is nothing unusual about this collection of 'causes': they are those typically discussed in the professional literature, and they constitute the everyday explanations invoked by members of the culture. In this context they were designed to read easily and — as far as possible — unambiguously, without the use of jargon or complicated sentence structure, and to be sufficiently general to cover a variety of similar beliefs and experiences.

All that has been said about the development of the 'aetiological' Q sort items applies equally to all the other items in the sort. Sentences were kept as short and simple as possible, and efforts were made not to offend, alienate or exclude women by their wording. And, whatever my influence on the interview, it was not sufficient to elicit entirely idiosyncratic responses. Other published interviews with lesbians contain very similar material, on the basis of which it is reasonable to conjecture that these lesbians, too, would have found Q sorting these items a meaningful exercise. Table 3.2 depicts the relevance of these Q sort items for a 'Miss Smith' interviewed by Charlotte Wolff (1971: 101–7), a psychoanalytically inclined psychologist, and quoted by her in full: despite the brevity of the interview (six pages) there are a fair number of comments relating to specific Q sort items, an observation which makes not implausible Brown's (1980: 189) claim that 'ultimately there would be little recognizable difference between a Q sample composed by a psychoanalyst and one composed by a radical feminist.'

Table 3.2   *The relevance of Q sort items to the interview protocol of 'Miss Smith' interviewed by Wolff (1971)*

I believe in romance. It's the most beautiful and important thing in life, and physical love is nothing compared with it. (p. 104)	16. If you truly love somebody then you put them first, before job, politics, children, everything. 27. The best thing about being lesbian is the sheer joy of the love we share; sex is secondary.
I feel and have felt male ever since my earliest memories. I always despised dolls and the sorts of games girls play. . . . Yes, I would still prefer to be a man. (p. 106)	11. I have never been very 'feminine' in the conventional sense. 12. I always felt different from other girls. 21. I would prefer to have been born male.
I think homosexuality is mainly biological. Anyway, that's how it seems to me. . . . To me, it's natural. You're born that way. (p. 106)	34. I believe I was born lesbian. 46. There are times when I feel that my lesbianism is unnatural.
I could never fall in love with a man. (p. 106)	9. I have been deeply in love with a man.

Administering the Q sort

The Q items so compiled are randomly numbered, typed out onto cards, shuffled, and offered to participants who are asked to use them to model their view or account by sorting them into categories from, in this case, 'Strongly Agree' (+5) to 'Strongly Disagree' (−5) with a central neutral category (0). Most Q sort investigations use 'forced' sorts — that is, the researcher tells Q sorters how many categories they must use, and how many items must go in each category — and the most common type of forced distribution is an eleven-point quasi-normal distribution of the type used in these studies (e.g. Eisenthal, 1973; Stephenson, 1964). Despite the existence of considerable debate about the merits of free versus forced distributions (Gaito, 1962; Cronbach, 1956; Jones, 1956; Block, 1956), leading Q methodologists have concluded that 'the shape of the distribution probably does not matter at all' (Brown, 1968), and because of the statistical advantages it yields, a quasi-normal distribution is employed in all these studies.

In Q methodology, the 'sample' is composed of the items in the Q sort, and the people who complete the Q sort are equivalent to, in R methodology, experimental conditions. The selection of items for the Q sort is thus a matter to which the logic of sampling techniques applies (as discussed in the preceding section), while the selection of sorters is guided by the requirements of subjecting the sample of statements to many *different* experimental conditions. People are not, therefore, randomly selected for sorting, but chosen on the basis of their presumed interests. A diverse subset of interviewees were therefore asked to complete each Q sort. The aim is to sample the range and diversity of views expressed, not to make claims about the percentage of people expressing them. Complaints about the non-randomness or small size of the so-called 'samples' of people used in Q methodological studies (Wittenborn, 1961; Kerlinger, 1973) are therefore entirely irrelevant.

Finally, despite the fact that 'the complexity of the Q sort task is generally felt to require in-person supervision of the respondent by trained interviewers' (Tubergen and Olins, 1979), no woman failed to correctly complete this procedure.

Data analysis
One Q methodologist compares human stituations to snowflakes saying:

> They are innumerable, they exhibit a multitude of forms, and above all they are highly perishable. Q methodology, Stephenson's great contribution to psychology, was designed to deal with this 'infinite variety', to make it accessible to scientific explanation without distorting it. (Duijker, 1979)

This is made possible through factor analysis. As Stephenson (1983) puts it:

> It would be remarkable if any two sorts, from different persons, were exactly alike; and unlikely that all will be totally different. It is the purpose of factor theory to determine which distributions, if any, are approximately alike, on the theory that they have the same 'eigen-werken', the same 'characteristic value', the same feeling.

In the first Q study reported here, on accounts of lesbian identity, 41 lesbians provided Q sort data. There are 820 correlation coefficients for 41 Q sorts (each Q sort correlated with every other), and since there are 61 items in this Q sample, there are $820 \times 61 = 50,020$ pieces of information in Duijker's snowstorm. It is to this that factor theory applies.

Factor analysis is based on the correlations between variables (in this case, women's Q sorts) and the computer program (SPSS Inc., 1986) starts by correlating each woman's Q sort with each other woman's Q sort, thus generating, in this case, a 41×41 correlation matrix. These correlations indicate the extent to which pairs of Q sorts resemble or are very different from each other. Factor analysis searches for family resemblances more generally, that is, for groups of Q sorts which, on the basis of their correlations, appear to go together as a 'group' or 'type'. The goal of factor analysis is to find a few underlying 'factors' which can summarize the pattern of correlations among a large number of variables. Despite the complex computational procedures involved, the basic principle is simple. Variables (Q sorts) which are highly positively correlated are apt to 'load on' or represent the same 'factor' or underlying dimension, while Q sorts having low correlations will probably be found to load on different factors.

Once factors have been extracted, they are then rotated to provide the best fit with the data: this can be accomplished according to purely statistical criteria (e.g. varimax) or can be carried out in accordance with theoretically derived criteria ('judgmental rotation', Stephenson, 1961: 10).

The *number* of factors extracted depends on the statistical conventions employed, the two most common of which, in R methodology, are to extract only those factors with eigenvalues in excess of 1.00 or, alternatively, to accept only those factors with at least two significant loadings. Neither convention can, however, be transferred unquestioningly to Q methodological factor analysis.

The eigenvalue of a factor is the sum of the squared loadings for that factor and as such is dependent on the arbitrary number of people associated with that factor who happened to be included in the study. As Brown (1980: 222) argues:

> Since an eigenvalue is a sum, it is affected by the number of variables included in the study, so is capable of producing spurious factors. Forty-five Q sorts, each with a very low loading of ±0.15, for example, will produce an eigenvalue of $EV = 45(0.15^2) = 1.01$.

If a factor such as the one exampled by Brown is extracted, it would not be possible to derive a factor array (i.e. to interpret it) because of the absence of high loading sorts from which such an array could be produced.

Equally, in Q methodology, factors with *fewer* than two significant loadings may be found to be meaningful. As discussed above, the *sample* in Q is the collection of Q items, and the Q sorters constitute the set of experimental conditions to which that sample is subjected. There is no special utility in having a large number of persons defining any one factor: after about four or five people have done so, further additions merely serve to fill up factor space without altering in any way the factor array or interpretation. As Brown (1979) has expressed it:

> Just as it is possible to distinguish a ruby-throated hummingbird from a kiwi without recourse to hundreds of each, so it is possible to distinguish one factor from another based on just a few observations.

A factor defined by only one person may, therefore, be sufficiently distinctive to be interpretable by the researcher, and certainly the arbitrary application of a rule that such interpretations should *not* be attempted is a mistake.

Once factors have been extracted and rotated to simple structure, a weighted average Q sort is calculated for each factor (the 'factor array'); this is derived from the individual sets of raw data obtained from each of the people defining a given factor, and is explained in more detail below with specific reference to this study. Factors are, then, theoretical Q sorts, 'idealized' from the Q sorts from which they are calculated.

In all the Q studies reported here, sorts were analysed using principal components (generally acknowledged to be one of the more statistically accurate methods, cf. Holzinger, 1946) and the resulting factors rotated to a simple structure using the varimax criterion. All factors with eigenvalues in excess of 1.00 were extracted, irrespective of the number of significant loadings with which they were associated, and efforts were made to interpret each. Where there were no significant loadings on a factor, this was obviously not possible, and so some factors were dropped from the analysis prior to the calculation of factor arrays. When a factor is defined by only one person, the factor array is simply that one person's Q sort. In this situation, attempts were made to explicate that person's subjectivity with recourse to interview material or other data as available. In some cases I found such interpretations satisfactory and have included these factors in the main body of my report, but on other occasions, especially when supplementary documentation was not available, and when the account represented by the factor was not one which I readily recognized as one I had encountered in the 'real world', I choose to describe these only very briefly, and to devote my discussion primarily to those factors whose interpretation I feel to be more secure.

Finally, it should be noted that the quotations from interviews used in illustrating the factor interpretations do not, of course, constitute, in any sense, a 'random' or 'representative' sample of all the comments made by those particular individuals. Interviewee comments are selected for presentation *if they are effective in illustrating the identity account on which that factor is based*: they constitute what Gerlach and Hine (1970) call 'apt illustrations'. Other authors have used interview material in a similar way; Collins (1983b: 74) for example, discussing his constructionist-based research on accounting procedures, comments:

> Since the aim in using these accounts and comments is unashamedly a matter of sharing an understanding, rather than presenting the results of certain measurements or measurement surrogates, the accounts and comments that should be selected for presentation are those that would be most effective for this purpose. To try to select a *representative sample* of speeches, accounts or comments is entirely misguided. (Collins, 1983b: 74, his emphasis)

Participants

One hundred and twenty women participated in the interviewing phase of this research. I began by interviewing my own friends and then asked each one whether they knew of others who might be willing to be interviewed ('friendship pyramiding' [Vetere, 1982] or 'snowball sampling' [Krausz, 1969]), sometimes specifying, especially near the end of the study, that I would like to meet women with particular interests or involvements not yet represented. This method was very successful in attracting volunteers and, because I was able to 'snowball' interviews from several different primary contact points (including academic contacts, a gay counselling service, feminist groups, and lesbian social meetings), I expected to find considerable diversity among them. They did not, of course, constitute a 'random' sample of lesbians, nor was it intended that they should do so, the aim being to achieve the breadth and diversity of response required in this study.

About one-half of the participants were living in or close to London (where I was based); the other half were interviewed in three Northern towns, and lived either in those towns or in rural or semirural settings near them. Most of the participants were English, although other nationalities include Scottish, Irish, Australian, American, Chinese, Indian, Israeli, Canadian, South African, Dutch, French and Belgian. Their paid jobs include nurses, secretaries, lawyers, psychologists, computer programmers, teachers, social workers, accountants, police officers, a bookbinder, an antenatal teacher, an archaeologist, a textile designer, a nutritionist, a silversmith, a farm worker, and a theatre director. Others were unemployed (some by choice, some by necessity), retired, working as full-time mothers and/or wives, or were school or college students. Their ages ranged from 15 to 73, with a mean of 35 and a standard deviation of 15.

Despite my efforts to obtain a diverse group of participants, there is a strong white, middle-class bias; only four black women, and twenty self-defined 'working-class' women participated in the research. Also only two Jewish lesbians were interviewed. This was, in part, their choice: politically conscious black lesbians I approached refused to be interviewed by a white woman, and radical working-class women declined to cooperate with the work of a hierarchical academic system from whose benefits they are systematically excluded. My own obvious whiteness and middle-classness (and self-definition as non-Jewish) severely limited the extent to which I could be perceived as an 'insider' by some women.

> Torn between the homophobia of the black community and the racism of the white lesbian movement, I need, as a black lesbian, to speak for myself and in my own voice, which is not the voice of the white world. I do not want my black experience filtered through your white academic language, the rage and passion edited out, explained away. I don't doubt your good intentions; I do doubt your ability to comprehend or accurately represent my lesbianism, which *cannot be taken out of the context of my blackness.* (Letter in response to my request for an interview; permission given to quote anonymously; her emphasis)

None of the twenty or so women I interviewed who did identify themselves as black, working class and/or Jewish were willing to discuss — and in fact often denied experiencing — oppressions other than those deriving from being a woman and a lesbian. If I had intended to use the interviews to make normative conclusions about lesbians as a group, the omission of these women would have invalidated or severely distorted my results. As it is, their absence is an important loss: the various different identity constructions of white middle-class gentile women are not invalidated or made untrue by my inability to tap the constructions of politically engaged black, working-class, or Jewish lesbians, but they are revealed as a limited and partial selection of the many different visions of the world and of themselves that lesbians as a whole have constructed.

The writings of Jewish (Beck, 1982a; Klepfisz, 1982), black (Blackdykewomon, 1981; Davenport, 1982; Clarke, 1983), American Indian (Brant, 1981; Chrystos, 1982) and Third World (Moraga and Smith, 1982; Hidalgo, 1984) lesbians are powerful suggestions of the existence of explicitly political lesbian identities evolved in part as a response to the 'fragmentation of loyalties' (Beck, 1982b: 81) that results when 'your lesbianism gets dealt with in an all-white atmosphere and your color gets dealt with in a straight context' (Moraga and Smith, 1982: 63). These accounts should, in theory, have been accessible using both interviewing and Q methodology.

Oppressed peoples (as Jews, people of colour, women and lesbians) are often convinced of the necessity for separatism, as a means of resisting assimilation into the dominant order, organizing politically, reclaiming our heritage and valuing our cultural differences. Membership of more than one such oppressed group means making decisions about where one's loyalties and priorities lie. In this particular study, many such lesbians chose to align themselves with their non-lesbian people and to exclude themselves from my research. While, as a middle-class white, I acknowledge and respect the political imperatives that guided this choice, as a woman and a lesbian I deeply regret the resultant loss to my understanding and description of the full richness of lesbians' experience, identities and ideologies.

There are also relatively few very young and very old lesbians in this study. Over two-thirds of the participants are aged between 20 and 50, with only thirteen women under the age of 20 (only one as young as 15), and only nine women over 60 (only one over 70). While this age spread is in fact considerably more wide-ranging than that of many other recent studies of lesbians (e.g. all the women interviewed by Ettorre [1980] are aged between 19 and 55), my failure to reach many younger and older women should be seen as indicative of the ageism — in society generally and in the lesbian and women's movements specifically — that prevents these women from identifying themselves as lesbians and/or from becoming involved in the lesbian counterculture. The oppression of ageism as it operates against younger lesbians is explored by, amongst others, Bieritz (1976), Ettinger (1976), Harris (1976), Donna (1978) and Alyson Publications (1980). The oppression of older lesbians is discussed with particular clarity by MacDonald and Rich (1983), and also by Batya (1978), Poor (1982), Almvig (1982) and Raphael and Robinson (1984).

Some other women refused to be interviewed, including some secretive, closeted lesbians who feared disclosure, and some radical lesbians by whom I, like a black interviewer in another study, was perceived as 'selling my people down the river for a few pieces of silver' (Josephson, 1970); many radical feminist lesbians were unconvinced as to the political utility of my decision to pursue an academic career. But because I used snowball sampling — i.e. asked each interviewee whether she could suggest others who might be willing to participate — I encountered relatively few direct refusals. As Mitroff (1974: 34) found using a similar recruitment technique, I had been 'previously certified by other members of their community as someone to whom they could open up.'

Except for two cases in which women specifically asked me to identify them using their real names (Jo and Shân), all the names used for research participants are pseudonyms and, although, in the interests of computerization, each woman was also assigned a number, I have in general supplied the pseudonym in addition to the number after each interview extract.

4

Lesbian Identities

In this chapter, a Q methodological study of lesbian identity accounts, the term 'lesbian identity' is intended to characterize the set of meanings ascribed by a woman to whatever social, emotional, sexual, political or personal configuration she intends when she describes herself as a 'lesbian'. A lesbian identity is a woman's subjective experience or intrasubjective account of her own lesbianism. I refer here to 'accounts' of lesbian identities as a reminder that the researcher has no direct access to that subjective experience, but must rely on what women are able and willing to say about it: an account of lesbian identity is the story (or one of the stories) a woman tells about her subjective experience of her lesbianism.

The research unit of this study is not the individual lesbian, nor her 'real', 'underlying' identity, but the identity account itself. This reflects, in part, the observation that it is only the account to which the social scientist has access (cf. Gilbert, 1983: 2–3). It also encourages a move away from the conceptualization of the account as derived from the psychology of individual lesbians, and suggests that the origins of accounts might be more readily located in their sociocultural and political contexts. For those researchers for whom the individual is the primary unit of study, the account is treated as the exclusive property of the individuals who provide it. When, as in this study, the *account* is defined as the primary unit of study, then, while account-gathering must depend initially upon individual account-providers, these people's psychologies are incidental to the research: because the account is no longer tied to the individual who provided it, the researcher can pursue her study of the account per se, broadening the research to find evidence of these accounts in the sociocultural milieu, to discover the ideologies with which they are associated, and the political interests which dictate their promotion or suppression. This approach serves to draw attention to the political, rather than the personal, features of lesbian accounts of identity.

Studies of the identity accounts elicited from members of other oppressed and socially marginalized groups have consistently revealed identity accounts which involve direct acceptance of the majority stereotype. Early studies on Jewish 'self-hate' (Lewin, 1948) or 'identification with the aggressor' (Sarnoff, 1951) were soon followed by similar work on black identities which located the same sort of 'self-hate' (Nobles, 1973) or 'negromacy' — a state 'ruled by confusion of self-worth and dependence upon white society for definition of self' (Thomas, 1971). This acceptance of the normative definition of one's own deviance has been widely noted: it is described as 'minority style indictment of one's own group' (Seeman, 1958) and characterized as 'acquiescence' by Rogers and Buffalo (1974), who note that 'the proverbial "shoe fits" and the deviant concedes his/her willingness to "wear it".' It has been speculated that 'lower status people generally find it less punishing to think of themselves as correctly placed by a just society than to think of themselves as exploited or victimized by an unjust society' (Lane, 1959, quoted in Adam, 1978: 52). It is identity accounts of this type which are accorded the lowest stage in the hierarchical models of lesbian identity discussed in Chapter 2.

One lesbian identity account that would, then, be expected to emerge from this study is an account reflecting the traditional version of lesbianism as a sickness, a sin, or a 'sorry state'. Other researchers have reported accounts of this nature among lesbians who 'admit regretfully that they still regard their homosexuality as a "weakness" ' (Kleinberg, 1977: x) and have 'introjected a sickness model of their identity and behaviour' (Hart, 1981: 64). Overall, as Adam (1978: 77) has noted, 'the literature still abounds with documents of internalized self-contempt among gay people,' and an identity account corresponding to this was expected to emerge here.

Equally, since Merton's (1957) distinction between the 'ordinary deviant' (or 'criminal') and the 'non-conformist', a number of researchers (e.g. Gusfield, 1967; Scott, 1969; Shoham, 1966) have conceptualized members of socially marginalized groups as facing a choice between basic acceptance of the majority culture norms they infract (with a tendency to concealment of transgressions), or, conversely, open challenge to and public dissent from the legitimacy of these norms (and attempts to change them). This literature, combined with my own lived experience as a 'non-conformist' lesbian, suggests that a second identity to emerge will be based upon a major challenge to the normative definition — a radical feminist construction of lesbianism.

It was also expected that identity accounts would be elicited which incorporate contemporary liberal humanistic reappraisals of the lesbian and her place within an 'enlightened' and 'pluralistic' society. There is very little explicit discussion of such identity accounts in the literature, most of which simply assumes the existence of such accounts in the 'mature' and 'mentally healthy' person and explores neither their content nor their implications. Related research does, however, offer a patchy and disjointed picture of some of the accounting mechanisms that can be employed. Briefly, these include the following.

1. 'Deviance disavowal', in which, at its most extreme, the person denies membership of the marginalized group (e.g. the name-changing Jew, the black who 'passes'). If concealment of this kind is impossible, then the person attempts to dissuade others from noticing her or his group membership. One study illustrates, for example, how the physically handicapped may assert that 'the handicap is only a small part of who I am' and draw attention away from their disability using books, religious symbols, badges, knitting etc. as cues to more socially valued labels and roles (Levitin, 1975).

2. 'Minstrelization' (Broyard, 1950), in which the person procures the approval of the dominant social group by behaving in exact conformity with the stereotype others have of such group members, thus being a 'predictable' or 'safe' deviant. The limp-wristed and effeminate gay man at least has the virtue of not disturbing the onlookers' preconceived notions about male homosexuality.

3. 'Role inversion', the reverse of the above, in which the person attempts to demonstrate in her or his own behaviour that her or his group is not what the stereotype says it is, e.g. Jews who are deliberately and overtly generous because Jews are typically characterized as being avaricious (Sartre, 1948).

4. 'Concern with in-group purification' (Goffman, 1963), which is manifested by behaviour and language guided by the idea that the minority's troubles are rooted in the misguided ways of a small faction among them, and the person attempts to purge from the group people thought to exhibit undesirable characteristics which might 'alienate' members of the dominant order, such as 'effeminate' or 'promiscuous' gay men (Hodges and Hutter, 1977) or aggressive, pushy, financially successful Jews (Sarnoff, 1951).

5. 'Fear of group solidarity' (Seeman, 1958), in which the person feels a strong resistance to any clearly identifiable group action on the group's problems, arguing that the answer lies, rather, in individual goodness.

It was expected, then, that elements such as these, found in the accounts of other oppressed groups, might emerge in some lesbians' accounts, but the way in which each relates to other aspects of an identity construction to form a cohesive account has not been documented.

Like those researchers whose work on lesbian identities is

discussed in Chapter 2, I have strong beliefs about which of the identities presented here is the 'best'. Unlike them, I do not glorify this identity account by designating it as the most 'well-adjusted', or placing it at the apex of some developmental hierarchy, with all other identity accounts trailing behind, indicative of psychological immaturity, but instead argue for my value claims explicitly, and from an overtly political perspective. I illustrate which of the identity accounts conform to liberal humanistic ideology, and argue that they thereby function to privatize lesbianism, removing it from the political domain. When women use these accounts, they are undermining radical feminist claims for lesbianism as a major political force, and for those of us who share those aims, such accounts are a tactical error. Liberal humanistic accounts of lesbianism are neither 'inaccurate' nor 'developmentally immature': they are politically inexpedient from a radical feminist perspective.

This first study, then, describes some of the different accounts of lesbian identity currently available, and speculates on the political interests and ideologies underlying each. In discussing the results of the Q sort study, I move away from reliance on specific Q sorts and interview protocols towards an examination of the ways in which these identity accounts are constructed and presented in the 'real world', the arguments and assumptions upon which they depend, and the political uses to which they are put.

Method
Following the principles described in Chapter 3, a sixty-one item Q sort was constructed (see Table 4.1), and mailed to forty-one self-defined lesbians, aged between 17 and 58, all but two of whom had also been interviewed. The sixty-one Q sort items were randomly numbered, typed on to 3″ × 5″ cards, shuffled, and posted, along with a standard set of instructions, to all participants. They were asked to distribute the items along a scale from +5 (most agree) to −5 (most disagree), with a central neutral category, in conformity with a quasi-normal distribution as follows:

Score	−5	−4	−3	−2	−1	0	+1	+2	+3	+4	+5
No. of items	(3)	(4)	(5)	(6)	(8)	(9)	(8)	(6)	(5)	(4)	(3)

As discussed in Chapter 3, the principles of random sampling are inappropriate in selecting Q sorters, and I was guided by my knowledge of the likely interests and allegiances of the potential participants, aiming to achieve breadth and diversity rather than randomness.

Table 4.1 *Q sort items for 'accounts of lesbian identity' study*

1. Being a lesbian gives me a sense of freedom.
2. I have enjoyed sex with men.
3. My relationship with my mother helps to explain why I am a lesbian.
4. I don't think it's necessary for me to tell everyone that I'm a lesbian.
5. I usually see myself as either 'butch' or 'femme' in my relationships with women.
6. I get on well with men.
7. I now find the idea of sex with men repugnant.
8. If I had a choice I would never have chosen to be lesbian.
9. I have been deeply in love with a man.
10. I came to lesbianism through feminism.
11. I have never been very 'feminine' in the conventional sense.
12. I always felt different from other girls.
13. Being a lesbian is *not* one of the most important things about me.
14. I would like to think that I would be faithful to my lover.
15. I feel an affinity with gay men.
16. If you truly love somebody then you put them first, before job, politics, children, everything.
17. I find it hard to feel sisterhood towards aggressive women.
18. I am/have been deeply in love with a woman.
19. Unless you have had, and rejected, sex with a man, you can never be certain that you are a genuine lesbian.
20. I find my lesbianism difficult to come to terms with.
21. I would prefer to have been born male.
22. Sometimes I wonder whether I am really a lesbian.
23. Any woman who has sex willingly with a man, and enjoys it, thereby stops being lesbian.
24. I think that all lesbian relationships contain an element of mother/daughter.
25. I enjoy sex with women.
26. You cannot choose to be a lesbian; if you are, you are.
27. The best thing about being lesbian is the sheer joy of the love we share; sex is secondary.
28. I feel good about being 'different'.
29. Sex with a woman is much more physically satisfying for me than sex could ever be with a man.
30. If a woman has never enjoyed sex with a woman, she cannot know she is a lesbian.
31. Part of my pleasure in being a lesbian is the way it shocks people and makes them disapprove.
32. There was nothing in my childhood that predisposed me to be a lesbian.
33. I would be a lesbian whatever my political and ideological beliefs.
34. I believe I was born a lesbian.
35. Even if I never had sex with a woman I would still be a lesbian.
36. Being a woman is very important to me.
37. My relationship with my father helps to explain why I am a lesbian.
38. My underlying sexual orientation is bisexual.
39. If I loved her I would stay with a partner even if we were sexually incompatible.
40. I don't like my sexuality being categorized and labelled.

41. I am *not* interested in a long-term monogamous relationship.
42. Being a lesbian is much more than having sex with women.
43. My relationships with women are more equal than any I had with men.
44. I think I would regret it if I never had my own children.
45. I feel angry towards heterosexual women.
46. There are times when I feel that my lesbianism is unnatural.
47. Basically I dislike men.
48. Being a lesbian has enabled me to grow up.
49. Sexual enjoyment is essential to any enduring lesbian relationship.
50. I find masculinity (hairy chests, hard muscular bodies) somewhat repulsive.
51. I enjoy the sensuality of the female body.
52. There are things I don't like about my sexuality.
53. Being a lesbian has enabled me to feel at home with my body.
54. I dislike 'macho' behaviour.
55. However hard I try not to, there are times when I feel ashamed that I am a lesbian.
56. I feel uncomfortable in the company of men.
57. I think that lesbians shouldn't have children.
58. Whatever happens, I will never change my mind about being lesbian.
59. Many lesbians I meet don't live up to my idea of what a lesbian should be.
60. I feel most relaxed and comfortable with just women around me.
61. I think I would have a happier life if I were not a lesbian.

Results

The forty-one completed Q sorts were analysed using factor analysis (principal components) (SPSS Inc., 1986), and resulted in seven factors which were rotated to simple structure (varimax criterion). The results indicated that the original 41 sets of rankings reduce to seven independent orderings. That is, seven accounts of lesbianism can be differentiated from these women's Q sort data. Factor loadings for each participant are given in Table 4.2. For each factor, the separate defining Q sorts (as indicated in Table 4.2) were merged, taking account of factor weight (Spearman, 1927), leading to a single set of factor scores for the statements. This comprises the factor array, as given in Table 4.3. Interpretation of the identity accounts relied upon an examination of relative factor scores in the factor arrays, supplemented by the use of interview accounts given by these same participants. Detailed discussion of the first five factors is presented in the Discussion section; the remaining two factors are only briefly discussed, and their interpretation was felt to be less secure, each being defined by only one woman.

Discussion

Factor I

As indicated in Table 4.2, participants 49, 58, 63, 69 and 79 define this factor, and although fifteen others (e.g. No. 3, my own sort)

Table 4.2 *Factor loadings for the 'account of lesbian identity' Q sort*[1]

Q sorter no.	I	II	III	IV	V	VI	VII
49	61 [2]	36	19	22	06	08	00
58	68	04	21	39	36	−01	17
63	65	36	18	23	08	−04	18
69	69	16	39	30	12	17	−04
79	75	20	16	35	00	12	10
72	26	64	24	−11	12	07	13
57	10	82	15	00	09	02	09
33	36	14	65	26	10	07	06
38	23	28	70	11	12	04	18
01	28	14	11	74	05	05	04
05	33	13	15	75	11	02	00
09	15	36	26	63	13	08	06
37	32	03	34	67	27	07	02
71	−05	05	14	−07	78	02	17
65	00	12	06	−18	58	12	03
12	16	26	14	18	01	75	12
10	34	00	09	05	15	24	62
02	65	36	21	46	08	05	03
03	51	00	22	55	03	11	23
04	30	55	12	48	07	00	−04
22	48	13	43	05	13	−11	25
27	49	19	30	36	14	12	21
52	00	27	11	45	27	02	65
59	51	52	02	24	−17	16	−02
61	65	19	41	11	25	17	07
70	06	28	29	02	17	22	12
74	57	20	11	48	−22	−06	08
75	61	18	00	46	−01	35	14
19	14	20	53	36	41	10	09
25	18	51	03	05	39	24	21
26	18	46	25	11	06	07	57
28	65	33	04	44	−12	21	09
29	36	00	26	45	−01	23	34
31	36	−12	28	42	−05	28	22
54	43	13	15	63	−15	12	−02
50	31	58	45	32	22	13	15
51	49	18	61	20	07	14	05
64	64	03	39	43	−02	14	19
80	72	03	26	41	06	00	09
81	52	40	00	18	45	06	24
90	24	29	43	12	54	04	05

[1] Loadings rounded off to two significant figures and decimal points omitted.
[2] Boxed loadings indicate those defining factors.

Table 4.3   *Factor arrays for 'accounts of lesbian identity' Q sort (Factors VI & VII omitted)*

Q sort item	I	II	III	IV	V
1	+5	+1	−1	+3	−4
2	0	+3	+1	−1	−2
3	−1	+1	−2	0	+4
4	+1	+2	+2	−1	+3
5	−3	−5	−5	−4	−1
6	0	+4	0	−3	0
7	+2	−3	0	+2	+1
8	−4	0	−2	−4	+5
9	−1	+3	−1	+1	−2
10	0	−3	−2	+4	−4
11	0	+2	−1	0	+2
12	+1	−4	−1	−1	+4
13	−3	+3	+3	−5	+1
14	+3	+4	+3	+1	+3
15	+1	+1	+1	−3	−1
16	−2	0	+2	−2	−1
17	0	−2	+3	0	+2
18	+5	+5	+5	+3	+4
19	−3	−2	−3	−2	−1
20	−4	−1	−4	−3	+1
21	−4	−4	−3	−5	−1
22	−4	+1	−2	0	0
23	−1	−3	0	0	−2
24	+1	0	−4	0	0
25	+3	+4	+2	+2	+2
26	−1	+1	+2	−5	+5
27	+2	0	+4	+4	0
28	+1	−2	+1	−1	−3
29	+2	+3	+5	+1	0
30	−2	+1	−3	−2	−4
31	−2	−1	−3	0	−5
32	−1	+1	0	+2	−5
33	+3	0	+3	−1	+1
34	−2	−1	+3	−4	−5
35	+1	−2	+4	+3	+3
36	+4	+2	+1	+5	−2
37	+1	0	−2	−1	+4
38	0	+2	−2	+1	−2
39	−1	−1	−1	+2	+2
40	0	+5	+4	0	0
41	−2	−4	−5	−2	−4
42	+3	0	+5	+5	0
43	+3	+4	+2	+4	+2
44	0	+5	+1	−1	−1
45	−3	−5	0	−2	−3

Table 4.3   *cont.*

Q sort item	I	II	III	IV	V
46	−5	−1	−4	−1	0
47	−1	−5	−1	+2	−1
48	+4	+1	−3	0	−3
49	+2	0	+1	−2	−1
50	+1	−3	0	+1	+2
51	+4	+3	+2	+3	0
52	−3	−2	−1	+1	+3
53	+2	+2	0	+1	−3
54	+2	+2	+1	+4	+1
55	−5	−3	−5	−3	+1
56	0	−4	0	+3	−2
57	−2	0	−1	−3	+1
58	+4	−1	+4	+2	+1
59	−1	−1	0	+1	−3
60	+5	−1	+1	+5	+3
61	−5	−2	−4	−4	+5

load significantly on this factor, they also have high loadings on other factors, and thus cannot be said to give 'pure' Factor I accounts of their lesbianism.

Women loading heavily on this factor emphasize the personal fulfilment they have achieved as a result of their lesbianism. All the five women defining this factor are or have been married (p<0.01), and they stress the advantages they have gained by rejecting their heterosexual lifestyles. (Factor scores are given to the right, under the factor number.)

		I
8.	If I had a choice I would never have chosen to be a lesbian.	−4
1.	Being a lesbian gives me a sense of freedom.	+5
48.	Being a lesbian has enabled me to grow up.	+4
60.	I feel most relaxed and comfortable with just women around me.	+5
61.	I think I would have a happier life if I were not a lesbian.	−5

Their accounts typically incorporate 'before-and-after' stories in which their pre-lesbian past is characterized as a life of conformity, attention to duty, and sexual unresponsiveness, while their lesbian present is depicted as fulfilling, rewarding and passionate.

> I'd been through all the other things; I'd been married, I'd done everything I was meant to do and so on. I had *tried*, you know. I had really *tried* to be heterosexual and to do all the correct things and I just knew then that it wasn't possible and the only way I could conceivably be happy was to be this way. Francesca (58)

> I thought for years, you see that I was frigid and I didn't love Richard

and I was frigid and unresponsive and a non-sexual kind of being. . . . It really didn't occur to me that maybe I was making the wrong kind of . . . or going in the wrong direction for me. I just thought, you know, that that was the nature I was. And it's been extraordinarily liberating for me to find that I'm not as I thought I was. I am actually much more passionate and much more of a sexual being than I'd thought. Pippa (49)

I think for about three years I lived in my own imagination and I hadn't met any lesbians at all, ever, in my life, although, you know, I must have done, but I didn't recognize them as such. I just had the growing feeling that I wanted . . . well, I didn't know what I did want. I wanted to know women closely and, clearly, sexually, and yet I didn't and couldn't believe it. It seemed too extraordinary, too way out, too unlike my life, which was a secure middle-class life with a husband and two children. There didn't seem to be any room for my fantasies and imaginations and they were well tucked away . . . The growth process took many years. Helen (63)

The personal fulfilment which their lesbianism accords them is central to these accounts:

I have never stopped feeling relief and happiness about discovering myself and, you know, accepting about myself and finding all these other women, and it means that I'm happy almost every day of my life. . . . Well, I mean, obviously one's had unhappy moments, but I've never regretted being a lesbian, or becoming a lesbian, if you want to put it that way, or coming out, or whatever. I mean, at least one was alive, you know, and doing the things that one was meant to do, doing the things that were natural to one. Francesca (58)

These women are very sure that they are indeed lesbian, and that they will never return to heterosexuality:

I

22.	Sometimes I wonder whether I really am a lesbian.	−4
58.	Whatever happens, I will never change my mind about being lesbian.	+4

I'm sure I'm a lesbian. I don't have any doubts. I mean, I made up my mind late, but I made it up very definitely. Helen (63)

I certainly know very clearly that I'm not going back into relating sexually with men. Pippa (49)

Now I don't think there's any possibility of me having a heterosexual relationship. Angela (69)

These women are not ashamed about their lesbianism, nor do they think it unnatural, and there's nothing they dislike about their sexuality. (All the following items have higher negative scores for Factor I than for any other.)

I

55.	However hard I try not to, there are times when I feel ashamed that I am a lesbian.	−5
46.	There are times when I feel that my lesbianism is unnatural.	−5
52.	There are things I don't like about my sexuality.	−3

The account represented by Factor I, then, depicts lesbianism in very positive terms as a route through which happiness, personal growth and fulfilment can be attained: through lesbianism a woman 'discovers her true self', 'gets in touch with her own feelings' and becomes a more fulfilled and emotionally healthy human being. The 1970s has produced a large proportion of lesbian (and lesbian–feminist) literature which draws on this theme, and stresses, in sharp contradiction to Radcliffe Hall's 'well of loneliness', the positive nature of lesbianism as a source of self-fulfilment. Coming out as lesbian, 'I am whole, a rediscovered self' (Faye, 1980: 178), and through lesbianism 'I am reclaiming my true womynhood, learning to truly know and love myself and other wimmin' (Toll, 1980: 29).

This account can be characterized as a laywoman's version of Self Theory and the pursuit of positive psychological health (cf. Jahoda, 1958; Rogers, 1959; Maslow, 1962) which became socially sedimented during the decade 1965–75, and which is well-represented by the wide selection of glossy American psychology textbooks of that era, with titles like *Born to Win: Transactional Analysis with Gestalt Experiments* (James and Jongeward, 1971), *The Way to Fulfillment: Psychological Techniques* (Bühler, 1971) or *Growth of Personal Awareness: A Reader in Psychology* (Stricker and Merbaum, 1973) and illustrations showing couples running through fields of daisies, or silhouetted against a setting sun, and naked children playing on seashores. The explanation 'I'm doing it because it makes me happy and fulfilled' has consequently acquired considerable socially persuasive power as a justification for otherwise questionable behaviour.

From the perspective of the lesbian, this account is important not only in explaining and justifying lesbianism to a potentially hostile audience but also in presenting it as a positive and attractive option. It explicitly challenges the traditional image of the lesbian as a shadowy creature haunting a seedy twilight world and enduring a life of unmitigated misery — 'the very antithesis of fulfillment and happiness' (Kronemeyer, 1980: 7). According to this traditional account, the lesbian leads a 'lonely, difficult and unhappy life' (Kenyon, 1978: 112) of 'frustration and tragedy' (West, 1968: 261) troubled by all the 'personal confusion, anguish and fruitless search for love which may be the products of maldevelopment' (Pattison, 1974): 'agony, sorrow, tragedy, fear and guilt of both unconscious and conscious nature . . . pervades the homosexual's life' (Socarides, 1972). According to this version:

> The label 'gay' behind which they hide is a defence mechanism against the emptiness, the coldness, and the futility of their lives. (Romm, 1965)

Kriegman (1969) claims that, 'despite propaganda to the contrary, there is no such thing as a well-adjusted, happy homosexual'.

Apologists for homosexuals have increasingly argued that, despite social discrimination, it *is* possible for homosexual men and lesbians to be happy and healthy human beings. In the early 1970s, a spate of psychological testing on non-patient lesbians revealed them to be significantly less neurotic than heterosexual women (Wilson and Greene, 1971), possessing more 'inner direction' and 'spontaneity' (Freedman, 1971: 78), 'goal-direction' and 'self-acceptance' (Siegelman, 1972), and scoring significantly higher than control heterosexual groups on tests designed to measure independence, resilience, composure and self-sufficiency (Hopkins, 1969). Freedman (1975) argues that 'homosexuals may be healthier than straights' because their sexual 'orientation' encourages them to 'centre' ('discover and live according to their own values'), to transcend limiting and restricting sex roles, and to enjoy a freer sexuality.

In its feminist form, this account uses the 'inner peace and self-fulfilment' rhetoric as part of its recruitment campaign. Radicalesbians (1969) describe lesbianism as leading to 'liberation of self . . . inner peace . . . love of self and all women': through lesbianism we 'find, reinforce and validate our real selves'. In a recent statement, the Leeds Revolutionary Feminist Group (1981) argues:

> . . . yes, it is better to be a lesbian. The advantages include knowing that you are not directly servicing men, living without the strain of a glaring contradiction in your personal life, uniting the personal and the political, loving and putting your energies into those you are fighting alongside rather than those you are fighting against, and the possibility of greater trust, honesty and directness in your communication with women.

However, this account, while ostensibly employed to justify lesbianism, is in fact drawn from and supports a more fundamental aspect of the dominant ideology — the focus on personal change as a substitute for political change. Lesbianism, in this account, is a product sold on the basis of what it is supposed to offer the individual: like psychodrama, encounter groups, rebirthing therapy, psychoanalysis and fantasy workshops (all of which are described by Cohen and Taylor, 1976: 103) as being 'deliberately directed towards accommodation rather than resistance to paramount reality'), lesbianism is represented as a route to self-awareness, self-actualization, happiness and inner peace.

The use of the ideologies of self-fulfilment and self-awareness as justifications for apparently 'deviant' actions is a relatively new phenomenon (Tedeschi and Reiss, 1981: 293), and a number of

recent authors (e.g. Jacoby, 1975; Schur, 1976) have described this
new 'awareness movement' as a reactionary force.

> Self-awareness is the new panacea. Across the country, Americans are
> frantically trying to 'get in touch' with themselves, to learn how to
> 'relate' better, and to stave off outer turmoil by achieving inner
> peace. . . . While the movement provides middle-class consumers with
> an attractive new product, attention is diverted away from the more
> serious problems that plague our society — poverty, racism, environ-
> mental decay, crime, widespread corporate and governmental fraud.
> (Schur, 1976: 5)

As Jacoby (1975) points out, the ideology of 'self-awareness' and
inner peace relegates social products to the position of private
pleasures and woes. The role of political or institutional processes is
de-emphasized.

Finally, if the attainment of personal happiness is made a priority,
then the forgoing of immediate gratification, or actual self-sacrifice,
that can be necessary parts of a political struggle, become
incomprehensible — may even be dismissed as 'masochistic'. It is
this very ideology that is used to discredit radical members of
oppressed groups. Greenberg (1950), for example, opposes Jewish
activism on the grounds that self-definition in terms of a social group
leads us to 'do violence to ourselves as personalities and interfere
with that self realisation which I conceive as one of the primary
goals of human striving', and Broyard (1950) has similarly argued
that 'today the anti-Negro is a secondary problem; their first
problem is their individual selves, their own authenticity'.

As Schur (1976: 180) has remarked — with reference to
homosexuality — '"out of the closets and into the growth center" is
no substitute for the militant rallying cry, "out of the closets and
into the streets".'

To conclude, then, an explanation of lesbianism in terms of
personal happiness and self-fulfilment serves to remove lesbianism
from the political arena and to reduce it to a private and personal
solution. This, then, is an account clearly acceptable in terms of the
dominant patriarchal order.

Factor II

Factor II is defined by participants 72 and 57 (and six other women
also have significant loadings on this factor). The theory on which
this account of lesbianism depends is based on the beliefs that
women respond to 'the person, not the gender' and 'it all depends
who you fall in love with'.

One of the most striking differences between these factor scores
and those of other factors is on items relating to men; these women

describe their social, emotional and sexual interaction with men very favourably.

		II
47.	Basically I dislike men.	−5
56.	I feel uncomfortable in the company of men.	−4
6.	I get on well with men.	+4
9.	I have been deeply in love with a man.	+3
2.	I have enjoyed sex with men.	+3
7.	I now find the idea of sex with men repugnant.	−3
50.	I find masculinity (hairy chests, hard, muscular bodies) somewhat repulsive.	−3

These items have nothing like the same salience for any other factor. (The sums of the absolute values of the factor scores for items 47, 56, 6, 9, 2, 7 and 50 are: Factor I = 5; Factor II = 25; Factor III = 3; Factor IV = 13; Factor V = 10.) All the women loading on this factor have had sexual relationships with men ($p<0.05$), and none rules out the possibility of doing so in the future, because the possibility remains that they might 'fall in love' with a man.

For women who define this factor, the crux of the matter is 'true love':

> For me it's so rare that I find someone with whom something magic happens . . . I can't think of a way of saying it that doesn't sound totally one hundred percent corny, but I suppose I might meet a man I'd feel that way about, and I might meet a woman. Alison (57)

> I think that having reached my age and stage now, that if I got involved with somebody then that would be *it*. But I mean, it could be a male or a female. I think that whatever it would be, it would be a commitment. . . . I've had three major relationships in my life. The first was with the man I married, who is overtly heterosexual; I mean, he's flirtatious and . . . I won't say chauvinistic, because I don't think he is — he's a very sensitive and interesting man, but nevertheless, very male. And during that relationship — and I was married for twenty years — I had a long-standing affair with a man who lived with us, in the same house, who was a transexual. And then I met a woman who I just fell absolutely head over heels in love with. So at the stage where I am at the moment, I have no sexual relationships, but I would just as happily have a relationship with a man as with a woman. Wendy (72)

Because they see the possibility of a relationship with a man in the future, and because they've enjoyed relationships with both men and women in the past, women presenting this account feel that their sexuality cannot be classified as truly lesbian, and are consequently reluctant to label themselves, or to invest too much in a lesbian identity. Their scores for the following items are quite different from those of Factor I (given to the right in parentheses for comparison), who feel strongly that they don't want sexual relationships with men again and have invested a great deal in their lesbian identities.

	II	(I)
40. I don't like my sexuality being categorized and labelled.	+5	(0)
13. Being a lesbian is *not* one of the most important things about me.	+3	(−3)
58. Whatever happens, I will never change my mind about being lesbian.	−1	(+4)
22. Sometimes I wonder whether I am really a lesbian.	+1	(−4)

More than women defining any of the other first five factors, these women present an account of themselves as bisexual:

> Bisexual can sound like such a cop-out. I think it generally does apply to me probably. Not totally, but yes . . . I certainly wouldn't emphasize heterosexual. I think bisexual is more acccurate, but I usually just say I'm gay. Alison (57)

> I definitely do think that I'm bisexual. Wendy (72)

	II
38. My underlying sexual orientation is bisexual.	+2

According to this account, then, lesbianism is the result of 'falling in love' with a person who happens to be a woman: it is not an essential state of being, and the 'lesbian' can become 'heterosexual' if her next 'true love' is male.

Like the 'true happiness' account of Factor I, this construction of lesbianism is widely documented by lesbians, as in this extract from an interview with Charlotte Wolff:

> S.R. Some of the women I'm thinking of would say — not — 'I've fallen in love with a woman, so I'm a lesbian' — but — 'I've fallen in love with this *person* who happens to be a woman.' It's often a very romantic view: I've found my Ideal Lover. You're saying that we're all potentially capable of falling in love with any human being irrespective of gender.
> C.W. Yes, why speak of falling in love with a sex, when it is a *person* and the sex is secondary.
> (Wolff, Charlotte [1977] 'Falling in Love Again', interviewed before the publication of her book on bisexuality, *Spare Rib* 63: 38–9)

Similar accounts are manifested in a number of autobiographical and fictional works: Rule (1975: 10) quotes lesbians as saying: I'm not a lesbian really. I'm living with a woman now, but I might be living with a man next year; why should I be labelled?'; Schwartz

(1978) makes one of her characters say: 'Don't use that word! I hate that word — I'm no lesbian, I just happen to love Doris and both of us happen to be women,' and Baetz (1980: 15) comments that 'I had always felt that I was in love with a person who just happened to be a woman.' In one study of lesbian-identity development, it was found that 45 percent of respondents did not see themselves as lesbian as an immediate result of their first relationship, and the authors explain this finding in terms very similar to the identity account described here: a woman's first homosexual relationship, they say, is seen as 'special' and she thinks of herself as a person who loves a particular woman, without that having any particular implications for identity (DeMonteflores and Schultz, 1978).

Within lesbian feminist literature, Cartledge and Hemmings (1982) have described a process they call 'Cupid's Dart (the romantic conversion)' which largely parallels pair-bonding themes presented in this account, and Johnston (1973: 92) describes 'the dark ages of our political consciousness' when

> the person you were involved with was first and foremost a person or special love object with no certain significance as to gender so that if it happened to be a woman it could as well be a man the next time if the right *person* came along.

There are strong parallels between this account and the normative construction of bisexuality. The liberal defence of bisexuality is often expressed in terms of the bisexual's supposed openness to people as people, irrespective of gender, her liberating capacity for transcending the artificial and restricting categories of 'hetero-sexuality' and 'homosexuality': unlike the lesbian, who is unable to relate fully to men, and unlike the heterosexual woman who is unable to relate fully to women, the bisexual can love everyone.

Responding to suggestions, commonly made by both lesbians and heterosexuals, that the bisexual should 'choose which side of the fence she wants to be on', Jem (1975: 66–7) says, 'I'm not on the fence at all. I chose both sides; I chose in my life not to build that particular fence,' and she ends with the rallying call, 'Down with fences, up with love.'

In terms of the dominant order of Western culture, the rhetoric of romantic love offers a powerful source of justification and provides a legitimating context for sexual activity (Gagnon, 1977: 180). The dominant value system implicitly depicts 'true love' as a moral imperative, the overpowering effects of which may excuse, but the incapacity for which must condemn, homosexuals and our relation-ships. Many psychoanalysts who present lesbianism as a sickness deny the homosexual's ability to form loving relationships:

Instead of union, cooperation, solace, stimulation, emotional enrich-
ment, and a maximum opportunity for creative interpersonal maturation
and realistic fulfillment, there are multiple underlying factors which
constantly threaten any ongoing homosexual relationship: destruction,
mutual defeat, exploitation of the partner and the self, oral-sadistic
incorporation, aggressive onslaughts, and attempts to alleviate anxiety
— all comprising a pseudo-solution to the aggressive and libidinal
conflicts that dominate and torment the individuals involved. (Socarides,
1972)

The pathologists have described homosexual relationships as
'inherently self-limiting' (Moberly, 1983: 84) liaisons which 'do not
contribute to the individual's need for stability and love' (Wilbur,
1965: 281) and, 'although basic sexual urges may . . . be fulfilled to
varying degrees, a feeling of complete attainment of romantic
longings probably never occurs' (Bieber, 1971). According to one
author, 'homosexuality is not another form of loving but an
alternate way of expressing hostility . . . an erotic form of hatred
(Hendin, 1978).

Some of those who defend lesbianism draw on the same moral
rhetoric to argue the basic equality or isomorphism of heterosexual
and homosexual or lesbian love, and homophobia scales often
demand that the 'unprejudiced' person reject the 'pathological' view
outlined above (e.g. 'I find it hard to believe that homosexuals can
really love each other' [Price, 1982]), while accepting that homosexual partnerships are fundamentally similar to heterosexual ones
and should be recognized as such (e.g. 'Homosexual "marriages"
should be officially recognized' [Dunbar, Brown and Amoroso,
1973]; 'A homosexual's partner should have the same legal status as
does a heterosexual partner' [Cuenot and Fugita, 1982]). Items such
as these continue to affirm the value of the romantic pair bond, but
de-emphasize the importance of the gender of the individuals
involved.

Authors who adhere to the liberal humanistic 'lifestyle' model
reject the notion that homosexuals are incapable of love and stress
the existence of romantic love between lesbians:

To say that the homosexual *by definition* cannot love is the Big Lie, a
gigantic hoax compounded for too many centuries. . . . Love is love.
How can you put a limiting value judgment on orgasm, ecstasy, bliss, or
the euphoric state, whether it is heterosexual or homosexual, if it
culminates from the love of one human being for another human being.
(Martin and Mariah, 1972: 126)

The sex researchers Bell and Weinberg (1978) describe five 'types'
of homosexual, but confer their scientific approval on those they
label 'close coupled', who approximate to the heterosexual ideal of

a happy marriage: they have tastefully furnished homes, radiate warmth, provide the interviewer with freshly baked chocolate chip cookies, and are discovered to have 'superior adjustment' (p. 220), being the 'least depressed or lonely' and the 'happiest' of all homosexual types. Introducing a survey of such closely coupled homosexuals (whom she refers to as 'married'), Mendola argues that

> the essence of a committed relationship is the same whether the union is between two men, two women, or a man and a woman. . . . Love and commitment transcend sexual orientation. They are universal experiences that are shared by all people. (Mendola, 1980: 2)

This same rhetoric of romantic love can also be used to assert the *superiority* of lesbianism over heterosexuality. Several authors have argued that, because of social inequalities between men and women, 'the conditions for learning to love fully and without fear are at present met only in a homosexual setting' (Kelly, 1972). A leaflet produced by the Campaign for Homosexual Equality (CHE, n.d.) claims that, unlike heterosexual love:

> Love between women is not a relationship of subordination and domination, of activity and passivity — it is a love between complete equals which profits from each woman's knowledge of her own, and therefore her lover's body.

Interviewees often interpreted their own experience in these terms:

> I just feel that two women really can understand each other so much better, and women are so much more able to talk about their feelings and really to be open with each other. I think in some ways you do get a much deeper relationship than you do with at least most heterosexual couples that I've observed. Rita (6)

> I just came to the final conclusion that women just cannot have equal relationships with men. They just can't. And what I wanted from him he could never give me — and what women want from men generally they can never really give us, not really: and that is this emotional identification, an emotional support and understanding. Vicky (24)

As the preceding extracts imply, this argument can be extended to query the possibility of 'true love' between *heterosexuals*, thus reversing the traditional formulation:

> Is love possible between heterosexuals; or is it all a case of women posing as nymphs, earth-mothers, sex-objects, what-have-you; and men writing the poetry of romantic illusions to these walking stereotypes? (Shelley, 1972)

However, this superiority of lesbianism is bought at a heavy price. An account of lesbianism which draws, as does the account discussed here, on the ideology of 'true love' is clearly borrowed from the official morality. The argument that lesbians are as (or more) capable of romantic love than heterosexuals serves to grant legitimacy to and reinforce the reification of love as a powerful and authentic expression of a person's 'true self', and disguises its socially constructed nature (Averill, 1985: 94). The social construction of romantic love depends, moreover, on precisely the privatization and personalization that contributes to the oppression of lesbianism:

> Only in a society with an enormously powerful ideology of the individual, in which the 'alienation' of the individual from the larger society is not only tolerated but even encouraged and celebrated, can the phenomenon of romantic love be conceivable. (Solomon, 1981: 136)

'Falling in love' is represented as a fundamentally personal experience, an expression of inner drives, needs and passions independent of social control: the euphoria of romantic love — the idealization of the beloved, the sense of 'floating on a cloud', of feeling 'giddy and carefree' (see the 'romantic love' scale by Kanin et al., 1972: 46) is considered particularly appropriate for women, who are 'subjected to a highly romanticized anticipatory socialization for love and marriage that begins in early childhood' (Kanin et al., 1972). And if two people really love each other, then in an important sense their actions are beyond moral censure — at worst they are exonerated as 'crimes passionels': 'the only intrinsic evil is lack of love' (Robinson, 1963: 118). Women who account for their lesbianism in these terms are, then, borrowing from, and affirming this aspect of the official morality, and in so doing achieve a form of social acceptance. As Sprey (1972: 81) points out, with reference to premarital sexual intercourse, 'violations of our [sic] traditional sex code seem easier to rationalize with "affection" than without such an association.' The affirmation of the centrality and importance of intimate couple relationships facilitates the acceptance of lesbianism as a variation on love's theme.

An account of lesbianism in terms of romantic love, then, serves the purposes of the lesbian in that it enables her to present her supposedly 'deviant' experience in conformity with the idiom of the dominant culture, relating her own experience to that presumed to be enjoyed by heterosexuals, and presenting her lesbianism in a morally unimpeachable light.

From the perspective of the dominant order, this account of lesbianism is useful in that it affirms the pervasive moral rhetoric of romantic love fundamental to the official morality which serves to remove personal relationships from the political arena, and to legitimate the institution of marriage. The effect of this ideology is to privatize sexual/romantic love, as a kind of opium of the masses:

> the narrow enclave of the nuclear family serves as a macrosocially innocuous 'play area', in which the individual can safely exercise his [*sic*] world-building proclivities without upsetting any of the important social, economic and political applecarts . . . . The marital adventure can be relied upon to absorb a large amount of energy that might otherwise be expended more dangerously. The ideological themes of familism, romantic love, sexual expression, maturity and social adjustment . . . function to legitimate this enterprise. (Berger and Kellner, 1964)

The irony of this account of lesbianism (and its usefulness to the dominant order) is that the lesbian deviates from the dominant order but then achieves assimilation (in some measure) into it, by articulating its morality and, paradoxically, providing evidence of its wide scope and applicability: the idiom of romantic love is seen to explain the experience even of those who are, theoretically, least committed to upholding the official ideology of which it forms a part. In this way the lesbian is no longer an embarrassment to, but a vindication of, the dominant morality. In fact, an account demonstrating her allegiance to the dominant order, in the face of her apparent defiance of it, is the price exacted for social acceptability:

> The more a stigmatized individual deviates from the norm, the more wonderfully he [*sic*] may have to express possession of the standard subjective self if he is to convince others that he possesses it, and the more they may demand that he provide them with a model of what an ordinary person is supposed to feel about himself. (Goffman, 1963: 141)

The lesbian, in invoking the culturally approved rhetoric of romantic love is accredited with a fundamental humanity and similarity to heterosexuals; and the morality of the dominant order is articulated, vindicated and reinforced.

Factor III
The women who define this factor (Nos. 33 and 38) account for their lesbianism as a personal sexual orientation and express their dislike of being defined solely in terms of this small part of themselves. This account emphasizes the other facets of their personalities, their other interests and involvements. This reflects their basically 'apolitical' stance; they value personal relationships, love, commitment and fidelity between individuals over and above what they see as 'political dogma' or 'group movements'.

III

13. Being a lesbian is not one of the most important things
    about me.   +3

40. I don't like my sexuality being labelled and categorized.   +4

I don't like labels. I wouldn't say 'I'm a lesbian,' because I'm a hell of a lot of other things besides. I'm interested in art; I'm a bit of a philosopher; I'm a bit of a poet, right? I wouldn't say 'I am a lesbian,' because that seems to exclude everything else. Charlotte (33)

I'm me — I'm Phyllis Jones (Ps.); I'm a social worker; I'm a mother; I've been married. I like Tschaikowsky; I like Bach; I like Beethoven; I like ballet. I enjoy doing a thousand and one things, and, oh yes, in amongst all that, I happen to be a lesbian; I love a woman very deeply. But that's just a *part* of me. So many other lesbians seem to have let it overtake them, and they are lesbians first and foremost. Phyllis (38)

Whereas the women who define Factor II don't like being labelled 'lesbian' because they find the label inappropriate, women presenting this account, on the other hand, are very clear that they are indeed lesbian, and believe that they were born lesbian.

III

58. Whatever happens I will never change my mind about
    being lesbian.   +4
34. I believe I was born a lesbian.   +3

I think I was born this way. I just think some people are born this way and some people are born that way. Some things are shaped in the way of a tree and others become cabbages, and yet other things become birds; and I just happen to be a lesbian. Charlotte (33)

It is part of me as is the colour of my hair and the colour of my eyes. That is what I am. That is my sexual preference. It's what turns me on. So I believe that it's something genetic. Phyllis (38)

This account relies on a firmly essentialist conception of lesbianism:

III

26. You cannot choose to be a lesbian; if you are, you are.   +2

The past is reconstructed so that a woman was really 'always' lesbian; rather than choosing lesbianism, she 'discovers' or 'accepts' what she was all along.

I knew I had feelings for women and when I found out what being a lesbian was, how it was defined, I thought, 'oh yes, so that's what I am.' Charlotte (33)

I had this bit of me which I didn't really accept and I didn't like. I *didn't* like it. You know, I wished it would go away, and it wouldn't. Once I got to the stage of thinking that it would be rather nice, you know . . . that what was wrong with lying in another woman's arms?, that there was nothing wrong with it if it was what *she* wanted and what *I* wanted. So having accepted my sexuality for what it is, and having discarded, if you like, the heterosexual role, which I now do believe was a cover which I hid behind for twenty-two years, I'm more at peace with me. Phyllis (38)

The account represented by this factor explains lesbianism as a private sexual preference or orientation, innately determined, and as natural and normal as heterosexuality. Lesbianism is characterized as a personal matter which describes only a small and relatively insignificant part of the 'whole person': lesbians are *people* first and foremost.

This account is widely represented in lesbians' own writing. The earliest British magazine for lesbians, founded in 1963, *Arena Three*, its now defunct successor, *Sappho*, and a more recent arrival, *Special K* (magazine of an organization, Kenric, which advertises itself as a 'non-political group for gay women'), all offer rich documentation of this account. Readers' letters (sandwiched between the horoscopes, recipes, driving tips, and articles on topics ranging from tourism in Yorkshire to investing in Georgian silver — the standard fare of many women's magazines) are largely devoted to rejecting the 'extremist' views of their more militant sisters, and articulating and justifying their own individualistic account of lesbianism:

> We too are normal human beings. We only differ from them in as much as our emotional and sexual needs are fulfilled by members of our own sex. . . . I am heartily against GLF's slogan 'Gay is Good.' It isn't, neither is it bad. It just *IS*. When oh when will people accept homosexuality as a fact of life which, when all is said and done, has existed for thousands of years. (Letter in *Arena Three* 8(6), 1971, her emphasis)

> We, together with many others, consider ourselves people in the first instance. Our sexuality is incidental and does not set us apart from our fellow men and women. Therefore we do not find it necessary to put labels on ourselves setting us apart by saying 'we are lesbians' and then begging for acceptance. We agree with Myrtle . . . that a large section of the population are ignorant, fearful and lacking in understanding about us. For years we and others like us have quietly beavered away in society, just being ourselves with certainty and without fear. We have many friends and acquaintances who must know of our gayness though this is only discussed with close friends, not because we are afraid, but because we believe that such a personal matter as one's sexual preferences should be private whether one be homo or heterosexual. So, dear Myrtle, you do your thing — wear your badges and labels, proclaim your sexuality to the Universe as childlike you shriek for acceptance and approval (or is it martyrdom?) — but don't knock us well-adjusted gays by calling us cowards! (Letter in *Sappho* 6(11), 1978)

The emphasis is on the fundamental similarity between the lesbian and the heterosexual, and the (ideally) minor or incidental nature of sexual preference in everyday human interaction: 'I'm the same as thee,/Just differently orientated sexually' (Gill, 1977, untitled poem in *Close Encounters of the Lesbian Kind*, Journal of the Aberdeen Lesbian Group).

Accounts drawing on themes similar to those discussed here have been referred to by other researchers on lesbianism (e.g. Peplau et al., 1978) and employed by other oppressed groups (Sarnoff, 1951; Kaye, 1982: 29) and this account is very successful in its elicitation and promotion of a form of social acceptance. Women who behave in accordance with this account are 'nice' or 'well-adjusted' lesbians: they are following exactly the guidelines laid down for them by representatives of the dominant moral order. Discussing the social management of stigmatized persons, Goffman (1963: 140) says:

> The individual is advised to see himself [*sic*] as a fully human being like anyone else, one who at worst happens to be excluded from what is, in the last analysis, merely one area of social life. He is not a type or a category, but a human being.

This advice is reflected in much of the literature prepared by heterosexuals for consumption by lesbians and homosexual men: it can be understood as instructional material designed to inform us how to construct our homosexuality so that it will be found acceptable on their terms. The following extract, taken from a book produced in association with the Samaritans and designed to help troubled young people, is clearly designed to promote this individualistic account of homosexuality:

> It's very bad to define people by their sexuality alone. I don't mind people saying 'Westall hates buying new clothes' or even 'Westall picks fluff out of his navel for a hobby.' But if they started cocking an eyebrow and saying 'He's a *heterosexual* of course' I would start getting narked. My sexuality is only a small part of me; it *doesn't* explain my whole being. . . . Homosexuals are *persons* first. (Westall, 1978: 117, his emphases)

Factor III, then, represents an account well-adapted to the demands of the heterosexual social system. Drawing on socially sedimented themes concerning the privatization of sex, the concept of 'sexual orientation' as a fixed and given entity, and the liberal reluctance to identify ('label') 'people' as members of oppressed groups, this account justifies, for the lesbian, the need to think and act in accordance with the recommendations of the dominant culture.

Factor IV

The women defining Factor IV (Nos. 1, 5, 9 and 37) present their lesbianism within the political context of radical feminism, and two of these women are the only self-defined Political Lesbians who completed this Q sort. Only Factor IV gives a positive score to the item:

		IV
10.	I came to lesbianism through feminism.	+4

It was only through feminism, through learning about the oppression of women by men and the part that the enforcement of heterosexuality, the conditioning of girls into heterosexuality plays in that oppression, it was through that that I decided that whatever happens I will never go back to being fucked by men. My resolution to choose sexual partners from among women only, that decision was made because I'm a feminist, not because I'm a lesbian. I take the label 'lesbian' as part of the strategy of the feminist struggle. Alice (1)

Feminism was the catalyst that enabled me to see myself as a lesbian. Josie (5)

I came really to feeling warmth and sisterhood and enjoying the company of women through the Women's Movement. Isobel (9)

I think that by joining the Women's Movement and having my consciousness raised I realized that there was more than just hetero-sexuality. . . . By coming into contact with other ideas where lesbianism is valid, where lesbianism isn't something sick and horrid and perverted and deviant, it sort of meant I was free to choose. Lesley (37)

These women report playing an active part in the creation of their own lesbianism — they were *not* born lesbian, or made lesbian by early environmental factors.

		IV
26.	You cannot choose to be a lesbian; if you are, you are.	−5
8.	If I had a choice I would never have chosen to be lesbian.	−4
34.	I believe I was born lesbian.	−4
32.	There was nothing in my childhood that predisposed me to be a lesbian.	+2

This is a fundamentally *constructionist* account of sexuality: it is argued that heterosexuality is constructed in a patriarchal society for the benefit of men.

I think I was brought up in a heterosexual society and took in male definitions of sexuality. You know, I was brought up as a heterosexual and I really sort of soaked in the patriarchal values. It wasn't until I got into the Women's Movement that I saw that there could exist a different value system, a different way of looking at things which was better for me as an individual and for womankind in general. You know, that the things I'd been brought up to believe were very much for the benefit of men, and I realized that there was another way of looking at things which was sort of a woman-centred, woman-identified way. So no, I don't think I was a latent lesbian. I do think every woman can be a lesbian, but I . . . . No, I just don't believe in an essential sexuality. I think sexuality is constructed in terms of ideas and consciousness. Lesley (37)

The radical feminist argument is that men have forced women into heterosexuality in order to exploit them, and that lesbians, in rejecting male definitions of sexuality, are undermining the patriarchy.

> I do think being a lesbian is a political thing. I do think it's to do with consciousness. I do think the ruling ideas of every age are the ideas of the ruling class, and I do think the sex-class of men has defined sexuality. And I do think it's by male definitions of sexuality that women are oppressed under patriarchy. I think of lesbianism as being a political challenge to male definitions of sexuality. Lesley (37)

For these women it is central to their identity that they are women and lesbians:

		IV
13.	Being a lesbian is *not* one of the most important things about me.	−5
36.	Being a woman is very important to me.	+5

Being a lesbian is being a 'woman-identified woman', and it is this aspect that is seen as most important: they do not identify as 'gay women' or feel any solidarity with gay men.

		IV
15.	I feel an affinity with gay men.	−3

> I resent being put in a category with men when my sexuality is referred to, when the vital part of that sexuality is that it specifically excludes men. Lesbianism has nothing to do with men and that includes male homosexuals. What have I got to do with their promiscuous cottaging, their measuring up of one another's bodies the whole time, their exploitative, youth-based sordid little escapades. They're just as bad as heterosexual men — worse really. They're what heterosexual men would be if they didn't have to present a veneer of civilized and mature behaviour in order to attract the women they need to service them. Homosexual men are men without the civilizing effects of women. Ugh! Alice (1)

> I identify much more with feminist women than with gay men, so I'd prefer to label myself as a *woman* with a sexuality, as a woman-identified woman, rather than a gay person or a female homosexual. Josie (5)

> No, I don't feel like I'm a gay woman, and in fact the women I go round with, mix with, we are . . . when we're together in lesbian feminist circles . . . we're quite contemptuous about men, gay men, and we'll talk about 'queers' and be quite pissed off with the idea that gay men might claim some sort of solidarity with us. And also gay men are into casual sex and cruising and sadomasochism and pornography and drag and stuff like that. I find that quite sickening. I don't have anything to do with gay men. Lesley (37)

More than the women on any other factor, women presenting this account express a distaste for men:

	IV
47. Basically I dislike men.	+2
56. I feel uncomfortable in the company of men.	+3
6. I get on well with men.	−3

You have to sort of pander to their egos, and you have to just do so much that I can't be bothered with them. No, I hate all men. You know, I just don't like men. Lesley (37)

I'm more interested in getting on well with the girls than with the boys, because the boys are just *so* immature — telling dirty jokes, and balancing milk bottles on doors so they fall on the teachers when they come in, and smoking in the loos. So childish. I just can't get on with them, and basically dislike the majority of them. Josie (5)

The Q sort for this factor also reveals a general de-emphasis on sex:

	IV
42. Being a lesbian is much more than having sex with women.	+5
35. Even if I never had sex with a woman I would still be a lesbian.	+3

Lesbianism to a feminist is much more than just a question of sex. It's a question of lifestyle; it's a question of sexual politics. It's much wider than the sexual act. Isobel (9)

The important thing about being a lesbian is not the sexual act itself. It's the self-definition in that way as a woman-identified woman, and the commitment to women. Josie (5)

In this account, then, lesbianism is located firmly within a political context. Lesbianism is not a personal pathology, a private sexual orientation, or, primarily, a source of 'true love' or 'true happiness'. It is fundamentally a challenge to patriarchal definitions of women.

The greatest insight that lesbian feminism provided the world is that the institution and ideology of heterosexuality (in its historical development) is a cornerstone of male supremacy. (Valeska, 1981)

In the heterosexual couple, 'love and sex are used to obscure the realities of oppression, to prevent women from identifying with each other in order to revolt, and from identifying "their" man as part of the enemy' (Leeds Revolutionary Feminist Group, 1981). Lesbianism, then, 'signals the limits of patriarchy' (Wood, 1981).

Lesbianism is . . . above all a practice of fundamental solidarity between women. All our emotional life is invested in women, for women, with women; we give no benefits to the oppressor. . . . All women must become lesbians, that is, gain solidarity, resist, and not collaborate. As long as lesbianism is considered a different kind of sexuality, as long as 'desire' is thought to come from an unknown impulse, the idea of lesbianism as a political choice will seem unacceptable. (Monique, 1980)

Where the preceding three (liberal humanistic) accounts incorporate lesbianism into the dominant order as a source of personal fulfilment, or 'true love', or as a sexual orientation), this account explicitly presents lesbianism as a departure from, and challenge to, the dominant social system.

The central assertion that lesbianism poses a threat to the dominant social order — and that, in this sense, 'the personal is political' — is in direct contradiction to the assurances common in other accounts to the effect that 'private lives of individuals do not change the moral or social values and cannot hurt public health' (Daniel, 1954). These other accounts, in their various ways, present lesbianism in terms derived from and acceptable to the dominant order into which the lesbian hopes to become assimilated: the radical feminist account is a challenge to that order. Where another account presents lesbianism as an inferior or pathological state, this account questions social definitions of sickness and health; where another account describes lesbianism as a sexual orientation, this account discusses the socially constructed nature of sexuality; where another account offers lesbianism as a source of true love, this account examines the role of romantic love, coupledom and monogamy in the oppression of women; where another account promises personal fulfilment through lesbianism, this account places the goal of individual happiness secondary to the political goals of women's liberation. It is precisely this rejection of socially sedimented notions that generates so much incomprehension of and hostility to this radical feminist account. Opposition to the radical feminist account of lesbianism is derived from, and can be understood in the context of, the ideologies underlying the other accounts of lesbianism presented in this chapter.

The radical feminist account fails, for example, to accord personal fulfilment and self-actualization, the vitally important role considered socially appropriate (and which is fundamental to the account of Factor I): there is often, instead, a focus on anger at our oppression: 'to be female and conscious is to be in a continual state of rage' (Morgan, 1978: 312). Lesbianism, it is stressed, is less a source of personal fulfilment (although it may also be that), and more a blow against the patriarchy: 'lesbianism is a necessary political choice, part of the tactics of our struggle, not a passport to paradise' (Leeds Revolutionary Feminist Group, 1981). And it is precisely this emphasis on the political, rather than on personal growth, that is attacked: feminist ideology, it is suggested, is a constraining dogma which inhibits personal development. One male gay author writes of his 'discovery' that:

There was as much danger in losing the integrity of my individual identity in conforming to the radical gay partyline as in conforming to establishment values. The real enemy was unmasked as *orthodoxy of any kind*. Liberation does not lie in the direction of seeking the right set of rules to govern one's life. On the contrary, individual identity and freedom require the relinquishment of all dogmas. (Rochlin, 1979: 166, his emphasis)

Such critics rarely consider it necessary to explain why radical ideologies should be more constraining and limiting than their own (unrecognized) liberal humanistic ideologies. Instead they insist that, for example, 'a personality which needs polemics and provocation cannot develop to a higher level than the world it chooses to defy' (Rosenfels, 1971: 137–8) and describe political involvement as a kind of escape from the struggle of self-actualization.

The concept of lesbianism as a private sexual preference or orientation, as natural and normal as heterosexuality (fundamental to the account of Factor III) is also rejected in the radical feminist account. If heterosexual intercourse is 'a political construct reified into an institution' (Atkinson, 1974: 42), then women's refusal of it is also political, and the notion that either heterosexuality or lesbianism are 'natural' is a product of the reification of a patriarchal structure. It is this construction of lesbianism as a 'natural' sexual orientation that is often used to attack radical lesbian feminists, particularly those who came to lesbianism through their feminism:

When the straight women became lesbians, I was sure it was for 'political reasons'. I was repelled by them. They could not possibly understand a 'real lesbian' like me. They hadn't suffered like me. They had been accepted and acceptable all their lives. They didn't live a lie, with the fear and self-loathing I had. Their lesbianism must be a gimmick. (Shea, 1979)

Sex, for women constructing this account, is often described as being merely an obligatory political act: Chrystos (1982) is typical in asserting, 'I wouldn't want to make love with a woman who felt that she was doing her political duty.'

Finally, the radical feminist account also rejects the ideology of romantic love. The various feminist critiques of romantic love present it as an objectifying and individualistic construction of the patriarchy which functions as a means whereby men have justified their dominance over women. 'Romance, like the rabbit at the dog track, is the illusive, fake, and never-attained reward which, for the benefit and amusement of our masters keeps us running and turning in safe circles' (Jones, 1970), and 'under the name of Love, a willing and unconditional servitude has been promoted as something ecstatic, noble, fulfilling, and even redemptive' (Frye, 1983: 72). 'Love, perhaps even more than childbearing, is the pivot of women's oppression today,' asserts Firestone (1971), adding that 'the panic felt at any threat to love is a good clue to its political significance.' In replacing the primacy of romantic love with passionate friendships and sisterly solidarity in the face of oppression, women who account for their lesbianism in these terms are often accused of 'over intellectualizing', of living by their heads rather than their hearts, and of ignoring what, to other women, is the central aspect of lesbianism.

> I cannot understand the lesbian liberation movement except as an assertion that ardent love, fervent love is essential to healthy functioning; we have a right to love because we have a right to be healthy. Liberation will save the original purity and joy of this love and let our inner child go on generating it as birds go on singing. . . . I am bewildered by lesbians who will shout in the streets for liberation and then reject ardour in favour of something more bland that won't interfere with other parts of their lives. Why be an outcast except for something essential? Why not marry a man and have a house in Westchester if you don't know that ardent love is essential? (Routsong, 1978: 50–1)

Adherents of this 'true love' ideology often attack radicals:

> You're worse than the blacks. Don't you ever get tired of telling others and reminding yourselves that you're being oppressed and insulted? . . . I still say: 'Stick oppression down the loo-hole, and up with good old love.' (Breinberg, 1977)

Alternatively, they may attempt to defend 'blatant gays' by suggesting that beneath the militance lies a desperate need for love:

> The zaps, the demonstrations, the disruptions, the hostilities used by those blatant gays toward heterosexual society and all its institutions, which often appear to be destructive and offensive, are mere defence mechanisms in order to survive in a world which denies our beingness, our being permitted to love. Underneath these violent arrays, if anyone will take the time, can be found a stillborn love, willing, waiting and wanting to be birthed, but rejected at all past turns. (Martin and Mariah, 1972: 133)

The frequency with which lesbianism is assessed in terms of ideology of romantic love is a good indication of its central role in the dominant moral order.

The great achievement of the radical feminist lesbian account of lesbian identity is to alienate and disturb proponents of all other lesbian identities. This hostility is derived from the fact that this account of lesbian identity fails to explain and justify lesbianism in terms familiar and acceptable to the dominant order: instead it attacks that order, presenting lesbianism as an explicit threat to society.

Factor V
The last factor, Factor V, represents the traditional account of lesbianism as a 'sorry state', a personal inadequacy or failing. It combines both the traditional religious objection to lesbianism as a sin (both of the women who define this factor are Roman Catholics — one is a nun), and the traditional scientific objection to lesbianism as pathology. In this account, lesbianism is not something chosen or welcomed, but 'a cross to bear' (Elizabeth [65]).

		V
61.	I think I would have a happier life if I were not a lesbian.	+5
8.	If I had a choice I would never have chosen to be a lesbian.	+5
55.	However hard I try not to, there are times when I am ashamed that I am a lesbian.	+1
20.	I find my lesbianism difficult to come to terms with.	+1

More than women on any other factor, women presenting this account dislike feeling different and disapproved of.

		V
28.	I feel good about being 'different'.	−3
31.	Part of my pleasure in being lesbian is the way it shocks people and makes them disapprove.	−5

Not surprisingly, these women give the highest factor score to item 4:

		V
4.	I don't think it's necessary for me to tell everyone that I'm a lesbian.	+3

Unlike the Factor I account, women loading on Factor V stress that they do *not* get personal fulfilment from their lesbianism.

		V
48.	Being a lesbian has enabled me to grow up.	−3
53.	Being a lesbian has enabled me to feel at home in my body.	−3
1.	Being lesbian gives me a sense of freedom.	−4

And in the interviews they stress the limitations they feel their lesbianism imposes on them:

> My friends had been gay, you see, and they were trying to convey to me that the world had more to offer than just that. Why cut out half of humanity? They were right. It's just that gap I can never bridge. . . . I suspect we're in a slightly retarded state. Well, 'retarded' is perhaps not quite right. It's a fear, an inability to relate to the opposite sex. There's nothing you can do about it. Jane (71)

The aetiological explanation offered by these women is that of 'nurture', as opposed to 'nature' (Factor III) or 'political choice' (Factor IV).

		V
26.	You cannot choose to be a lesbian; if you are, you are.	+5
32.	There was nothing in my childhood that predisposed me to be a lesbian.	−5
37.	My relationship with my father helps to explain why I am a lesbian.	+4
3.	My relationship with my mother helps to explain why I am a lesbian.	+4
34.	I believe I was born lesbian.	−5

Why do I think I am lesbian? I don't know. I mentioned earlier this sort of mother relationship business, which, well, maybe it's just coincidence but I have found that an awful lot of other gay women have poor relationships with their mothers, so perhaps that's a contributory factor. Maybe psychologically it does something to you that reinforces your feelings in a certain direction . . . I think, in fact, if you look for reasons, I think the rape incident that I had was quite a significant one, which gave me very ambivalent feelings toward men. Elizabeth (65)

Oh, I certainly don't think I was born lesbian. I think that a whole chain of circumstances, goodness knows what it is, triggers it off and leaves you in this somewhat retarded state. Jane (71)

Certainly feminism is not seen as relevant.

	V
10. I came to lesbianism through feminism.	−4

There you find what people call the political thing, which I don't understand. I don't see the link. Jane (71)

In this account, then, lesbianism is a fixed, essential state, an unfortunate condition largely unrelated to the public and political.

This account can be seen as reflecting traditional constructions of lesbianism in terms of sin and sickness, common in both academic and folk-theorizing from the early twentieth century on, and given wide publicity by Radcliffe Hall's (1928) novel, *The Well of Loneliness*. Published with a sympathetic preface from the sexologist Havelock Ellis, testifying to its scientific accuracy, the book's social impact was such that it has been described as 'the Uncle Tom's Cabin of homosexuality' (Martin and Mariah, 1972) and 'the Lesbian Bible' (Lyon and Martin, 1972). The notorious prosecution and banning of the book as obscene promoted it as a major source of how to 'be' a lesbian in real life, and 'helped to convince subsequent generations of lesbians that they would be honorable freaks at best, lonely outcasts at worst' (Sand, 1982). Throughout the novel, Hall insists on the terrible suffering of her lesbian protagonist, and imparts the message that 'God's cruel; He let us get flawed in the making' (p. 204). Because of its historical roots, this construction of lesbianism as a flawed state is often attributed to 'older' (i.e. 50+) lesbians (Laurie, 1978; Plummer, 1981), for whom Hall's novel and the early sexological models provided the major explanatory resources upon which they could draw in constructing their accounts. Its continuing availability as an interpretative framework is evident from the fact that the younger of the two women who define this factor is twenty-nine.

Unlike the other accounts discussed — all of which, in varying degrees, assert the positive value of lesbianism in the face of claims to the contrary — the account of Factor V involves a basic acceptance of the cultural definition of lesbianism as a 'sorry state', and embodies socially approved vocabularies for mitigating or relieving responsibility for this socially questionable conduct by appealing to the coercive forces of environmental control ('excuses', Scott and Lyman, 1968) and the effects of a dismal past ('sad tales', Scott and Lyman, 1968). Similar acceptance of the cultural definition of their deviance is manifested by some blind people (referred to by Scott [1969] as 'true believers') and accounts have been collected from both prostitutes (Goffman, 1963) and sex offenders (Taylor, 1972) which are structured similarly to the account of lesbianism presented here in their use of 'atrocity tales' to explain the 'fallen state'. These are all, in Poussaint's (1973) terms, 'surrendered identities'.

This self-acceptance of inferiority clearly serves the purposes of the dominant order: it nihilates (cf. Berger and Luckmann, 1967: 132) lesbianism as a threat to the reified norm of heterosexuality: in assigning lesbianism an inferior ontological status, the institution of heterosexuality is validated and reinforced. While the utility of this account from the perspective of the dominant order is patent, it is less obvious why lesbians themselves should accept this version. Clearly, there must be powerful explicit and implicit social mechanisms leading some lesbians to construct their experience in this way, and a corresponding inaccessibility of alternative versions. One possibility is that lesbians employing this account can be characterized as the victims or dupes of a heterosexist social system — women so terrorized or indoctrinated that they passively accept, absorb and reflect back society's image of themselves. This is, in fact, a very common retrospective explanation offered by women charting their autobiographical progression from this to other accounts of lesbianism (cf. Cruickshank, 1980; Stanley and Wolfe, 1980). But rather than characterizing these women as just passive recipients and relayers of accounts foisted onto them by the oppressors, as mere puppets of the patriarchy, it can be useful to see them also as active participants in the process of account construction. Women who provide this account of their lesbianism are involved in a good deal of interpretative effort in, for example, pathologizing their personal histories — selecting and applying a particular aetiological explanation, constructing an appropriate autobiography and, in the case of many lesbians presenting this account today, simultaneously resisting, invalidating or denouncing alternative accounts (e.g. radical feminist) which compete with their own. Far from representing mere 'acquiescence' to the dominant version of lesbianism, then, this account is now seen as the product of energetic and ingenious efforts at account construction.

The advantage of this identity construction for lesbians lies primarily in its attenuation of personal responsibility or culpability for the deviance, and in the attainment of limited social privileges as reward for confirming the dominant ideology. In employing this account, a woman herself undermines any suggestion that she is a threat to society or to the heterosexual hegemony. She depoliticizes her lesbianism in a bid for acceptance.

Factors VI and VII

Factors VI and VII were each defined by only one woman — not in itself a barrier to explication, particularly if the account is expected to emerge on theoretical grounds. In the case of these two factors, however, I did not feel confident that I had an adequate understanding of the accounts, and they are presented here only in outline.

Factor VI shares some of the bisexual self-construction of Factor II, but with the emphasis on not romantic love but sexual attraction. This nineteen-year-old participant raised in interview that her's is an uncertain and fluid account which she herself sees as subject to change.

The account of Factor VII was derived from a woman in her fifties who has identified as lesbian since her early teens and who, until ten years ago, saw her lesbianism as a sickness, since when she has come into contact with feminist ideas. This identity account has a binary quality in which two self-stories — one effectively radical feminist, the other the traditional approach to lesbianism as pathology — relate in an inner dialogue. During the eight years that I have been friendly with this participant, she has maintained this bifurcated account, and her interview protocol shows high tolerance of ambiguity.

Both women also define factors in the Q sort presented in Chapter 5, and are further discussed in that context.

Four of the five identity accounts discussed in this chapter rely on the construction of lesbianism as a personal and private sexual orientation or lifestyle. The account of lesbianism as pathological (Factor V) is well represented in the psychological literature, as well as in much of lesbians' own writing prior to the late 1960s, and its role in maintaining the institution of heterosexuality is self-evident. The three liberal-humanistic accounts represented by Factors I, II, and III all draw on certain aspects of the official morality as justifications for the infringement of other aspects of this same morality.

The account of Factor I relies particularly on socially sedimented notions of personal fulfilment and the pursuit of positive psychological health; the account of Factor II invokes the culturally approved rhetoric of romantic love; and the account of Factor III focuses on the construction of lesbianism as a private 'sexual orientation' as 'natural' for some women as heterosexuality is supposed to be for others. Each of these accounts can be seen, then, as explaining lesbianism in terms borrowed from the dominant order. While such accounts serve the purposes of lesbians by assuring relative social acceptability, by the same token, they serve the purposes of the dominant order by reinforcing and validating its moral rhetoric.

When lesbians use such accounts, or when aspects of liberal humanistic accounting are employed within a predominantly feminist discourse, attention is distracted away from the central (political) aims of radical feminism towards individual (private) solutions in terms of personal happiness, self-fulfilment and true love, thus supporting the privatized ideologies of the dominant culture. Moreover, exaggerated claims are often made for lesbianism as a private solution, with lesbians:

> portraying their lives with all the reality of a 1950s movie in which once the lovers find each other, they go off into the sunset to the strains of organ music to live happily ever after, unbeset by the ills that afflict us lesser mortals. (Mainardi, 1975: 122)

In response to such propaganda, more than one lesbian has asked, like Rickford:

> What's the secret? My 'personal life' (I'm a lesbian) is riddled with glaring contradictions, dubious motives, irrational and compulsive needs and desires. I have very few friends I really trust and none of them is a lover. (Rickford, 1981: 11)

Finally, the use of science to support claims of lesbian health, normality, happiness, or capacity for sexual and romantic satisfaction serves to ensure lesbian reinforcement of and loyalty to the concept of science as a privileged way of knowing.

5

Lesbian Politics

When speaking of ideology, sociology suddenly loses its hushed voice and opaque language; its technical language suddenly joins forces with blunt and lively common parlance. It characterizes ideology as the mind-inflaming realm of the doctrinaire, the dogmatic, the impassioned, the dehumanizing, the false, the irrational and, of course, the 'extremist' consciousness. (Gouldner, 1976: 4)

The study reported in this chapter serves basically as an extension and elaboration of the preceding study (Chapter 4) which elicited a selection of accounts of lesbian identities. These identity accounts suggest the existence of a parallel set of ideological or political frameworks which underlie and sustain them. The terms 'politics' and 'ideology' are used interchangeably here to denote all 'belief systems' or 'theoretically articulated propositions about reality' (Berger et al., 1973), whether normative or counternormative in nature. This definition permits the recognition not only of the political status of 'deviant' acts and beliefs (often excluded from the political arena through a highly formalistic vision of politics as confined to the formal juridical aspects of social life, cf. Horowitz and Liebowitz, 1968), but also allows the identification of the taken-for-granted dominant versions of reality as being ideological and political in their implications. This is in contradistinction to the more usual approach in which 'ideologists' are seen only as those holding *counter*-normative ideologies, thus obscuring the fact that a normative belief system is *also* an ideology. Liberalism is typified by a reluctance to identify itself as ideological.

> Liberalism is generally regarded by its defenders as an anti-ideological, and anti-metaphysical approach, which, unlike its doctrinal rivals, eschews a comprehensive world-view in favour of the principle of attempting always to see and to grasp the facts as they are, free from the distortions imposed on them by mediating ideologies. (Arblaster, 1972: 89)

The 'received wisdom' is that ideologies (i.e. counternormative ideologies) are, by definition, a Bad Thing: mirroring this conventional approach, one writer comments that

> The trails that ideologists have blazed have led to the fires of the Nazi

crematoria, and to the Arctic wastes of the Soviet labour camps. Men's [*sic*] visions have been warped by ideology; their hatreds have been exacerbated; and every anointed elite has felt itself anointed to misuse human beings. (Feuer, 1975: 191)

In both academic and folk-theorizing, the ideologist or political radical is typically discredited in three ways: through the riffraff theory, the equivalence theory, and through an attack on the structures that support and uphold the counternormative ideology. Most of the psychological research on lesbianism relies on one or more of these methods (usually implicitly rather than explicitly) when describing radical lesbian feminist ideology.

In the first of these, the behaviour or thought patterns of the ideologist are said to demonstrate his or her underlying pathology: 'many studies conclude that the radical attitude, in contrast with other types of political attitude, indicates a basic personality disturbance' (McCormack, 1950). The term 'riffraff theory' is taken from Caplan who discusses the way in which black militants are dismissed as irresponsible deviants, criminals or emotionally disturbed:

> By attributing the causes of riots to individual deficiencies, the riffraff theory relieves white institutions of much of the blame. It suggests that individual militants should be changed through psychotherapy, social work, or, if all else fails, prolonged confinement. If protesting militants can be publicly branded as unable to compete successfully for personal reasons, then their demands for system changes can be declared illegitimate with impunity. (Caplan, 1970)

The activist is supposed to be anomic, estranged, neurotic, discontented, disoriented, frustrated, anxiety-ridden and self-rejecting, the sum of these constituting the classic symptoms of 'alienation' (Zygmunt, 1972). The 'neuroticism' (Feuer, 1975: 135), 'insecurity' (Rudin, 1969: 9) and 'paranoia' (cf. Thomas, 1973) of the radical together contribute to the pathological syndrome called 'rebellionitis', the main symptom of which is 'fantasies of oppression' (Greenwald, quoted in Schur, 1976). 'All important fanatics,' says Kretschmer (quoted in Rudin, 1969) 'bear even in their bodily structure the characteristics of the schizothymic-schizoid syndrome', while Eaves and Eysenck (1974) emphasize the importance of a 'largely inherited personality configuration [which] makes some people emphatic, dogmatic, authoritarian and Machiavellian, thus predisposing them to extremist ideological positions'. Radical lesbians are described as exhibiting 'a chronic attitude of resentment against society' (Scharfelter, 1980) and as 'compulsively provoking and unconsciously "enjoying" the same suffering they experienced with the disappointments of infancy' (Kronemeyer, 1980). As Bergler puts it:

> The entire personality structure of the homosexual is pervaded by the unconscious wish to suffer; this wish is gratified by self-created trouble-making. This 'injustice-collecting' (technically called psychic masochism) is conveniently deposited in the external difficulties confronting the homosexual. (Bergler, 1956)

Through imputing pathology to adherents of ideologies other than liberalism, the riffraff theory avoids the open acknowledgement and discussion of political differences.

The equivalence theory, whereby the thinking and behaviour of the radical is said to resemble in fundamental respects (or to be an inverted or reflected image of) the ideologies of the radical's political opponents, is another technique whereby radical ideologies are often discredited. The simplest way in which this claim is advanced is by postulating identical psychological mechanisms as underlying both radical and reactionary ideologies, as in Rokeach's dogmatism scale, which is supposed to measure dogmatism of both the right and the left (cf. Smithers and Lobley, 1978). Similarly, it may be claimed that a person with a particular personality configuration is equally likely to become a Fascist, a Nazi, a Phalangist (or whatever other right-wing possibility presents itself), *or*, a Communist, a Maoist or a Trotskyist; but is psychologically incapable of becoming a liberal (Eysenck and Wilson, 1978: 309–10). Associated with this theory is the argument based on the notion of 'overcompensation' — the claim that the radical oppressed, far from having achieved the 'raised consciousnesses' sometimes claimed, are in fact manifesting symptoms of self-hate and internalized self-oppression. This argument has been advanced in relation to Jewish activists:

> By projecting it upon others and attacking it in them, these 'positive' Jews may be exorcising from their own consciousness an image of the Jew that is no less negative than that in the mind of the most cringing 'assimilationist'. . . . Jewish separatism intensifies self-hatred by concealing and dissembling it, by sinking it into the depths of the psyche where it becomes all the more malignant because out of sight. Remaining invisible, retreating at most, but not disappearing, self-hatred prompts us to go to ever greater lengths to convince ourselves that we have extirpated it — to strut and posture and boast. Yet we succeed no better than before in coming to terms with ourselves, and only exchange one expression of self-hatred for another, more indirect and deceptive one. (Greenberg, 1950)

Similarly homosexuals have been described as developing 'a protective brazen front, an "I'm as good as the next one" attitude. Such overcompensation,' says West (1968: 54–5), 'has a lot to do with the aggressively brazen behaviour of those groups who . . .

affect outrageous manners.' This can be interpreted as a tactical move to discredit the radical account of oppression by asserting its fundamental similarity to the 'self-hating' account to which it sets itself up in opposition.

Finally, commitment to radical feminist ideology involves a 'conversion' experience which catapults the person into commitment to a counternormative construction of lesbianism. Lacking the institutionalized support and professionally constructed legitimations of normative (especially liberal humanistic) reality constructions, counternormative ideologies must rely on alternative methods of support and legitimation. Foremost among these, in a variety of movements of social transformation, are separatism, name-changing, use of kinship terms and movement slogans.

Separatism functions to insulate the radical (to some extent) from normative ideologies which contaminate and undermine the counternormative ideology to which a commitment is made (Poussaint, 1973: 364; Goodman et al., 1983: 79). Name-changing signifies the 'rebirth' that occurs with the conversion process: as Saul becomes St Paul, and Stokely Carmichael becomes Kwame Ture, so many radical lesbians (22 percent of those responding to a survey in *Innerviews* [1982]) take new names for themselves, usually to avoid being labelled by their father (or husband) and to reflect some attribute of their 'reborn' selves (e.g. Sarahschild, Helensdaughter, Freespirit, Blackdykewomon). The use of kinship terms — Pentecostals are brothers and sisters in Christ, Black Power radicals are 'soul' brothers and sisters, feminists are united 'in sisterhood' against patriarchy — reinforces the converted individual's acceptance of a new reference group in which the movement ideology constitutes the taken-for-granted version. Finally, counternormative ideologies are generally codified into a common rhetoric or 'party-line', with slogans which summarize or evoke large segments of the movement's underlying theoretical framework: within radical feminism these include 'Any woman can be a lesbian', 'The personal is political', 'Feminism is the theory; lesbianism is the practice'. A major function of such slogans is in providing patterned answers to the (patterned) questions raised by members of the established order who oppose the movement, so that 'converts have ready, effective, and oft-tested answers to most questions' (Gerlach and Hine, 1970: 162). The codification of movement ideology also facilitates its transmission to new converts and to those seeking the commitment experience.

These various supports for counternormative ideologies are all necessary props or facilitating aids to the maintenance of alternative versions of reality which have none of the benefits of institutionalized support and professionally constructed legitimations of the normative reality construction. And it is precisely these aids to the maintenance of counternormative ideologies which are often singled out for attack by members of the established order: separatism is 'counterproductive' or is labelled 'reverse sexism/ racism/homophobia'; solidarity with one's sisters is interpreted as retreat into a 'ghetto' or 'clique'; and codifications of the ideology are dismissed as 'mindless jargon' and 'empty slogans'.

This collection of techniques for discrediting counternormative ideologies should be familiar from the earlier discussion of the 'well-adjusted' lesbian (Chapter 2) and they are discussed in more detail as they arise in the context of the accounts elicited in this study. The aim is to elicit accounts of lesbian politics without the automatic and implicit reliance on the discrediting formulae previously cited which pervade liberal humanistic psychology. Unlike liberal humanistic psychologists, who typically refuse to acknowledge their own ideological roots, I am explicitly writing this chapter from within the 'radical feminist' perspective, and am particularly concerned to explore and contrast the various accounts rooted in liberal human-istic ideology with that derived from radical feminist ideology.

As in the previous study, it is the account, and not the account-provider who is the unit of study, although when (as in the case of the last two factors presented in this study) a factor is defined by only one woman, I draw more freely on aspects of personal biography as presented in interviews. There is an unavoidable overlap between the 'identity' accounts of the previous study, and these accounts of ideology, because identities are constructed and transacted in the context of the underlying ideological frameworks which sustain them. In this chapter I present each account, document its existence in the 'real world', consider its relationship with the other accounts of ideology and identity, and discuss its political implications.

Method

The sixty-one item Q sort (Table 5.1) was completed by twenty-seven (two-thirds) of the women who participated in the previous study, plus an additional six women who had been recruited too late for inclusion in the preceding study. Care was taken to ensure that representatives of all seven 'identity' factors were included amongst these: of the seventeen women defining factors in the 'identity' Q sort, thirteen completed this Q sort. The distribution used was identical to the previous study. All participants were also interviewed.

Table 5.1   *Items in the 'politics of lesbianism' Q sort*

1. People should not be pigeon-holed just according to their sexual orientation.
2. Lesbians and gay men should work together for their mutual benefit.
3. Being a lesbian means more than just engaging in sexual activity with a woman.
4. Being a lesbian sets you free from male exploitation.
5. Without society's sexual indoctrination many more women would choose to be lesbian.
6. No matter what I feel, or how attracted I am, I will never have sex with a man again.
7. To conform to society's values is to support a system that oppresses women.
8. True equality in a relationship is never possible between a man and a woman.
9. I feel angry with women who draw attention to their lesbianism.
10. Lesbianism is a private thing; what I do in bed is my business.
11. Romance and 'falling in love' are quite separate from politics and ideology.
12. Sex between two women is not in itself a political act.
13. Most women want to have children even if they deny it.
14. Lesbianism is a blow against the patriarchy.
15. Heterosexual women are collaborators with the enemy.
16. The oppression of other groups, like blacks and the working-class, is at least as important to me as the oppression of women.
17. Every woman has the potential to be a lesbian if she chooses.
18. Men have forced women into heterosexuality in order to exploit them.
19. As a lesbian I am not especially interested in women's rights issues such as abortion and contraception.
20. Most women are, by nature, heterosexual.
21. Feminism is the theory; lesbianism is the practice.
22. Penetration is inevitably an act of domination.
23. Lesbians should seek alternatives to monogamy.
24. As a lesbian I see myself as a member of a minority sexual-interest group, in common with people like transexuals and paedophiles.
25. I disapprove of separatist man-hating lesbians.
26. Being a woman is very important to me.
27. Men are 50 percent of the human race; it is silly trying to live separately from them.
28. Most women who claim to have chosen lesbianism as a political decision were probably really lesbians anyway.
29. It is wrong to alienate people by being too militant.
30. I resent it when people assume that I am heterosexual.
31. Sisterhood with all women should come before your love for one woman.
32. If we want to change social attitudes to lesbianism a gentle approach is likely to be more effective.
33. Being a lesbian is *not* one of the most important things about me.
34. Monogamous lesbian couples are imitating heterosexual patterns.
35. Men are as oppressed by social expectation as women are.
36. You cannot choose to be lesbian: if you are, you are.
37. Whatever your sexuality, it is a cop-out to call yourself a bisexual.
38. I have more in common with, and greater allegiance to, *any* woman, whatever her politics (e.g. National Front) than to any man, however ideologically similar.
39. Whatever the time in history, wherever the place in the world, in every culture women are exploited by men.

40. In my heart of hearts I believe women are superior to men.
41. Women exploit men as much as men exploit women — they just go about it in a different way.
42. I wouldn't want to live in a woman-only world.
43. It is not men who exploit women, but their institutions (the Law, the Church, the Educational system), so it is wrong to hold individual men responsible.
44. Young people should be taught about lesbianism within their sex education at school.
45. I don't want to change society; I just want the freedom to be myself.
46. I don't think it's necessary to me to tell everyone that I'm a lesbian.
47. Putting pressure on heterosexual feminists to be lesbian is wrong.
48. There is no such thing as an unnatural sexual act.
49. The love of one woman for another is the most sublime form of love.
50. I reject the notions 'butch' and 'femme'; they are irrelevant to lesbianism.
51. Sexual orientation is a poor foundation on which to build your political ideology.
52. I believe that most people are basically bisexual.
53. If a woman genuinely wishes to stop being lesbian, facilities should be available to help her to change.
54. I would like to see a law similar to that against racial prejudice which would aim to protect lesbians against prejudice and abuse.
55. A woman who is willingly having sex with a man has no right to call herself a lesbian.
56. Lesbian couples should be treated exactly the same way as married couples with regard to housing, benefits etc.
57. Many lesbians don't live up to my idea of what a lesbian should be.
58. Books which portray lesbianism as a sickness or aberration should be withdrawn from schools and public libraries.
59. It's hard to understand how feminist women can justify having heterosexual relationships.
60. There is no such thing as 'sexual orientation': we all have the potential to be *anything* sexually.
61. I think lesbians shouldn't have children.

Results

The raw data were analysed exactly as in the previous study, and the varimax rotated factor matrix is given in Table 5.2. Factors VII and VIII have no 'pure' loadings, so factor scores were calculated only for the first six factors. Table 5.3 presents these factor scores.

Table 5.2   *Factor loadings for the 'politics of lesbianism' Q sort*[1]

Q sorter no.	I	II	III	IV	V	VI	VII	VIII
01	82 [2]	14	−14	−10	01	−19	−08	−06
03	82	14	−14	00	13	−03	−24	08
43	82	08	−04	12	16	16	20	06
95	80	04	−06	09	−24	−14	09	−03
05	77	10	−01	01	03	08	07	03

Table 5.2 *cont.*

Q sorter no.	I	II	III	IV	V	VI	VII	VIII
74	77	24	12	02	10	21	−04	−03
75	77	08	−20	11	21	17	12	10
29	76	00	−15	19	28	13	−05	−10
37	74	22	−14	−08	05	03	18	05
08	27	78	−01	01	03	08	07	03
33	19	66	19	29	15	04	−10	01
12	27	63	−23	14	−02	38	13	09
71	−15	00	72	−09	−01	−01	11	06
70	−31	29	61	31	−04	12	06	18
61	14	11	−09	80	02	11	16	04
58	−09	29	35	60	28	05	−15	14
10	28	14	−05	09	76	22	05	18
57	03	37	15	19	22	64	−05	12
02	68	33	08	04	20	06	21	−13
04	64	35	09	−05	12	−24	34	09
25	24	57	29	01	21	00	32	02
26	10	44	17	24	54	−17	18	−03
49	68	18	−02	02	−12	36	22	00
50	44	57	38	17	23	19	13	01
51	55	53	−01	26	08	29	22	−11
54	65	−13	15	18	−11	01	26	19
63	22	05	19	42	21	08	11	50
65	−06	33	37	34	34	31	17	02
72	−25	60	24	01	14	20	−02	53
81	49	44	−10	36	11	−06	31	36
88	38	28	30	27	04	09	37	07
92	−35	28	45	36	27	08	−08	−19
93	07	36	25	15	18	02	46	08

[1] Loadings rounded off to two significant figures and decimal points omitted.
[2] Boxed loadings indicate those defining factors.

Table 5.3 *Factor arrays for 'politics of lesbianism' Q sort*

Q sort item	I	II	III	IV	V	VI
1	+1	+5	+4	0	+2	+5
2	−1	0	−1	0	+1	+3
3	+5	+2	0	+5	+5	0
4	0	−4	0	+4	−5	−1
5	+4	+4	−4	+2	+2	+3
6	+2	−2	−1	−1	+1	−2
7	+4	+5	0	0	+5	+1

8	+4	−1	0	−1	−1	−2
9	−4	−5	+1	−1	−2	−2
10	−4	−1	+5	+3	−4	−1
11	−2	+1	+3	+1	0	+2
12	0	+1	+5	−1	−4	+1
13	−2	−1	−1	−4	+1	−1
14	+4	0	0	−2	+4	0
15	0	−1	−5	−4	−4	−2
16	0	−2	+2	0	−2	−3
17	+5	+1	−3	−3	+1	−1
18	+3	−3	+2	−3	0	+2
19	−3	−4	−4	−5	+4	−4
20	−5	−5	−2	+2	0	0
21	+2	−2	−1	−3	−3	0
22	0	−3	−3	−1	0	−2
23	+1	0	−2	0	0	−3
24	−5	−4	−3	−1	−5	−1
25	−3	−2	+2	+3	+3	+1
26	+5	+2	−3	+5	+5	0
27	−2	+2	+1	+2	+3	+3
28	−1	0	+2	+1	0	0
29	−2	−4	+5	+1	+3	+4
30	+3	+3	−4	+1	+1	−1
31	+1	−2	−2	−2	0	−3
32	−1	−3	+4	+1	+1	+5
33	−4	+3	+3	−5	−4	+1
34	0	−3	−1	−1	−1	−5
35	−3	+2	0	0	−1	+2
36	−5	+1	+3	+4	−3	+1
37	+1	−2	+1	0	−3	−4
38	−1	−1	+1	−3	−3	−5
39	+3	+1	+1	+4	−1	+3
40	+2	+1	−2	+1	−1	−3
41	−3	0	0	0	−2	−3
42	−2	0	−1	−1	+4	+4
43	−2	+5	0	+1	−1	+2
44	+3	+4	−2	+3	+2	+4
45	−3	0	+4	+3	−5	−4
46	−1	+4	+4	−3	+2	+1
47	0	+2	+3	+1	+2	+2
48	−1	−1	−1	+3	0	+5
49	0	0	−1	+2	−3	−1
50	+2	+1	+1	+2	+4	+2
51	0	+1	+3	−2	−2	0
52	+1	+2	0	−2	−1	+1
53	−1	−3	+2	−2	+1	+1
54	+2	+3	−4	+4	+2	+4
55	−1	0	−5	0	−1	−1
56	+1	+3	−3	+2	+3	+3
57	+1	−1	−2	−5	−2	−2
58	+2	+3	+1	+5	+3	0
59	+1	−1	−5	−4	−2	−4
60	+3	+4	+2	−2	−1	0
61	−4	−5	+1	−4	0	−5

Discussion

Factor I

The Q sorts completed by nine women (Nos. 1, 3, 5, 29, 37, 43, 74, 75, and 95) define this factor, and of the seven who also completed the 'Accounts of Lesbian Identity' Q sort (reported in Chapter 4), all have significant loadings on the 'radical feminist' factor (Factor IV).

The involvement of these women in the Women's Liberation Movement and related activities far exceeds that of women defining any other factor: of the nine, six live in (different) women's collective houses, three work with (different) lesbian telephone contact services, two are on the collectives of feminist publications, one runs a woman-only cafe, another is well-known for her political activity around the issue of lesbian motherhood, and one is the author of this book.

This account of the politics of lesbianism locates it firmly within the framework of radical feminist ideology. The role of hetero-sexuality as an institution of patriarchal control, and the potential of lesbianism for subverting male domination are made explicit:

        I

18. Men have forced women into heterosexuality in order
    to exploit them.   +3
14. Lesbianism is a blow against the patriarchy.   +4
21. Feminism is the theory; lesbianism is the practice.   +2

In this account, personal relationships between individuals are interpreted in terms of the political context in which they take place. It is argued that a relationship between any individual woman and man cannot be understood without reference to the political structure of male supremacy and male domination, which invests each man with power over each woman.

        I

8. True equality in a relationship is never possible between a
    man and a woman.   +4

Thus the 'personal' (including romance, falling in love, sexual attraction, fantasy, and personal relationships generally) is 'political' in at least two senses: firstly that it is the personal experience of women that generates and informs feminist theory, and secondly in that feminist theory offers a structure within which individual experience can be interpreted and understood.

        I

11. Romance and 'falling in love' are quite separate
    from politics and ideology.   −2

And you can try over and over with different men to have equal and caring relationships, and you find over and over again that it's impossible. And so many women take the blame for that and say, 'there's something wrong with me.' And because there's nothing they can do about it, because they can't make relationships with men work, they say they were born incapable of it, instead of seeing that they were born into a society which makes all women incapable of having equal relationships with men. They make it a personal failing instead of a social and political injustice. That's what feminism means, I think, about 'the personal is political.' Lesley (37)

In this account, men (rather than merely 'society', 'institutions' or 'conditioning') are seen as the enemy:

	I
43. It is not men who exploit women but their institutions (the Law, the Church, the Educational system), so it is wrong to hold individual men responsible.	−2
35. Men are as oppressed by social expectation as women are.	−3
41. Women exploit men as much as men exploit women — they just go about it in a different way.	−3

In this account, the blame is put squarely on men, and separatism is represented as a legitimate strategy:

	I
25. I disapprove of separatist, man-hating lesbians.	−3
6. No matter what I feel, or how attracted I am, I will never have sex with a man again.	+2
27. Men are 50 percent of the human race; it is silly trying to live separately from them.	−2

Some men I find sexually attractive, but I don't think I'd ever sleep with them, because, having got involved in feminism, I get very angry at the way men treat women at a very general level, and so, although physically I might be attracted to them, mentally I don't want to, and I don't like the relationships that often seem to build up. I don't like the unequal side of it, and the imbalance of power. Samantha (29)

Once you realize about the power struggle and the role of men as oppressors, you *can't*, you just *can't* find men sexually attractive any more. Alice (1)

These are views which underlie the theory of political lesbianism — the theory that women can and should choose lesbianism as part of the political strategy of feminism — and this account endorses constructionist theories of sexuality:

	I
20. Most women are, by nature, heterosexual.	−5
17. Every woman has the potential to be a lesbian if she chooses.	+5
36. You cannot choose to be lesbian; if you are, you are.	−5
60. There's no such thing as 'sexual orientation'; we all have the potential to be anything sexually.	+3

In interviews, women providing this account came up with

various constructionist arguments, but essentialist notions are always rejected.

> I think possibly I can imagine that if I was in a healthier society, where men were not brainwashed into being such subhuman creatures, I could possibly enjoy things a bit more with men. Because, I mean, it's not as though men have such monstrous bodies. They're not terribly interesting physically, but I mean, they're not *awful*. If they were a bit nicer in their *heads*, then you could have relationships with them. Shân (95)

> I think that lesbianism *can* be a choice for some women, and I think that for other women it isn't a choice. I think that some women are emotionally bound up in lesbianism, in loving other women, and almost instinctively reject the patriarchal values, before they know what it is, or experience it, or whatever. And then there are other women who are not emotionally bound up in it, who come to it via the head, via their politics I suppose. And I think both ways are valid. And I think it *is* about making choices. Sally (75)

When asked about lesbians from whom they felt different, liberal feminist lesbians were commonly mentioned.

> I felt different from that woman who seemed to think that her sister was definitely heterosexual and she was a lesbian, as if . . . you know, as if women *are* heterosexual or lesbian. I do see it as a case of a choice and an attained consciousness. And I do feel very different from lesbian women, like my first lover, who just think they were born that way and that everyone, you know, every person ought to get on with what they want to do, you know. They just see it as a personal issue. And that's the difference, I would have thought, between a political lesbian, and a 'real' or 'straight' lesbian. Lesley (37)

> It was interesting that those women immediately jumped to the defence of the male sex, and said, 'oh, but you're writing off half the human race', and 'how can you say that about half the human race?' and 'but there are some nice men, you know.' All the usual arguments, you know, anti-man-hating. And it was a roomful of *lesbians*! . . . And this was a roomful of lesbians who were terribly anxious that men shouldn't be insulted, that men shouldn't be put down. Shân (95)

This factor, then, involves a constructionist version of sexuality in which heterosexuality is seen as imposed by men on to women, and in which lesbianism represents a challenge to male supremacy. Feminism, in this account, relates fundamentally to personal relationships, experiences and emotions, and lesbianism is a central and intrinsic aspect of this conceptualization of feminist ideology.

The 'hard line' version of this account of the politics of lesbianism has achieved wide representation in lesbian feminist publications. The often reprinted 'political lesbianism' paper reads:

> Men are the enemy. Heterosexual women are collaborators with the

enemy. All the good work that our heterosexual sisters do for women is undermined by the counter-revolutionary activity they engage in with men. Being a heterosexual feminist is like being in the resistance in Nazi-occupied Europe where in the daytime you blow up a bridge, in the evening you rush to repair it. . . . Every woman who lives with or fucks a man helps to maintain the oppression of her sisters and hinders our struggle. (Leeds Revolutionary Feminist Group, 1981: 7)

Earlier American writers had used much the same imagery: 'Can you imagine a Frenchman, serving in the French army from 9am to 5pm, then trotting "home" to Germany for supper and overnight?' asks Ti-Grace Atkinson (1974: 132); 'That's called game-playing, or collaboration, not political commitment.' Any attempt to improve the quality of heterosexual relationships is rejected: as Rita Mae Brown (1976: 11) says, 'You do not free yourself by polishing your chains', and Jill Johnston argues:

Many women are dedicated to working for the 'reconstructed man' — or any translation into movement rhetoric of the old saw of a woman with clout in the home who gently prods her provider and protector into being a more thoughtful oppressor. . . . Feminists who still sleep with the man are delivering their most vital energies to the oppressor. To work out a suitable compromise or *apparent* equality, at any private level, is an exceptional solution between exceptional people, and . . . remains an effort in isolation from the groundthrust of the most fundamental social revolution in the world. A personal solution or exceptional adjustment to a political problem is collusion with the enemy. (Johnston, 1973: 180–1)

The defensiveness generated by this argument amongst hetero-sexual women is often seen as preventing productive discussion and analysis of the institution of compulsory heterosexuality (Franklin and Stacey, 1986: 3). Feminist critics of the theory have argued that it contravenes the Women's Liberation Movement demand for the right to a self-defined sexuality (Pettitt, 1981), that it denies the principle that each woman's experience is valid and real (Rickford, 1981; Laws, 1981) and that it supports a new elite of right-on radical lesbians with 'raised consciousnesses' (Cloutte, 1981).

Factor II
The account represented by this factor (defined by Q sorts 8, 33 and 12, Table 5.2) shares much of the feminist ideology of Factor I, but does not attribute individual men with responsibility for the patriarchy, or see personal relationships between individual women and men as necessarily flawed by the social structure of male domination. Women are oppressed not by men, but by social institutions and conditioning, and men and women should work

together for a non-sexist society in which people are *people* first and foremost, and in which the full range of sexual expression (from pure heterosexuality, through varying degrees of bisexuality, to pure homosexuality) are permitted and accepted. Lesbianism is neither intrinsic to nor necessary for the feminist cause, and the anti-male, separatist position of some radical lesbians simply results in a 'ghettoized' existence which leads nowhere.

While supporting at least some of the feminist ideology of Factor I (e.g. item 7 is scored at +5; item 26 at +2), and identifying themselves as feminists, the women presenting this account hold not individual men but the social system and its institutions responsible for women's oppression.

		II	(I)
43.	It is not men who exploit women, but their institutions (the Law, the Church, the Education system), so it is wrong to hold individual men responsible.	+5	(−2)
35.	Men are as oppressed by social expectations as women are.	+2	(−3)
27.	Men are 50 percent of the human race; it is silly trying to live separately from them.	+2	(−2)

Feminism, in this account, means seeing people first and foremost as human beings, rather than as members of a gender:

> I'm important as an individual, not as a sexual being, and you should treat everybody on the same level as an individual, not depending on whether they're a man or a woman. Jill (12)

This version of feminism is one which does *not* incorporate lesbianism as an intrinsically political identity. In this account, there is no necessary link between the theory of feminism and the practice of lesbianism: heterosexuality represents neither exploitation nor domination, and lesbianism is not seen as posing any particular challenge to male supremacy.

		II	(I)
21.	Feminism is the theory; lesbianism is the practice	−2	(+2)
18.	Men have forced women into heterosexuality in order to exploit them.	−3	(+3)
22.	Penetration is inevitably an act of domination.	−3	(0)
14.	Lesbianism is a blow against the patriarchy.	0	(+4)

Because lesbianism is not, in this account, central to feminism, a lesbian identity is not considered centrally important:

		II	(I)
33.	Being a lesbian is *not* one of the most important things about me.	+3	(−4)

The aetiological theories of this account rely heavily on the popular version of Kinsey's 'heterosexual-homosexual continuum' as endorsing notions of universal bisexuality.

> There are several degrees of sexuality, ranging from heterosexual to pure homosexual, but there are *several*, not just 'heterosexual', 'homosexual', and 'bisexual'. And people are somewhere along a range. Jill (12)

> Everyone is bisexual, and there's all sorts of different levels of heterosexuality and homosexuality, and then in the middle the perfectly bisexual person who couldn't care less. People are all sorts of shades, but at either end there are people who *have* to be heterosexual or *have* to be homosexual. I have known women in the Women's Movement who have made the political decision to become lesbian, but when it came down to doing it, they were forced to admit that it did nothing for them, and were forced to accept that they were heterosexual, and that was it. Which means that the ones who *did* manage to do it for political reasons had a lot of lesbianism in them anyway. Mary (8)

So compared with the radical feminist account, this account rejects the 'hard-line' version of the interdependence of lesbianism and feminism, stressing that men, too, suffer in a non-egalitarian society, and providing a traditional essentialist (albeit 'bisexualized') explanation of sexuality.

In answer to interview questions as to how they see themselves as different from other lesbians, women providing this account distinguish themselves particularly from lesbian separatists, and express fears about living a 'ghettoized' existence:

> When they're saying they wouldn't consider a relationship with a man, I feel different. And when they're generally being anti-male and dismissing them as people . . . I don't think you can do that. They're 50 percent of the population and all that sort of thing, you know . . . I dislike . . . like, if you start a society for gay and bisexual women, and then you go to it or go to a gay society to meet lesbians, I dislike that attitude, that set-up. Because the only reason you're meeting together is because you're all gay or bisexual. So I start off resenting these groups, resenting it that I'm meeting these people, so I mean, the only reason they become my friends is because they're gay, rather than meeting the way other people meet friends. Jill (12)

> I don't believe that the only people I should go out with or relate to should be lesbians. I've got a lot of heterosexual friends, female friends mainly. I like mixing with heterosexual people who are not feminists. I don't believe in living in a lesbian ghetto. I'm not a separatist — some lesbians are, and I'm different from them. What else? I don't know . . . I'm not terribly political, that's another kind of difference. Charlotte (33)

This liberal feminist ideology is generally represented as an 'acceptable' face of feminism (in, for example, the hierarchical models discussed in Chapter 2), especially for its rejection of separatism as a political strategy:

> The very concept of turning away from men becomes the dreaded 'separatism': the dustbin into which all the 'bad' lesbians are dumped, while the 'good' ones remain those who will hotly deny any allegiance to such an outrageous idea. (London Lesbian Offensive Group, 1983)

The ideology represented by this account has also been described as a self-protective reaction to male oppression:

> Some women continue to be intimidated by the label 'anti-male'. Some feel a false need to draw distinctions, for example: 'I am antipatriarchal but not anti-male'. . . . This deception/reversal is so deep that women — even feminists — are intimidated into self-deception, becoming the only self-described oppressed who are unable to name their oppressor, referring instead to vague 'forces', 'roles', 'stereotypes', 'constraints', 'attitudes', 'influences'. (Daly, 1979: 28–9)

The difference between the political theory of this factor, and that represented in Factor I has been discussed by a number of feminist writers who have described two basic perspectives on the roots of sexism: 'there is the perspective that men oppress women. And there is the perspective that people are people, and we are all hurt by rigid sex roles' (Justice, 1977). The latter position comes closest to that represented by this factor, and as such is in conflict with the political position adopted in the former account, as represented by Factor I.

Factor III

In this account (defined by Q sorts 71 and 70, with 65 and 92 also having significant loadings), lesbianism is a private sexual orientation, not something to announce to the world or to transform into a political act and the militance of radical lesbians is strongly opposed. The political stance of this factor account is entirely compatible with the 'sorry-state' identity discussed in Chapter 4, elicited from two of the women (Nos. 65 and 71) who also contributed to this account of ideology.

The account insists on the private and personal nature of lesbianism, which is unrelated to political concerns:

		III
10.	Lesbianism is a private thing; what I do in bed is my business.	+5
11.	Romance and 'falling in love' are quite separate from politics and ideology.	+3
12.	Sex between two women is not in itself a political act.	+5

In this account there is no connection between politics and sexuality, oppressions other than the oppression of women are of at least equal concern, and personal freedom, rather than social revolution, is the goal:

		III
51.	Sexual orientation is a poor foundation on which to build your political ideology.	+3
16.	The oppression of other groups, like blacks and the working class, is at least as important to me as the oppression of women.	+2
45.	I don't want to change society; I just want the freedom to be myself.	+4

They do not identify strongly as women:

		III
26.	Being a woman is very important to me.	-3

And they oppose the militance of some radical lesbians:

		III
29.	It is wrong to alienate people by being too militant.	+5
32.	If we want to change social attitudes to lesbianism, a gentle approach is likely to be more effective.	+4
9.	I feel angry with women who draw attention to their lesbianism.	+1

As one woman (a retired police officer) said in interview:

> I resent the flamboyant lesbian. I think they bring it into mockery and alienate any understanding. Lynne (92)

Finally, these women present a firmly essentialist account of lesbianism as a 'sexual orientation':

		III
5.	Without society's sexual indoctrination, many more women would choose to be lesbian.	-4
36.	You cannot choose to be a lesbian; if you are, you are.	+3
28.	Most women who claim to have chosen lesbianism as a political decision were probably really lesbian anyway.	+2

> Lesbianism is not something you choose; not something anybody in their right mind *would* choose. But if you're stuck with it, then you just have to put up with it, and live your life with as much dignity as you can. Certainly things aren't helped by exhibitionists who run round screaming about their lesbianism and somehow link it to politics, as though you could vote Labour, Conservative, or Lesbian. Many of these women aren't even lesbians at all, but Women's Libbers jumping on the lesbian bandwagon for dubious motives of their own. They don't really have a clue what lesbianism is about. Lynne (92)

Similar antifeminist ideology is expressed by those writers who refer to radical feminist lesbians as 'the extremist fringe' exhibiting 'latter-day lesbian fascism' (Lewis, 1979: 174), or as 'the aggropedlars of the movement' (Evans, 1977). In the recent issue of the lesbian magazine *Artemis*, one woman writes:

> I am quite conservative, and find publications such as *Spare Rib* depressing . . . I am glad that in *your* publication, lesbianism has been portrayed as feminine and fun, instead of an angry political backlash. (Letter in *Artemis* 5, 1984)

And Elula Perrin, who runs the famous Katmandou lesbian nightclub in Paris, has written of feminist lesbians:

> They give the world a totally false image of the lesbian, and they presume to speak in our name — they are bisexual, nothing but lesbians of opportunity, ostentatious and indecorous lesbians at best. And we are assumed to be like them, in filthy jeans and rumpled shirts, with flopping breasts and greasy hair. Once they have 'become lesbians' they are relieved to think they will never again have to wear pretty clothes or curl their hair. Nonsense! (Perrin, 1980: 12–13)

Factor IV

The account of Factor IV (defined by Q sorts completed by lesbians 58 and 61, both of whom have significant loadings on the 'true happiness' factor (Factor I) of the 'identity' Q sort) represents lesbianism as a private solution to a political problem. In a world in which most women are 'naturally' heterosexual, some women have the good fortune to have a lesbian sexual orientation, and this affords them a great deal of personal happiness and freedom from male exploitation.

In interview both women talked about their happiness as lesbians:

> I'm extremely glad that I'm a lesbian. I can think of nothing nicer. It suits me perfectly: it suits my lifestyle, my career, to be a lesbian. I don't want to be tied by family; I can move around, I can be free, I can have a good social life. And in my particular work there aren't any problems with being gay. Virginia (61)

> Being lesbian is just totally and completely natural — for me, it's absolutely right. Everything I do as a lesbian is . . . comes naturally to me, and is the way I should be, that's all. And I think amongst the people that I know, we have a very pleasant life, really. It's just . . . *me*; it's just me being me, and therefore it's right, and therefore it's easy and relaxing, and it's just totally fulfilling for me, being a lesbian. Francesca (58)

Lesbianism is, for women presenting this account, fundamentally a private solution, a personal idyll, a source of happiness and contentment, and they are aware of their own privilege in experiencing it as such — a privilege made possible, in part because of their relative wealth and independence. (One of the two women whose sorts define this factor works as a self-employed and successful businesswoman, the other is a theatre director.)

> I have a sort of cocoon-like existence, I suppose, because . . . I mean, I have a certain amount of capital, and a large enough income to be able to create this cocoon, and so I'm very lucky. And I've found the sort of people I like, and we're all more or less independent — you know, lawyers, lecturers, businesswomen, whatever; you know, we *can* be independent. We can choose the way we want to live, and we can go to restaurants, good restaurants, as groups of women, and really you can go from week to week, month to month, even year to year, totally unaware that most people, if they knew you were lesbian, would hate you. So I'm very privileged and lucky in that sense. You know, I know some of these little eighteen-year-old kids go to pubs and stuff and get beaten up by the locals because they're lesbians, and I think that's tragic. You know, I don't know what to do about it; there's nothing I *can* do about it. . . . But I am aware, don't think I'm not, that I'm very privileged. Francesca (58)

In this account, 'sexual orientations' are seen as powerful controlling forces organized such that most women are neither lesbian nor bisexual, but firmly heterosexual in constitution:

		IV
60.	There is no such thing as 'sexual orientation'; we all have the potential to be anything sexually.	−2
17.	Every woman has the potential to be a lesbian if she chooses.	−3
36.	You cannot choose to be a lesbian; if you are, you are.	+4
52.	I believe that most people are basically bisexual.	−2
20.	Most women are, by nature, heterosexual.	+2

The analysis of lesbianism as a political phenomenon is largely limited, in this account, to the desire for 'freedom to be oneself':

		IV
45.	I don't want to change society; I just want the freedom to be myself.	+3
10.	Lesbianism is a private thing; what I do in bed is my business.	+3

While the oppression of women is acknowledged, the women presenting this account are notable for having, apparently, found a private solution to male oppression, believing that through lesbianism they are avoiding male exploitation:

		IV
39.	Whatever the time in history, wherever the place in the world, in every culture women are exploited by men.	+4
4.	Being a lesbian sets you free from male exploitation.	+4

Unlike the 'antifeminism' of Factor III, moderate social reforms are supported (e.g. the passing of antidiscrimination laws [item 54, scored +4], the extension of legal rights and duties associated with marriage to cover lesbian couples [item 56, scored +2]), but neither of the women presenting this account is involved in political activity:

> I feel really I ought to do more, but I just . . . well, sink back into happiness I suppose. Francesca (58)

> I'm concerned about what's happening to women, and where we're going, and the way that we're second-class citizens; I'm very concerned about that. But not concerned enough to get up and do anything about it. Even in my work in the theatre. People say, 'well, you're in a perfect position, you know, you have a platform!' but it just isn't uppermost in my mind. Virginia (61)

Ideologies incorporating sentiments not dissimilar to Francesca's statement that she 'just sinks back into happiness' are discussed, usually critically, by a number of feminist authors. A feminist poet complains: 'My lesbian friends kept saying/ I like my job/ No one bothers me/ I'm happy/ My private life is my own business' (Winant, 1971), and another poet asserts that 'those who lie in the arms of the "individual solution"/ the "private Odyssey"/ the "personal growth"/ are the most conformist of all' (Morgan, 1978). The happiness and contentment that can come from lesbianism are identified as inhibiting political action:

> There *is* a danger for women, however, in the fact that lesbian relationships are often so much more fulfilling than heterosexual ones. Sometimes when a lesbian discovers the joy of loving women, she feels that she has arrived, that she has made it, and that this is the individual solution to all her problems. She is tempted to put more and more energy into her personal relationships and lose her militancy as a feminist. . . . It is crucial for a feminist who becomes a lesbian to keep her political analysis in mind and not to imagine her oppression as a woman has ended just because she now has a woman lover. (Goodman et al., 1983: 81)

In contrast to the account presented here, the radical feminist or political lesbian account does *not* usually incorporate the belief that through lesbianism a woman can attain personal liberation:

> A heterosexually identified woman who chooses to become a lesbian does not choose liberation over oppression. She chooses a public relationship with the oppressor over a private feudal one. Moving out of the heterosexist family, she identifies herself and her interests with women as a class. As a class, women are still oppressed, but as lesbians, we are no longer tied to a private master/servant relationship. This explains for me why lesbianism, while not a liberated lifestyle, is still a positive choice. What I have chosen, as a lesbian, is the *form* my oppression will take. (Peterson, 1980)

Factor V

Factor V is defined by just one woman's Q sort (No. 10), and she also defines Factor VII in the 'identity' accounts study, in which it was suggested that her's is a bifurcated account in which two self-stories, one effectively radical feminist, the other the traditional version of lesbianism as pathology, relate in inner dialogue. This is made explicit at various points in her interview, as in the following example:

> There's still a bit of me that can be thrown back at times into thinking 'is it still, after all, some kind of fear or immaturity, some kind of fear of male sexuality?' Of course, that's funny, because whereas at one time you could see fear of male sexuality as being just a negative thing, just an immaturity, with the reinforcement of the feminist movement now you can see that as being perfectly valid. You know, perfectly valid because men are bloody aggressive and violent and all the rest of it, and it's perfectly reasonable to be fearful of that. That's all valid, whereas for years and years I thought that was a lack of appreciation on my part, for not being able to appreciate the maleness of men. Rachel (10)

Rachel herself makes explicit the extent to which she holds contradictory views about her lesbianism:

> I think what you do all the time is to hold two things at the same time, in a way, concurrently almost. That is partly to hold at a very, very deep level that, yes, you're a lesbian and you're not anything else. And at another level, to think, almost equally, that you're not really a lesbian, and that you've just got into the way of thinking that you are, and it might be because you need to feel different, or it might be because you feel you're unlovable by a man, or because what you'd really like is maternal love, and if you had a big enough dose of that then you'd be cured, as it were. So, yes, in a sense, all those ideas you can hold at the same time.

In this Q sort, she certainly endorses a number of items salient to the radical feminist account, meaning that her account differs markedly from the 'antifeminism' of Factor III.

		V	(III)
45.	I don't want to change society; I just want the freedom to be myself.	−5	(+4)
10.	Lesbianism is a private thing; what I do in bed is my business.	−4	(+5)
26.	Being a woman is very important to me.	+5	(−3)

But this account also *differs* significantly from many of the radical feminist scores, especially those relating to political lesbianism and lesbian separatism (e.g. items 21 [−3], 27 [+3], 42 [+4]). Compared with the liberal account of Factor II, this account is far more radical, particularly in its theoretical conceptualization of lesbianism as a blow against the patriarchy (item 14 [+4]), and in its analysis of oppression as perpetrated by men (not merely their institutions) (item 35 [−1] and 43 [−1]).

The striking differences between Rachel's account and those of other women in this study can be interpreted with reference to aspects of her biography which, while they distinguish her from the other women included here, are common experiences of many lesbians who so defined themselves in the 1930s, 1940s and 1950s (Almvig, 1982). Born in 1929, Rachel describes how she identified herself as a lesbian in her early teens, and adopted a 'stone butch' role in which she refused sexual reciprocation: not until the early 1970s did this change for her:

> There's no doubt that in my early days when I was in love with women who were never in love with me — they kind of put up with me — there's no doubt about it that I felt in a *male* role toward them, because I tended to fall in love with women whom I saw as being more feminine than myself, and I *certainly* didn't want them to pay any attention to the female aspects . . . to my female physical . . . the female bits of my body. I didn't want them to be attracted to me as a woman, or to pay any attention to me sexually. I wouldn't have wanted them to touch my breasts . . . or anything like that. And in that sense, yes, I've undergone a complete change, and I feel that sexually the relationship I have with Helen is very equal in that sense. It was the relationship with Janice that broke the pattern. But before that I might as well have been fully clothed, really, for all the interest I wanted the other person to take in my body as such. I mean, I wanted to be the one taking an interest in *their* body.

With her exposure to the Gay and Women's Liberation movements, Rachel says now:

> I *hate* any notion that we do that butch/femme thing. I mean, I totally reject it. Those words strike the kind of horror in me that the word 'lesbian' did twenty, thirty years ago, and I absolutely detest them, these notions. I *hate* any idea of role-playing.

The priority she gives to rejecting butch/femme role-playing in her Q sort is presumably derived from the fact that this item has considerably more salience for her than it does for the other women defining factors, none of whom have reported being personally involved in role-playing, and many of whom say that they have encountered it only in fiction.

V

50. I reject the notions 'butch' and 'femme'; they are irrelevant
    to lesbianism.   +4

In summary, this factor can be seen as reflecting the politics of someone who initially constructed a lesbian identity in the 1940s (as 'sick' and male-identified), and who has subsequently, in the context of the Gay and Women's movements, constructed a radically different — in many ways, diametrically opposed — identity, but has relinquished only in part, or only spasmodically, much of her original construction, while firmly rejecting some aspects of it.

Current radical feminist theory (especially that of political lesbianism) provides an elaborate interpretative framework within which erstwhile *heterosexual* women can reconstruct their biographies, but has evaded issues necessary to many *lesbians* who so defined themselves before the current wave of feminism. Where the ex-heterosexual woman can talk of her own past in feminist terms, analysing its oppressions and detailing its exploitation, the ex 'butch' is met with a resounding and embarrassed silence from her radical feminist sisters. The evasion, within much of the Women's Liberation Movement, of any attempt towards understanding (rather than simply dismissing) the particular oppressions endured by 'butch' lesbians has been described as one of the manifestations of the widespread and reactionary acceptance of male-defined 'femininity', rife in lesbian and feminist communities as well as in society generally:

> Because femmes — in varying degrees — fit more closely the male-created ideal of 'real woman' we are more privileged than butches, both in the het world and in Lesbian communities. Because butches have rejected feminine conditioning more completely, they are treated as being more Queer, more suspect, more 'unnatural'. (Strega, 1985)

There has been relatively little attempt to incorporate the complexities of butch and femme roles into a radical feminist framework in a way that could recognize the courage of the butch (and femme) lesbians of the early decades of this century and which might provide a political perspective on their importance to lesbian history and identities. To refuse to acknowledge the (continuing) existence of butch and femme roles, to avoid discussing their meaning, is to discount and dismiss the survival strategies of many of our lesbian sisters and foresisters. Until the experience of 'butch' and 'femme' lesbians is acknowledged, accepted and analysed with as much clarity as is the experience of the heterosexual woman, both they and feminism will be the poorer.

Factor VI

The woman whose Q sort defines this factor is Alison (57), who also defines the 'true love' account in the 'identity' study, and many of the themes that distinguished that factor are reiterated here, including an emphasis on romantic love and sexual exclusiveness:

VI

11. Romance and 'falling in love' are quite separate from
    politics and ideology.   +2
31. Sisterhood with all women should come before your love
    for one woman.   −3
23. Lesbians should seek alternatives to monogamy.   −3

In line with Alison's bisexual self-construction, she expresses here a relatively favourable attitude to men:

VI

42. I wouldn't want to live in a woman-only world.   +4
35. Men are as oppressed by social expectation as women are.   +2
27. Men are 50 percent of the human race; it is silly trying to
    live separately from them.   +3

Alison's perception of the need for social change is tempered by her belief that militant action is counterproductive:

VI

45. I don't want to change society; I just want the freedom
    to be myself.   −4
32. If we want to change social attitudes to lesbianism, a gentle
    approach is likely to be more effective.   +5
29. It is wrong to alienate people by being too militant.   +4

Her political approach to change is evident from her interview:

In my teaching, when people make silly remarks like 'Michaelangelo was a poofta,' I say, 'Yes, he was a homosexual; I'll show you some slides next week and see if you can pick up his love for men from his work.' And then we talk about his erotic paintings of men and we get very serious, and you can put across feminist ideas without ever spelling it out crassly — you know, without ever using words like 'Women's Lib' or . . . I never use words like that. I was showing a whole lot of slides of eighteenth-century artists, and I said, 'Do you realize that in every one of those the subject has been "The Rape of Europa", "The Rape of Philomel", "The Rape of this that and the other"?' And I said, 'Do you get a feeling of distress from *any* of those paintings? Do you feel in any one of them that someone's being dreadfully hurt?' And they said, 'Oh no!' for every picture. And I said, 'Whose point of view are you seeing it from?' And in that way you can put across a lot of . . . And I feel it always comes down to how you put it across. If I ever sort of spelled it out with labels. . . . I just think I'm doing it the way *I'm* best at. I'm just not really political. I think I really can do something in my own way.

This account is fundamentally a liberal feminism not dissimilar to that of Factor II, but with a still more notably pro-male slant, and with a strong emphasis on employing less militant, more 'sensitive' and 'non-polemical' tactics in promoting feminist ideas. However, while Alison identifies herself as sharing radical feminist politics but disapproving of their tactics, many radical feminists see the account she presents as adhering to an entirely different set of ideological principles, because the politics of radical feminism includes the belief that such tactics are necessary.

The gradualist concept of social change presented in this account contrasts drastically with the radical feminist demand with radical social change: this difference can be seen as representing a central distinction between those who participate in movements of social transformation and their supporters:

> The committed Black Power participant feels the same thing when he [*sic*] hears white liberals say 'I respect your goals and agree with them wholeheartedly, but I cannot go along with your methods.' Black Power ideology includes not only the long-range goals of equal opportunity, equal rights and self-respect for black Americans; it also includes the argument that if the means to these ends were actually available in the American political economic and social structure as it now exists, the goals would long ago have been reached. The belief that such means do not, in fact, exist, and therefore must be created by radical social innovation, constitutes an ideological glass wall between the Black Power militant and the earnest white liberal or the conservative black Civil Rights workers. . . . Participants in movements know the glass wall is there, and nonparticipants typically do not. (Gerlach and Hine, 1970: 176)

Like the liberal feminism of Factor II, this account is often awarded the seal of approval from many liberal members of the established order. It is a 'rational' and 'reasonable' approach, and they join with her in condemning radical ideologies as 'extremist', 'hostile' and 'violent'.

This study has elicited six different accounts of the politics of lesbianism: one radical feminist, two liberal feminist, an antifeminist account, a mixed account combining elements of both radical feminism and antifeminism, and a representation of lesbianism as a personal solution to a political problem.

The differences between the radical and the liberal feminist constructions of lesbianism have been brought to the fore and clarified in the context of the 'political lesbian' debate within the Women's Liberation Movement. Other commentators suggest that debate around the issue of political lesbianism reflects two different political positions, the first of which might be characterized as 'liberal feminism':

> If you accept feminism only as one part of a wider struggle for human rights; accept the politics of gradual reform of existing institutions and attitudes; believe that it is not only worthwhile, but proper work to be trying to change men, then there is nothing inconsistent about women sleeping with men, even if you don't do it yourself. Lesbians who hold

these views see their sexuality as merely a question of sexual preference. (Alderson, 1981: 57)

This position is reflected in Factors II, VI, and, to a lesser extent, Factor IV. The radical feminist position, from which the theory of political lesbianism is derived, is summarized as follows:

> If, however, you believe that the patriarchy is the root of all forms of oppression, that all men benefit from and maintain it and are, therefore, to be seen as the enemy; that the power balance cannot be changed by reason, patience and simply right being on our side; and further that women must build positions of autonomous strength through and with each other — then it is clearly a big inconsistency to, at the same time, be in close sexual/emotional relationships with men. (Alderson, 1981: 57–8)

The same split in political beliefs has been characterized as a division between separatists and radical feminists on the one hand, and assimilationists on the other:

> Separatists . . . maintain that the only way to free ourselves from male domination is for all females to withdraw from men, to withhold from them our energy, our nurturing, our care-taking of them; only in this way, we believe, can we erode the foundation of male power and control over us. . . . The Assimilationists, in contrast, maintain that the only way to liberate ourselves is to 'struggle' with men, educate them about their sexism, nurture them through the painful changes necessary to a thorough-going social revolution. (Penelope, 1986: 45)

This study provides evidence for the split outlined by Alderson (1981) and Penelope (1986) and clarifies a variety of different liberal political perspectives as they relate to lesbianism.

Contemporary psychology provides, as I have shown, support for liberal or assimilationist ideologies, while denouncing radical political ideologies as indicative of pathological disturbance or developmental immaturity. By way of conclusion, it is worth noting, however, a recent trend in psychological theorizing towards the ostensible legitimation of at least some aspects of the radical ideology. Compared with the liberal ideologies, radical feminism puts a great deal of emphasis on the importance of both the open assertion of one's lesbianism, and on involvement in the lesbian counterculture. Both are seen as furthering the political ends of radical feminism: as Rita Mae Brown says, discussing the need for disclosure of one's lesbianism, 'Every time you keep your mouth shut you make life that much harder for every lesbian in this country' (Brown, 1972: 190), and, on the need for involvement in lesbian groups: 'The more disparate we are, the more vulnerable we are. . . . Individuality is the luxury of the white man' (Brown, 1975).

Traditionally, psychology has represented involvement in the lesbian counterculture as leading a 'ghettoized' existence, and openness about one's lesbianism as 'flaunting' one's pathology (e.g. 'Most lesbian women are content to keep their homosexual inclinations hidden from general view and it is only the most psychopathic among them who make a show of their abnormality' [Munro and McCulloch, 1969, quoted in Hart and Richardson, 1980]).

Recent developments in the literature suggest that psychology is shifting towards a general approval of overt lesbianism and countercultural involvement. This reversal is in line with the other shifts in psychological opinion described in Chapter 4: lesbians once discovered to be unhappy are now proved to be personally fulfilled, once discovered to be incapable of 'true love' are now proved to have more egalitarian and sexually satisfying relationships. Similarly, coming out as lesbian and involvement in the counterculture, once proof of pathology, is now apparently essential for mental health.

Through presenting these *political* strategies in the individualized terms of mental health, psychology again seeks to depoliticize lesbianism, rendering even overt political activities politically innocuous. The message some psychologists are now offering is that it's okay to be politically active (to the extent of coming out and being involved in lesbian groups) because such activity has beneficial effects on our psychological health. Closeted gays are now described as 'pathological nondisclosers [whose] option to pursue a meaningful and productive life wanes' (Ehrlich, 1981: 134).

> The decision to conceal the homosexual identity from significant others may be detrimental to psychological wellbeing. Is it possible to achieve an integrated personal identity or have authentic relationships while concealing fundamental aspects of the self? Recent studies suggest that closeted homosexual men have negative attitudes to homosexuality and experience barriers to self-acceptance. (Minton and McDonald, 1984: 102)

Whereas in the past overt homosexuality compounded the original pathology, recent psychology ascribes it the whole panoply of liberal humanistic virtues. Similarly, involvement in the gay and lesbian communities is now considered an important aid to adjustment and 'some evidence suggests that homosexuals who are involved in their subculture exhibit higher levels of self-esteem than those only marginally related to it' (Troiden, 1984). One detailed study of the relationship between participation in the lesbian community and lesbian mental health demonstrates that 'happiness' (as measured on the 'affectometer') is positively correlated with involvement in lesbian groups (Rand et al., 1982).

Psychology, then, has either pathologized political involvement and 'extremist' ideologies, located them at lower levels in hierarchical models of development, or conceded that certain aspects of such ideologies are acceptable on the grounds that they enhance mental health. In all such cases, the emphasis is on the person and her or his individual characteristics, rather than on the ideology and its political content. This emphasis contributes to psychology's continuing relocation of the political in the realm of the private and personal. Even explicitly political actions and beliefs are described in terms of their presumed origination in or consequences for the private mental and emotional life of the individual.

6
The Social Construction of Prejudice

Psychological research on attitudes to oppressed groups has generally been carried out within the framework of the psychology of prejudice: that is, an operational definition of a negative or prejudiced attitude to the group in question is constructed, and this forms the basis of a rating scale which is then used to assess the degree of prejudice within individual subjects. Much of the classic research central to psychological understandings of prejudice relies on scales constructed in this manner (e.g. Bogardus's [1925] social distance scales, and Adorno et al.'s [1950] anti-Semitism and F scales). Research employing such scales can then 'calculate' the number of prejudiced people in the population (e.g. the percentage of prejudiced individuals in Britain was discovered to be 27 percent in 1968 [Rose, 1969, quoted in Littlewood and Lipsedge, 1982: 59]) or, more commonly, may attempt to uncover correlates of prejudice in terms of associated personality patterns, family background and psychodynamic factors. Such studies usually engage in character assassination of prejudiced persons:

> Racism and anti-Semitism are described as part of a pathological personality pattern characterized by sexual inhibition, anxiety, obsession, a strong tendency to acquiesce to authority and to impose authority on those in subordinate positions. (Adorno et al., 1950)

Where once science proved the inferiority of blacks and Jews, now liberal psychology proves the pathology of the racist and anti-Semite: in one study it was found that 'the anti-Semite group does not contain a single individual who can be regarded as normal' (Robb, 1954: 222) and racism has been hailed as 'America's chief mental health problem' (*Psychiatric News*, 1975).

Although more recent research on prejudice against blacks and Jews tends towards a conceptualization of racism as a social institution rather than a personal pathology (Jones, 1972; Sanford, 1973; Littlewood and Lipsedge, 1982), research on attitudes to homosexuals (male and female) is, overwhelmingly, modelled on the earlier individualized concept of prejudice employed in the classic studies of racism and anti-Semitism. Such research is generally formulated and implemented in terms of a hypothetical state supposedly manifested by people who are strongly prejudiced against homosexuals. This is the pathological condition of 'homophobia' introduced and discussed in Chapter 2, and also known as 'homoerotophobia' (Churchill, 1967), 'homophiliaphobia' (Cole, 1973), 'homosexism' (Hansen, 1982), 'antihomosexualism' (Dunbar et al., 1973) and 'gayism' (Henley and Pincus, 1978). In Chapter 2 I argued that homophobia research represents an explicit attempt to construct subjectivities about lesbianism in accordance with liberal humanistic ideology. I showed how this is achieved through the construction of an operational definition of prejudice, i.e. the designation of specific scale items as 'pro' or 'anti' gay, such that those consistent with liberal humanism are promoted as constituting the only 'unprejudiced' and mentally healthy attitudes. This chapter presents a Q study of attitudes to lesbianism which both avoids the a priori definition of certain attitudes as 'favourable' or 'unfavourable' and which explicitly addresses and renders problematic the issue of people's varying understandings of what it is to hold a 'favourable' or 'unprejudiced' attitude to lesbianism.

The early homophobia studies which appeared at the beginning of the 1970s (e.g. Smith, 1971; MacDonald and Games, 1974; Lumby, 1976) have been criticized by more recent authors on a number of counts. In particular, researchers have criticized their incorporation of a male bias, such that 'homophobia' is almost always understood as fear of *male* homosexuals (Plummer, 1981: 63), while lesbians are either ignored altogether (as in the scale constructed by Smith, 1971), or the word 'lesbian' is subsequently substituted for the word 'homosexual' in each item to create a scale supposedly suitable for studying attitudes to lesbians (e.g. MacDonald and Games, 1974); and criticism has also been made of their individuocentric description of the oppression of homosexuals as caused by the personal pathology of specific individuals who deviate from the supposedly egalitarian norms of society, thus obscuring analysis of our oppression as a political problem rooted in social institutions and organizations; the oppression of homosexuals is, like racism, 'not a disease but part of a political system' (Littlewood and Lipsedge, 1982: 10). Additionally, I have also argued (in Chapter 2) that, through its assumption of the right of psychological experts to define what counts as 'prejudice' and what counts as 'mental health', homophobia research serves the covert function of reinforcing the status of psychology as a scientific discipline. Moreover, like most research of this type (Gergen, 1973), it presents the academic psychologist in a highly favourable light. The more similar the respondent is to the researcher, the more likely she or he is to be discovered to be 'unprejudiced' toward homosexuals: homophobia is negatively correlated with higher education (Henley and Pincus, 1978; Hudson and Ricketts, 1980), left-wing political allegiances (Henley and Pincus, 1978) and Caucasian origin (Hudson and Ricketts, 1980).

The criticism on which I focus in this chapter, however, is related to the operational definition of homophobia, a concern reflected in much of the recent homophobia research. Recent writers have criticized the operational definitions of the earlier scales for their lack of balance (many were heavily weighted with 'anti' gay items, Weis and Dain, 1979), their lack of standardization (Kite, 1984), the lack of information as to validity or reliability (Serdahely and Ziemba, 1985: 111; Mosher and O'Grady, 1979) and their postulation of the existence of a single, unidimensional continuum, from 'prejudice' at one end to 'acceptance' at the other. Consequently a great deal of research is now structured around the perceived need to create an objective, valid and reliable operational definition of homophobia.

The search for an objective definition of 'homophobia' has led to the fragmentation of the original unitary concept of 'prejudice against homosexuals', as different aspects of what it means to be prejudiced are identified and labelled. Factor analytic studies of 'homophobia' items (R methodologically) have suggested that homophobia scales are not usually unidimensional instruments. An analysis of one early homophobia scale (MacDonald et al., 1972) revealed three factors ('moral condemnation and repression', 'denial of similarity between heterosexual and homosexual relationships', and 'personal revulsion and threat') (Herek, 1984). The first factor, with a positive pole of 'tolerance' and a negative one of 'condemnation' also emerged in a re-analysis of another homophobia study (Millham et al., 1976), and as in the previous study, accounted for the greatest percent variance (Herek, 1984). On the basis of these findings, Herek recommends that homophobia scales should in future be limited to items found to load on this factor, from which a unidimensional scale can be constructed. While Herek's resulting and, he claims, unidimensional definition of prejudice against homosexuals includes both items that characterize homosexuality as unnatural, disgusting, perverse and sinful, and also items advocating social sanctions against homosexuality, other authors have made a distinction between these two components. Hudson and Ricketts (1980), for example, use the term 'homonegativism' to describe the multidimensional set of possible cognitive and affective antihomosexual attitudes, and define homophobia as constituting only the *affective* component of prejudice against homosexuals (fear, disgust, anger, discomfort, and aversion), excluding cognitive responses (decisions and judgements about legality, personal and social relationships, morality etc.). In addition, other researchers have distinguished between 'homophobia' or fear of homosexuals, and alternative possible negative affective reactions which they label 'homosexual panic', 'homosexual prejudice' and 'homosexual threat' (Mosher and O'Grady, 1979).

All these various attempts to arrive at a valid and reliable definition of prejudice against homosexuals share a common problem — prejudice against homosexuals cannot be objectively defined. There exists only a range of different ideological positions, each positing its own definition of what constitutes a 'prejudiced' attitude towards homosexuals. People's definitions of what constitute 'favourable' (unprejudiced) or 'unfavourable' (prejudiced) attitudes depend heavily on their own opinions and beliefs. Competing beliefs about what constitutes a favourable or unfavourable attitude to a marginalized group can thus be seen as *data*. Traditionally, however, 'prejudice' has been defined in normative cultural terms, a fact which is most easily illustrated in historical perspective. An early study of attitudes to blacks (Hinckley, 1932, quoted in Roiser, 1974) included the following items, scored so that agreement was counted as having a favourable or unprejudiced attitude:

> A wide-awake Negro is physically superior and in other respects equal to the white man.

> The Negro is fully capable of social equality with the white man, but he should not be so recognized until he is better trained.

> The rich spiritual life of the Negro compensates adequately for the defects in his nature.

This scale had been pretested and the ratings of a subgroup of mainly black respondents, whose deviant judgements Hinckley considered indicative of 'poor discrimination and carelessness' had been excluded. Similarly, a study of the definition of prejudice incorporated into the Levinson–Sanford anti-Semitism scale found that many of the items scored by these researchers as indicative of a 'prejudiced' attitude to Jews were not interpreted in this way by Jewish activists, many of whom opposed the liberal-assimilationist definition embodied in the scale:

> Is it anti-Semitic to say that it is wrong for Jews and Gentiles to intermarry? Seventy-four percent of our Gentile subjects, who were apparently interpreting the statement to mean segregation, thought so . . . But less than half that percentage of Jews (difference significant) interpreted the statement as anti-Semitic because 'it is not in the interests of Jews to marry non-Jews.' (Kaye, 1947)

There is, then, consistent evidence that people's ratings of items as 'favourable' or 'unfavourable' depend heavily on their own opinions and beliefs about the topic in question. But the implications of this finding are applied only to those making *deviant* judgements, and the ideologies underlying *normative* ratings are never explored. For example, one author, summing up the accumulated evidence, comments:

> Evidence seems to indicate that the attitude of the judge may bias his [*sic*] judgement of statements; however, only judges with extreme attitudes will show substantial distortion. (Thomas, 1978: 10)

Thus, rather than treating competing beliefs about what constitutes a favourable or unfavourable attitude to a marginalized group as *data*, this traditional approach merely obscures these differences by explaining away the views of deviant judges as 'distorted'. The answer lies not in revising or refining these scales so that they better reflect some 'objective' standard of favourability but in recognizing that there *is* no such objective standard — only ideological positions which posit different beliefs as favourable or unfavourable.

Just as some blacks rejected the consensual definition of 'prejudice against blacks' incorporated into Hinckley's racism scale, and some Jews rejected Levinson and Sanford's definition of 'anti-Semitism', so many homosexuals may not accept the liberal definition of 'homophobia'. One male gay researcher, for example, comments on the notion, commonly incorporated into the operational definition of a 'favourable attitude' that 'gays are just the same as straights', arguing that this is in fact a profoundly antihomosexual view in that it represents the liberal refusal to notice and attempt to dissolve the specificities of homosexual existence, and contributes to the 'dehomosexualizing' of homosexuals (Dannecker, 1981). From a different theoretical perspective, another researcher argues that it is not necessarily 'unfavourable' to find homosexual acts disgusting:

> The heterosexual with a secure identity will usually experience disgust toward homosexual acts, but that need not imply an extension of that disgust to the actor or the class of persons who engage in such acts . . . nor does the ego-alien affect preclude a variety of positive feelings between heterosexual and homosexual. (Pattison, 1974)

However, these debates about the proper definition of homophobia miss the central point that prejudice against homosexuals can only be defined in the context of specific ideological frameworks: the liberal humanistic construction of a 'favourable' attitude towards homosexuals is thus one derived from a particular ideological perspective not shared by some traditional psychoanalysts, on the one hand, or some radical gays, on the other.

There is, however, very little professional discussion about what constitutes a 'favourable' view of lesbians (or male homosexuals). What does exist is usually phrased in terms of recommendations to the Gay Movement for improving its image. Arguing that prejudice against homosexuality is caused by fear of blurring gender divisions and, particularly, of losing the association between 'masculinity' and 'virility', some researchers suggest that 'increased visibility of "masculine" male homosexuals may do much to further the success of the Gay Liberation Movement', adding that

> The choice of the word 'gay' for male homosexuals may have been an unfortunate one. It is difficult to conceive of a strong association between 'gay' and 'potent'. (MacDonald and Games, 1974)

Similarly, lesbians are counselled to avoid both 'superfeminine' and 'butch-macho' appearance in order to reduce pejorative attitudes (Laner and Laner, 1980). Another researcher recommends that gay people should strive to counter three specific beliefs which, he says, are strongly associated with negative attitudes to homosexuals. People are apparently more 'negative', in Thompson's terms, if they believe that homosexuals are inappropriately identified with the other gender, if they believe that people can be 'made' homosexual through early seduction, and, most importantly, if they believe that we have a *choice* in our 'sexual orientation'. 'These people are very anti-homosexual. Some gay people write about sex *choice*, and when we do that we're feeding into this notion, and feeding into negative attitudes' (Thompson, 1983). Finally, Herek suggests that to change attitudes to gay people interactions between gays and straights should be carefully structured to meet certain criteria:

> Common group memberships other than sexual orientation should be made salient (e.g. religious, social, ethnic, and political); contact should occur on a one-to-one basis rather than group-to-group; and the lesbian or gay man should violate some commonly held stereotypes or several homosexual persons should be visible so as to demonstrate the diversity of the community. (Herek, 1984)

None of these authors considers the possibility that, for some lesbians, the maintenance of gender stereotypes and denial of choice in lesbianism might be seen as negative attitudes per se, or that a favourable attitude in radical feminist terms is possible only when so-called 'sexual orientation' is recognized as an important and salient feature of every interaction.

The aim of the research reported here is to elicit a diverse range of 'actual' attitudes about lesbians and to discuss these in terms of different constructions of the 'most favourable' view of lesbians. Q methodology is used here to elicit people's constructions of lesbianism and of the most 'favourable' view of lesbians. Unlike most research in this area, the items generated are specific to lesbians as distinct from male homosexuals; unlike rating scales and opinion-poll research (e.g. Levitt and Klassen, 1974) I am interested in the interrelationship of items and in their different meanings for different people; unlike research on prejudice which relies on electrophysiological measures (Cooper, 1959), or disguised techniques (Weissbach and Zagon, 1975; Snyder and Uranowitz, 1978), my concern is with what people are able and willing to *say* about their attitudes. It is not assumed that this has any necessary relation to action (LaPiere, 1934; Linn, 1965; Wicker, 1969). Finally, 'favourable' views of lesbians have usually been used as templates in terms of which all other views are assessed: if this were the procedure to be followed here, I could, for example, use my own Q sorting, or that of other radical feminist lesbians, as the model of the 'unprejudiced' attitude, and correlate the Q sorts of all other participants with this, correlations approaching +1 indicating increasing lack of prejudice, and correlations approaching -1 representing increasing prejudice. This is not so different from what psychologists normally do, except that they reserve for themselves the exclusive right to make the template. However, in this study, both 'actual' and 'favourable' Q sorts will be entered into the same data pool and factor analysed together following the procedure used in the preceding chapters. Factors that emerge may then be composed exclusively of either 'actual' or 'favourable' sorts, or may be defined by a combination of the two.

Method

A sixty-four item Q sort was derived from examination of the following sources: professional (scientific and religious) literature on homosexuality; professional literature on 'homophobia' or prejudice against homosexuals; explicitly gay literature on attitudes to homosexuals; comments made to me personally about lesbianism; sex-education books, and media presentations. A list of these items is given in Table 6.1.

Forty-three Q sorts were completed, thirty-seven by non-lesbians and six by lesbians. 'Actual' attitude Q sorts were obtained by asking non-lesbians to sort the cards so as to describe their views of lesbians. 'Most favourable' sorts were obtained by asking both non-lesbians and lesbians to use the Q sort to describe 'the most favourable (or unprejudiced) view of lesbians'. (Additionally, one lesbian

Table 6.1   *Q sort items for 'attitudes to lesbianism' Q sort*

1. I would be afraid for a daughter of mine to have a teacher who was a lesbian.
2. I find lesbianism difficult to accept because of my moral and/or religious beliefs.
3. I suspect that some lesbian women can be turned into heterosexuals by men who have enough sexual skill.
4. Lesbianism is clearly unnatural in that sex is intended for reproductive purposes and lesbianism clearly cannot achieve this.
5. People who have strong prejudices against lesbians are probably just trying to repress their own homosexuality.
6. I would probably find it a bit difficult to know just how to behave towards a lesbian.
7. Lesbianism is a blow against the patriarchy (i.e. society structured by men for men).
8. Lesbianism is a private thing; what people do in bed is their own business.
9. I'd like to see a law similar to that against racial prejudice which would aim to protect lesbians against prejudice and abuse.
10. It's probably true to say that some lesbians are just ugly women who can't get a man.
11. Lesbians differ from heterosexual women only in terms of their sexual preference.
12. I find lesbianism more acceptable than male homosexuality.
13. Most lesbians seem to hate men.
14. I think lesbianism is probably due to early environmental influences, such as the girl's relationship with her parents, and the kind of upbringing she had.
15. I think there are probably more lesbians these days than there were in the past.
16. There is no such thing as 'sexual orientation': we all have the potential to be anything sexually.
17. Lesbians are giving the Women's Movement a bad name.
18. I would like to have sex with a lesbian — just to see what it was like.
19. Some women who say they are lesbians are just trying to be different.
20. Fear of becoming pregnant and giving birth probably explains some lesbianism.
21. I think a lot of men feel very threatened by lesbianism.
22. Lesbians should count themselves lucky: there are other groups (like the unemployed, blacks, etc.) that are much worse off.
23. It would be upsetting for me to find that I was alone with a lesbian.
24. I think sadness and regret are the appropriate emotions of any parents who find they have a lesbian daughter.
25. I think that sex is probably not very important in most lesbian relationships.
26. I think the best approach to lesbianism is to hate the sin but love the sinner.
27. People should not be pigeon-holed just according to their sexual orientation.
28. There's too much fuss made about the whole topic of lesbianism.
29. There are probably good biological reasons for lesbianism — such as population control.
30. Lesbian couples should be allowed to adopt children if they want to.
31. Nowadays it seems as though it's trendy to be lesbian.
32. I have gained the impression that lesbians are sexually promiscuous.

33. Lesbians who insist on talking about their lesbianism all the time are just alienating people who might otherwise be on their side.
34. I am disgusted by the thought of two women having sex.
35. I believe that most lesbians are actually bisexual.
36. Lesbianism is fundamentally a political statement, not a sexual preference.
37. Lesbians pose a threat to the nuclear family and society as we know it.
38. I can't see how sex with another woman can be as satisfying as sex with a man.
39. I find the thought of a lesbian sexual act arousing.
40. I think lesbianism is probably genetic or hormonal in origin.
41. Lesbianism is a perfectly natural state for a small minority of women and probably always will be.
42. Lesbians seem to have 'got stuck' in what should be a passing adolescent phase.
43. Some people seem to have gone to the other extreme and be saying that lesbianism is actually *better* than heterosexuality.
44. I suspect most lesbians find the idea of sex with a man repugnant.
45. I would imagine that lesbian couples are usually made up of the 'butch' (the one taking the male role) and the 'femme' (the other).
46. I believe that most people are basically bisexual.
47. If a lesbian genuinely wishes it, facilities should be available to help her to change.
48. A woman who enjoys sex with a man is not a lesbian.
49. Lesbian couples should be treated exactly the same way as married couples with regard to housing, benefits, etc.
50. Books which portray lesbianism as a sickness or aberration should be withdrawn from schools and public libraries.
51. It's hard to understand how feminist women can justify having *heterosexual* relationships.
52. I don't mind lesbians, but I wish they weren't so blatant.
53. I'm not aware of ever having known a lesbian.
54. Every woman could be a lesbian if she so chose.
55. I have no sympathy for the man-hating kind of lesbian.
56. Many lesbians are in some sense 'masculine' — in the way they look or the way they behave.
57. I think a lot of lesbians are paranoid; they see prejudice and discrimination where there isn't any.
58. I am fairly sure that I would know if a woman I met was a lesbian without having to be told.
59. Lesbianism is a personal tragedy and lesbians deserve sympathy and understanding.
60. I don't think there is any simple or single explanation of lesbianism.
61. I'd bet there are more lesbians in this society than in more primitive cultures because we have moved further away from nature.
62. I find it hard to imagine what it must feel like to be a lesbian.
63. There isn't much prejudice against lesbians any more.
64. If two people really love each other, then it shouldn't matter whether they are a woman and a man, or two women.

participant completed a 'most unfavourable [or prejudiced]' sort.) The forced quasi-normal distribution employed in this study was:

−5	−4	−3	−2	−1	0	+1	+2	+3	+4	+5
3	4	6	7	8	8	8	7	6	4	3

Amongst the participants in this study were eighteen psychology undergraduates (divided into three groups of six), who participated as paid volunteers. They first completed individual sorts according to the appropriate condition of instruction ('actual' or 'most favourable') and then engaged in a group discussion lasting between 45 minutes and an hour. In order to provoke debate, I selected out Q sort items about which there was considerable disagreement between group members (i.e. items which some of the six participants in each group had scored so as to indicate strong agreement [or favourability] and others had scored so as to indicate strong disagreement [or unfavourability]). The group discussion then focused on these items (between ten and fifteen in number) which participants were asked to Q sort as a group along a five-point distribution. As these were all items which people had scored very differently in their individual sorts, their attempts to reach a consensus were very successful in provoking vigorous and sometimes quite heated debate between people with differing views (and were used only for this purpose, not being subjected to statistical analysis). These group discussions were tape-recorded and extracts are used to illustrate factor interpretations where appropriate.

Results

The forty-three Q sorts were analysed using the same procedure as in earlier chapters and eight factors emerged, of which only six were interpretable, as Factors VII and VIII have no significant loadings on which an intepretation might be based. The factor loadings are given in Table 6.2, and the factor scores for Factors I to VI are presented in Table 6.3.

Discussion

Factor 1

The Q sorts that load most heavily on this factor were all completed by lesbians representing accounts of 'the most favourable view of lesbians' (Nos. 1, 2 and 3 all with high positive loadings) or 'the most *un*favourable view of lesbians' (No. 5, with a high negative loading). All of the lesbians whose Q sorts define this factor had also completed both the 'Accounts of Identity' and the 'Accounts of

Table 6.2 *Factor loadings for the 'attitude to lesbianism' Q sort*[1]

Q sorter No.	I	II	III	IV	V	VI	VII	VIII
1	87 [2]	12	17	05	−05	−06	−12	−22
2	81	06	32	13	12	−07	−03	09
3	80	−10	32	19	02	06	23	02
4	80	−12	25	14	06	11	−07	−05
5	−79	07	14	26	05	10	14	00
6	79	−02	−26	−11	07	−08	01	07
7	79	−05	23	20	−02	−07	06	11
8	78	02	09	−09	−26	00	−11	−07
9	74	28	22	24	12	−23	12	10
10	02	73	16	−03	14	07	−06	06
11	−07	58	05	−04	−01	18	09	−02
12	08	56	08	10	03	−02	02	−06
13	−23	49	−03	24	17	09	06	−01
14	32	13	81	02	−02	−16	03	−04
15	22	10	71	06	−06	07	−06	10
16	01	20	14	70	11	11	03	−02
17	02	−06	33	63	08	−06	30	00
18	−02	19	−07	07	75	00	12	−01
19	−10	28	03	12	03	55	11	00
20	−03	23	69	27	10	37	13	−08
21	18	46	37	26	04	−31	09	31
22	36	51	33	08	13	−17	13	−08
23	11	08	35	36	32	−08	01	26
24	30	43	37	38	21	01	22	15
25	32	26	61	25	−05	−27	14	−02
26	77	09	40	12	22	00	00	−09
27	65	02	30	24	18	01	42	−04
28	24	27	44	19	12	17	21	21
29	22	08	45	15	46	13	10	04
30	45	40	37	28	03	−18	06	28
31	−23	31	24	18	23	16	35	−14
32	22	20	55	25	27	11	39	17
33	−05	50	11	12	20	22	49	19
34	60	40	38	24	08	13	05	17
35	30	28	48	00	04	−10	36	−05
36	77	−03	43	21	12	00	08	00
37	72	08	35	08	−02	−14	−05	00
38	73	28	15	−11	−02	06	21	14
39	31	−03	57	47	15	15	39	02
40	43	22	51	22	−02	−07	00	−36
41	41	18	52	26	−08	−36	−04	−08
42	64	31	35	30	00	02	13	−01
43	76	−05	14	18	01	−32	12	21

[1] Loadings rounded off to two significant figures and decimal points omitted.

[2] Boxed loadings indicate those defining factors.

Table 6.3   *Factor arrays for the 'attitudes to lesbianism' Q sort*

Q sort item	I	II	III	IV	V	VI
1	−4	−2	−1	−2	+3	+1
2	+1	−4	+2	−2	−3	+5
3	−4	−1	−3	+2	+1	0
4	−2	−3	+2	0	+4	+3
5	+2	+1	−4	−2	+5	−1
6	+1	−2	+4	−5	0	−4
7	+5	−3	0	+1	−1	−1
8	−2	+5	+2	+5	−1	−2
9	+3	+3	0	+1	+2	+3
10	−3	−3	−4	+3	+1	−3
11	−2	+3	−2	+1	−2	−1
12	+3	−2	−4	+3	−4	−2
13	+2	−1	−1	−3	−3	+3
14	0	+2	+2	+3	+3	−3
15	+1	−1	+1	+2	+1	0
16	+4	+2	0	−1	0	−2
17	−3	+2	−2	+1	+5	0
18	0	−1	−5	+2	0	−4
19	0	+1	+4	0	+1	+3
20	−1	−3	−2	0	+2	−3
21	+2	−1	+1	+5	+3	+1
22	−1	+3	+1	−1	−2	+3
23	+1	−4	−3	−5	−3	−5
24	0	−2	0	0	0	+1
25	+3	+1	+1	−2	+2	+1
26	−4	−2	−1	0	−3	+5
27	+1	+4	+4	+2	−2	0
28	−2	+2	+3	+3	−2	+1
29	−1	0	−2	−2	+1	−2
30	+3	+4	0	−2	−4	−3
31	−3	+3	−2	+3	+2	+3
32	0	0	−3	−3	−1	0
33	−4	+2	+1	+4	+4	+4
34	−1	−4	+2	−4	−2	−3
35	+1	+1	−1	+1	−1	0
36	+4	−5	+1	−2	0	−2
37	+5	−5	+1	−1	+1	+2
38	−1	−1	+3	−4	+3	+2
39	0	0	−5	+4	−4	−4
40	−5	+1	+2	−1	−2	−2
41	−1	+5	+4	+4	+2	−1
42	−3	−3	−1	−1	+4	0
43	+1	+2	0	0	0	+5
44	+2	0	0	−3	+3	+2

45	−3	−1	+2	−3	+1	−4
46	+2	0	−2	+1	+2	−2
47	−5	+2	+3	+2	0	+4
48	0	0	−3	−1	−1	0
49	+3	+5	+5	+1	+2	+2
50	+3	+3	−1	0	−5	−1
51	+4	−4	−5	−4	−3	−5
52	−5	+1	−1	+2	−4	+1
53	+2	−5	+3	−5	−1	−5
54	+5	+1	−3	+4	−1	−1
55	−1	+4	+5	+2	+3	+4
56	−2	0	−1	−1	+4	−3
57	−2	0	0	+1	+1	+2
58	−1	−2	+1	−4	−1	+1
59	−3	−3	−4	−3	−2	+4
60	+4	+3	+3	+5	+5	−1
61	0	−1	−3	+3	−5	−1
62	+1	−2	+5	−3	−3	+2
63	−2	+1	−2	−1	−5	+2
64	+2	+4	+3	0	0	+1

Politics' Q sorts, and all define the 'Radical Feminist' factor in each. Also defining this factor, albeit less strongly, are sorts completed by heterosexual feminists describing their *actual* view of lesbians (Nos. 6, 7, 8 and 9).

This account stresses the political importance of lesbianism:

> 36. Lesbianism is fundamentally a political statement, not a sexual preference. +4
> 7. Lesbianism is a blow against the patriarchy (i.e. society structured by men for men). +5
> 37. Lesbians pose a threat to the nuclear family and society as we know it. +5

In this account, lesbianism is central to feminism:

> 51. It's hard to understand how feminist women can justify having *heterosexual* relationships. +4

In accordance with this interpretation of lesbianism as a political force, a constructionist version of lesbianism is presented: lesbianism is not a given essence innately determined, but a choice theoretically available to all women.

> 54. Every woman could be a lesbian if she so chose. +5
> 16. There is no such thing as 'sexual orientation': we all have the potential to be anything sexually. +4
> 40. I think lesbianism is probably genetic or hormonal in origin. −5

Because lesbianism is a choice that all women could make, it is to be expected that those with power in a threatened male supremist order, would attempt to suppress all knowledge of it. This feminist account gives particular salience to items condemning attempts to silence lesbians. Items suggesting that lesbians should be relatively discreet about their lesbianism (shouldn't make a fuss about it, shouldn't talk about it or behave in a blatant way) on the grounds that lesbianism is a 'private thing', and that lack of discretion is, anyway, counterproductive (alienates people, gives the WLM a bad name) are firmly rejected:

52. I don't mind lesbians, but I wish they weren't so blatant.　　−5
28. There's too much fuss made about the whole topic
　　of lesbianism.　　−2
33. Lesbians who insist on talking about their lesbianism
　　all the time are just alienating people who might otherwise
　　be on their side.　　−4
　8. Lesbianism is a private thing; what people do in bed is
　　their own business.　　−2
17. Lesbians are giving the Women's Movement a bad name.　　−3

One woman who defines this factor said: (unless otherwise indicated, all quotations are from tape-recorded group discussions):

I think the problem comes when you think that the whole of the status quo is *heterosexual*, and therefore just adopting a sort of laissez-faire attitude towards lesbianism, I think that's . . . It's the same as oppressing them. I mean, I'm not saying that lesbians should *have* to go round shouting about the fact that they are, but to expect them to keep quiet about it, that's another form of oppression. Andrea (8).

Another woman whose sort defines this factor returned this comment with her Q sort.

One way they try to shut us up is by saying that we're not oppressed, so what are we making all that noise about? It's a fuss about nothing. If they ever let themselves see that we are oppressed, they'd have to accept that there's a need for us to fight back, so they refuse to see it. Josie (5)

It is quite clear, according to this account, that lesbians *are* oppressed, and that lesbianism is not an acceptable alternative in this society:

63. There isn't much prejudice against lesbians anymore.　　−2
31. Nowadays it seems as though it's trendy to be a lesbian.　　−3
57. I think a lot of lesbians are paranoid; they see prejudice
　　and discrimination where there isn't any.　　−2

Factor I, then, presents an explicitly political analysis of lesbianism and represents lesbianism as central to feminism. It is entirely compatible with the radical feminist accounts presented in earlier chapters.

Factor II

In the account represented by this factor, lesbianism is depicted as a perfectly natural and normal sexual orientation, adding to the rich variety of life. Great stress is put on the importance of accepting people as people regardless of gender or sexual behaviour, and legal reforms to this end are strongly supported. Three of these Q sorts represent 'the most favourable' view of lesbians, and were completed by two lesbians and a heterosexual woman. The fourth is a heterosexual man's 'actual' view of lesbians.

In this account, lesbianism is seen as a natural state, and it is, anyway, felt to be inappropriate to categorize people in terms of sexual orientation, sexual behaviour or gender. Note the large differences in score on the following items between this 'liberal humanistic' factor, and the 'radical' account of Factor I (given in parentheses to the right):

	II	(I)
41. Lesbianism is a perfectly natural state for a small minority of women, and probably always will be.	+5	(−1)
27. People should not be pigeon-holed just according to their sexual orientation.	+4	(+1)

Lesbianism is seen as a personal sexual orientation or private choice of lifestyle:

	II	(I)
8. Lesbianism is a private thing; what people do in bed is their own business.	+5	(−2)

It's ludicrous pigeon-holing people just for their sexual orientation; it's their own private business. Because it's not inflicting anything on anyone else. I mean, no one else need know what's going on; it's private, and it's two consenting adults, and it's not involving anyone else, it's not hurting anyone else. Hannah (12)

Lesbianism is seen as political only in so far as this account recognizes the need for, and indeed strongly supports, social and legal reforms. (The radical account of Factor I also supports social reforms, but because they give priority to explicitly feminist items, their scores on the following items are generally lower [see table 6.3].)

30. Lesbian couples should be allowed to adopt children if they want to.	+4
49. Lesbian couples should be treated exactly the same way as married couples with regard to housing, benefits, etc.	+5

9. I would like to see a law, similar to that against racial prejudice, which would aim to protect lesbians against prejudice and abuse.   +5
50. Books which portray lesbianism as a sickness or aberration should be withdrawn from schools and public libraries.   +3

Outside of this limited context, however, this account denies lesbianism any political implications, and is particularly concerned to disagree with items linking lesbianism to feminism. It is on these items that the disagreements between Factor I and Factor II are most obvious.

	II	(I)
36. Lesbianism is fundamentally a political statement, not a sexual preference.	−5	(+4)
37. Lesbians pose a threat to the nuclear family and society as we know it.	−5	(+5)
51. It's hard to understand how feminist women can justify having *heterosexual* relationships.	−4	(+4)
7. Lesbianism is a blow against the patriarchy (i.e. society structured by men for men).	−3	(+5)
17. Lesbians are giving the Women's Movement a bad name.	+2	(−3)

As one participant said:

> The gay *movement* may be somewhat political, but only in respect of getting certain laws changed. Matthew (13)

Because, in this account, there is no intrinsic political meaning to lesbianism, the people presenting it are at a loss to understand the 'extremism' of militant lesbians:

> I just don't think, if they want to change things, that the way to do that is through all this anger and bitterness and hatred of men. Lesbians will be accepted more easily if they just act like normal human beings, living ordinary dignified lives, which is what I expect most of them are doing. The minority who shout about it all the time are just making things worse and giving off a wrong impression. Hannah (12)

	II	(I)
55. I have no sympathy for the man-hating kind of lesbian.	+4	(−1)
28. There's too much fuss made about the whole topic of lesbianism.	+2	(−2)
33. Lesbians who insist of talking about their lesbianism all the time are just alienating people who might otherwise be on their side.	+2	(−4)

Unlike the Factor I account, the account of Factor II tends towards agreement with items suggesting that lesbians are not really very oppressed compared with the oppression suffered by other groups:

	II	(I)
31. Nowadays it seems as though it's trendy to be a lesbian.	+3	(−3)
63. There isn't much prejudice against lesbians anymore.	+1	(−2)
22. Lesbians should count themselves lucky; there are other groups (like the unemployed, blacks, etc.) that are much worse off.	+3	(−3)

In this account, then, lesbianism is presented as a personal sexual orientation or a private preference for a particular lifestyle. Any attempt to place lesbianism in a political framework is resisted, except in narrow terms as it relates to the need for sociolegal reforms. This is essentially a liberal humanistic view of lesbianism embodying a 'live and let live' philosophy of 'what you do in bed is your own business.' In giving primary importance to opposing the labelling, pigeon-holing and defining of people in terms of their 'sexual orientation', and in its emphasis on advocating sociolegal reforms which would protect the rights of individuals to live out their private lives however they choose, this account closely approximates the 'favourable' view of lesbians as defined by 'homophobia' scales and implicit in much of the research on lesbianism since the mid-1970s.

Factor III
Defined by Q sorts contributed by two heterosexual women (Nos. 14 and 15) the account represented by this factor is the only one of the six factors to give a positive score to the following item:

34. I am disgusted by the thought of two women having sex.   +4

(Scores for the other factors are: Factor I, −1; Factor II, −4; Factor IV, −4; Factor V, −2; Factor VI, −3.)

This account focuses on lesbianism as a sexual activity, and the affective response is reported to be one of disgust. High priority is given to commenting on items relating to lesbian sexuality, and the lesbian sexual act is described as personally distasteful and unlikely to be sexually satisfying for any woman:

18. I would like to have sex with a lesbian — just to see what it was like.   −5
39. I find the thought of a lesbian sexual act arousing.   −5
38. I can't see how sex with another woman can be as satisfying as sex with a man.   +3

It's just how I feel. It doesn't feel natural. I'm not against lesbians, it's just that I wouldn't want to do it myself. It sort of seems yucky and . . . not very nice. I've nothing against them as people, but, you know, the plumbing's all wrong. Nobody could say it was natural. Lucy (14).

Despite this emphasis on sex, the differences between lesbian and heterosexual women are seen as extending far beyond mere sexual preference:

11. Lesbians differ from heterosexual women only in terms
    of their sexual preference.   −2

The women presenting this account express a strong sense of being different from lesbians: they can't imagine what it must feel like to be a lesbian, they have never known any lesbians, they don't think they could choose to become lesbians, and they wouldn't know how to behave in the company of a lesbian. The overall picture is one of personal discomfort with the whole topic of lesbianism.

62. I find it hard to imagine what it must feel like to be
    a lesbian.   +5
53. I am not aware of ever having known a lesbian.   +3
54. Every woman could be a lesbian if she so chose.   −3
 6. I would probably find it a bit difficult to know just how
    to behave toward a lesbian.   +4

In fact, this discomfort seems to originate largely from their definition of lesbianism as a 'sexual preference', as the group discussion about item 6 above indicates. In the following extract, Sophie is one of the women defining this factor (No. 15).

Sophie: It would depend on the person. If she came on all sort of . . . I'd go 'ugh!!'

Tessa: Yes, but it wouldn't be any more difficult than with a heterosexual man who was behaving like that.

Sophie: But if you're being friendly, and they think you're going to sort of . . .

Richard: I'd find it harder with a homosexual man than with a lesbian.

Sophie: I'd feel the other way round! (Laughter)

Tessa: But why do you assume that just because she likes girls she's going to like all girls? It's like . . . You don't assume every guy likes all girls.

Sophie: I don't assume that at all. I just . . . It would still make me feel uncomfortable, not knowing quite how to . . .

Despite this feeling that lesbians are very alien to them, the women providing this account nevertheless support some legal and social changes in the interests of humanitarianism.

27. People should not be pigeon-holed just according to their
    sexual orientation.   +4

64. If two people really love each other, then it shouldn't matter
    whether they are a woman and a man or two women.   +3
49. Lesbian couples should be treated exactly the same way as
    married couples with regard to housing, benefits etc.   +5

This account, then, expresses a strong sense of personal unease with lesbianism — which is identified primarily as a sexual practice — although this is tempered by their liberal social concern.

While the 'liberals' of Factor II approximate to the 'favourable' attitude as defined by the homophobia research, the 'disgusted women' of Factor III probably come closest to manifesting the traditional concept of 'homophobia'. Similar responses have been described in earlier research. One researcher labels as 'revulsion' the attitude of women who said such things as 'terrible that is; it makes me feel sick', and 'revolting — not so bad in a man, but unforgivable in a woman' (Gorer, 1971), and another group of researchers has described some of their respondents as exhibiting 'disgust and avoidance of homosexuals' (a response they label 'personal anxiety') and comment that this 'most closely approximates the cognitive-emotional dimension often described as "homophobia" ' (Millham et al., 1976). This factor is also in line with the findings of several studies which report that for well-educated, young respondents, favourable attitudes towards civil liberties for gays often go hand-in-hand with repugnance toward homosexual activity (Sorenson, 1973; Sobel, 1976).

To women who define this factor, lesbianism is a cause of personal anxiety and threat because they fear lesbian sexual advances: this is a response familiar to most lesbians, and one which many choose to play upon rather than attempt to quell with reassurance. As one radical feminist lesbian said:

> You know how women say to you, nervously, 'of course, *I* don't think lesbians are all sex maniacs, ready to leap on any woman they see'; well, I used to say 'no, of course not . . . patriarchal emphasis on sexuality . . . etcetera etcetera.' *Now* I say 'Don't you be too sure. Don't take it for granted that I'm *not* interested in your body as well as your mind. Don't assume that I'm *not* attracted to you.' What that does, it makes them face up to their own fears, instead of being able to avoid them. It makes them really uncomfortable. Josie (5)

Factor IV

The two men who define this factor (Nos. 16 and 17) present lesbianism primarily in sexual terms: it is seen as an elected route to sexual gratification, chosen by women who want to be trendy, who have no other sexual outlets, or who are simply taking the opportunity to sample the erotic market in a 'sexually liberated' society. This sexual appetitive view of lesbianism is a favourite theme in pornography (Dworkin, 1981), and these men report reacting to it with sexual arousal. Nevertheless, as heterosexual men both married to feminist women, they also find lesbianism, particularly the theory and practice of political lesbianism, of which both these men were fully aware very threatening to themselves personally and to their marriages. They are notable for their strong agreement with the following item:

21. I think a lot of men feel very threatened by lesbianism.   +5

The scores assigned to the other items in the Q sort give one no reason to assume that they exclude themselves, as men, from their understanding of this statement. They are amongst those who most strongly agree that lesbianism is becoming a 'trendy' thing to do, and agree more strongly than any other factor that there has been an increase in the number of lesbians. This is combined with a strong agreement (equalled only by that of the feminists of Factor I) that any woman can be a lesbian if she so chooses:

31. Nowadays it seems as though it's trendy to be a lesbian.   +3
15. I think there are probably more lesbians nowadays
    than there were in the past.   +2
54. Any woman could be a lesbian if she so chose.   +4

Any *political* content to lesbianism is firmly denied:

36. Lesbianism is fundamentally a political statement,
    not a sexual preference.   −2
51. It's hard to understand how feminist women can justify
    having *heterosexual* relationships.   −4

Lesbianism is first and foremost a type of sexual behaviour (item 25) chosen by women whose primary aim is appetite satisfaction and who, under different conditions, might welcome the opportunity of sex with men.

35. I believe that most lesbians are actually bisexual.   +1
44. I suspect most lesbians find the idea of sex with a man
    repugnant.   −3
10. It's probably true to say that some lesbians are just ugly
    women who can't get a man.   +3
 3. I suspect some lesbian women can be turned into hetero-
    sexuals by men who have enough sexual skill.   +2

Unlike women presenting the Factor III account, who react to lesbianism with disgust and some bewilderment (see Factor III scores given in parentheses) these men report finding lesbianism a turn-on:

	IV	(III)
34. I am disgusted by the thought of two women having sex.	−4	(+2)
39. I find the thought of a lesbian sexual act arousing.	+4	(−5)

And they add that they themselves are interested in having sex with lesbians:

	IV	(III)
18. I would like to have sex with a lesbian, just to see what it was like.	+2	(−5)

One of these men reiterated this point in a discussion group:

> I *would*, yes. It's like that one about the idea of women doing it being exciting. Peter (16)

They would certainly not mind being alone with a lesbian, nor do they anticipate any difficulties in their interaction with her:

23. It would be upsetting for me to find that I was alone with a lesbian.	−5
6. I would probably find it a bit difficult to know just how to behave toward a lesbian.	−5

And unlike the account of Factor III, the men presenting this account report that they do not find it hard to imagine what it must be like to be a lesbian: as one man said, 'on the contrary!' In so far as they understand lesbians to be women who have sex with women, they, as heterosexual men, are, they feel, well placed to understand it:

	IV	(III)
62. I find it hard to imagine what it must feel like to be a lesbian.	−3	(+5)

In this account, then, as in the account of Factor III, lesbianism is defined primarily in sexual terms, but whereas the women of Factor III react with disgust and a sense of alienation, the men of Factor IV respond to the 'threat' with sexual interest. This is certainly one reading of a male journalist's comment (Llew Gardner, 1978, *Evening News*) that, after giving a talk at a lesbian meeting and encountering some opposition:

> A pretty girl apologized for the earlier hostility and said, 'I can't stand all this aggression. I'm a gay because I like looking at well-dressed, attractive women.' I murmured that already we appeared to have something in common.

Similarly, a lot of so-called 'soft porn' depicts women engaging in simulated lesbian sexual activities only until they find the right man: 'Ooooh, Dick, now that I've found a man with a REALLY BIG prick like yours I don't think I want to do it with girls anymore' (*Lovebirds,* 1979). By addressing itself to the lesbian threat and translating it into a male heterosexual masturbatory stimulus, the climax of which is women's return to the man, and more specifically the penis, this type of material can be seen as massaging the male ego and assuaging his fears.

A similar purpose can be read into a front page *Daily Star* 'exclusive' story of Miss World's valiant struggle against lesbian seduction in prison ('Staff even ogled me in the bath'), which describes how 'some nights she was woken by girls in the next bed making love, and was invited to join in,' but made it 'perfectly clear' that she didn't want to (*Daily Star,* 9 February 1984). Again the same theme is evident: although exposed to lesbian temptation, women prefer ('need') sex with men. In this way

> the lesbian is colonised, reduced to a variant of woman-as-sex-object, used to demonstrate and prove that male power pervades and invades even the private sanctuary of women with each other. (Dworkin, 1981: 47)

Factors V and VI
These two factors, each defined by one person (Factor V by No. 18 and Factor VI by No. 19), reflect similar attitudes to lesbianism in that both agree that lesbianism is unnatural:

	V	VI
4. Lesbianism is clearly unnatural in that sex is intended for reproductive purposes and lesbianism clearly cannot achieve this.	+4	+3

They differ in that Factor V, as I will show, justifies this belief with reference to science, whereas Factor VI defends it in religious terms.

	V	VI
2. I find lesbianism difficult to accept because of my moral and/or religious beliefs.	−3	+5

The 'religious' stance (Factor VI) focuses on sin and forgiveness:

	V	VI
26. I think the best approach to lesbianism is to hate the sin but love the sinner.	−3	+5
59. Lesbianism is a personal tragedy and lesbians deserve sympathy and understanding.	−2	+4

Being a lesbian is not a sin, but acting it out is. But I don't want to talk about sin without making it clear that God is always ready to forgive you. Sandra (19)

The 'scientific' defence of the unnaturalness of lesbianism (Factor V) involves a focus on aetiology. The following items all have higher scores on Factor V than on any other factor:

	V	VI
14. I think lesbianism is probably due to early environmental influence, such as the girl's relationship with her parents, and the kind of upbringing she had.	+3	-3
42. Lesbians seem to have 'got stuck' in what should be a passing adolescent phase.	+4	0
20. Fear of becoming pregnant and giving birth probably explains some lesbianism.	+2	-3

The accounts represented by both factors share a concern about the exposure of children to homosexuality, defending the wish to protect children from knowledge about lesbianism on the grounds that the children might then become homosexual themselves. From a religious perspective, 'they might be led astray into not realizing that God has forbidden homosexuality' (Sandra, 19). From a scientific perspective, the 'whole social process of identification and role-modelling needs to be taken into account' (Brian, 18).

	V	VI
1. I would be afraid for a daughter of mine to have a teacher who was lesbian.	+3	+1
50. Books which portray lesbianism as a sickness or aberration should be withdrawn from schools and public libraries.	-5	-1
30. Lesbian couples should be allowed to adopt children if they want to.	-4	-3

So the accounts of both Factors V and VI oppose the practice of lesbianism, the former because it is a sickness or immaturity, the latter because it is a sin.

The religious objection to homosexuality has been described by a number of other researchers. One researcher categorizes 5 percent of his male and 4 percent of his female respondents as demonstrating 'moral disapproval' (e.g. 'Disgusting; not only going against God's law but also defiling their bodies; using their organs for things they were never intended for, and reaping disease from it, which they do' [Gorer, 1971: 191–2]). And Millham et al. (1976) describe as 'moral reprobation' the attitude of people who agree with items such as:

The growing number of lesbians indicates a decline in American morals.

Homosexual behavior between women is just plain wrong.

Lesbianism is a sin.

While this represented the predominant response of institutionalized Christianity until very recently, the attitude finds its most
extreme expression today less among members of the established
churches, and more from certain fundamentalist and evangelical
sects, as illustrated in these quotations:

> Demonic activity is the basis of homosexuality to destroy that individual.
> When young people experiment with homosexuality they open them-
> selves up to these dark forces, like the days of Sodom and Gomorrah.
> (God is the Answer, Inc., quoted in *The Guardian*, 14 December 1982)

> The White People's Committee to Restore God's Laws is not embar-
> rassed to admit that we endorse and seek the execution of all
> homosexuals. We find that we must endorse and support the law of God
> which calls for the death penalty to the faggot slime. ('Gas Gays', *The
> Torch: The Revolutionary Newspaper of WHITE Christianity*, July 1977,
> quoted in Lewis, 1979: 4)

Within mainstream Christianity there has generally been a greater
emphasis on repentance, compassion, forgiveness and, especially
in recent years with the AIDS panic, celibacy as the morally proper
response. In reaction to the traditional Christian opposition to
homosexuality lesbians and gay men have countered with alternative biblical interpretations or translations (e.g. Gay Christian
Movement, 1978).

Just as Factor VI can be characterized as reflecting the religious
discourse of early writings of homosexuality, so Factor V can be
seen as representing the scientific discourse which, historically, has
increasingly replaced it: the rhetoric of moral disapproval is
replaced by the scientific jargon of aetiology and diagnosis. This
factor approximates to the traditional scientific conceptualizations
discussed in Chapter 2.

In this study, I elicited six different attitudes to lesbianism, and
discussed them with reference to their social context and political
significance. They do not, of course, represent all possible attitudes
to lesbianism, especially as the participants represent a far more
restricted group than those in the studies of earlier chapters, most of
the heterosexual participants being drawn from an undergraduate
population. Of the six factors elicited in this study, the accounts of
Factors I and II are both compatible with definitions of 'favourable'
attitudes to lesbianism, and both are endorsed as such by both
lesbians and heterosexuals. Whereas one account emphasizes the
fundamental humanity and normality of the lesbian (the 'liberal'
version of Factor II), the other emphasizes her revolutionary
potential (the radical version of Factor I).

The dialectic between these two accounts of lesbianism is part of a broader debate between radicals in any movement and their liberal supporters, and the unresolved differences lead to the 'ideological glass wall' (Gerlach and Hine, 1970) discussed in Chapter 5 in the context of the 'radical feminist' and 'liberal feminist' factors of the 'Politics of Lesbianism' Q sort, which parallel the accounts discussed here. The argument of this book represents one part of that continuing dialectic: lodged within a radical feminist framework, my arguments focus less on discrediting the traditional view of lesbianism as pathology, and more on demonstrating the reactionary political implications of the liberal humanistic position embodied in recent so-called 'gay affirmative' research.

7

The Future for Research on Lesbianism

The central argument of this book has been that recent liberal humanistic so-called 'gay affirmative' research, far from being a liberating force, represents a new development in the oppression of lesbians. The shift from 'pathological' to 'lifestyle' research has merely substituted one depoliticized image of the lesbian with another. Through the invention of 'homophobia' and 'the well-adjusted lesbian' psychology and its allied disciplines engage in energetic attempts to shape the subjectivities of both lesbians and non-lesbians in accordance with their individualized models, while, through the rhetorical techniques discussed in Chapter 1, the social sciences construct the conditions for their own legitimacy. Liberalism has taken the form of 'gay affirmative' psychology, proclaimed that the lesbian is amenable to rational and impartial scientific enquiry, only to discover the 'true nature' of the lesbian to be in exact conformity with the needs of a patriarchal social order. Gay affirmative research is, I have argued, intimately connected with the needs of a liberal patriarchal order to contain and control the political challenge of lesbianism.

First I consider how it has been possible for well-intentioned, scientifically competent researchers, often gay themselves, to have produced research complicit in the oppression of lesbians. I suggest that it is because 'gay affirmative' research has taken on board the positivist empiricist model of science, and sought to be no more than an addendum to social science as it stands, that it unwittingly reproduces, in its conceptual schema, the very categories that maintain dominant (heterosexual and patriarchal) reality. The developing alternative paradigm of social constructionism is offered as a way forward for research on homosexuality, and I argue that it is only through an explicit commitment to the deconstruction of normative reality that researchers can free themselves from the reproduction, elaboration and maintenance of that reality.

Gay affirmative research: the problem
The early 'gay affirmative' critiques developed in the 1970s suggested that the model of homosexuality as pathology and the results that seemed to support it were the product of 'bad' science or

'bad' scientists. Gay affirmative social scientists, and large segments of the Gay and Lesbian Liberation Movements more generally, believed that 'good' science (which meant science using random samples, matched control groups, unbiased tests etc.) produced by 'good' (which, increasingly, means 'gay') social scientists would vindicate the position of gay men and lesbians and contribute towards the goals of gay liberation. To some extent this dream has been realized.

Openly gay researchers have produced results challenging the traditional formulations, and their findings have been used to argue for — even sometimes to win — custody of their children for lesbian mothers, to prevent gay adolescents from being taken into care, to encourage the development of gay affirmative education in schools and colleges, and to enable the provision of counselling for gay couples (and for individual gay alcoholics, depressives, anorexics, etc.) that doesn't depend on the premiss that their homosexuality is the root cause of their problems. I do not want to deny that positive benefits have derived from or been associated with gay affirmative research, but I do want to suggest that we have paid heavily for them. The argument of this book is that the concessions gained are bought at the cost of the denial of any political meaning to lesbianism and the consequent relocation of lesbianism in the area of the 'private' and the 'personal'. Viewed from a radical feminist perspective, the ultimate effect has been not the liberation of the lesbian but a new form of oppression.

This new form of oppression has been very successful in eliciting the willing co-operation of lesbians. By shifting its emphasis — in response to consumer demand — from 'affliction' to affirmation, and by replacing the heterosexual with the homosexual expert, psychology and psychiatry have gained or retained the allegiance of lesbians to its individualized and depoliticized models. Increasingly, in the West, psychiatry and psychology are not imposed coercively upon lesbians incarcerated and subjected to scientifically legitimated torture in mental hospitals. Rather, many lesbians are actively seeking out psychology and its related disciplines (in the form of psychoanalysis, assertiveness training, Rogerian therapy, trans-actional analysis groups, and the like), using its concepts (such as 'homophobia'), drawing on its findings (as in recent lesbian custody cases), and seeing it as a route to the discovery of their real selves and the fulfilment of their human potentials. As Allen (1986: 104) points out, in her discussion of the rapid increase of feminist therapies, however valuable a contribution may be made by such therapies to individual happiness or well being, nevertheless, 'their development can only be viewed as in some way *extending* the existing field of the psychiatric system, and not as subverting or supplanting it.'

The personalization of the political intrinsic to psychological approaches to lesbianism is too high a price to pay for the individual benefits gained, and is fundamentally incompatible with radical feminist goals. I suggest that the oppressive nature of both the pathological and the lifestyle schools of research on lesbianism is due neither to 'bad' science nor to 'bad' scientists, but must be attributed to features basic to the very nature of the science itself.

It is important to differentiate my argument here from the ad hominem attacks more usually made by gay radicals. The early demands from the Gay Liberation Movement for the abolition of psychiatric and psychological involvement in lesbianism and male homosexuality were often predicated on a presumed dichotomy between 'psychiatrists' on the one hand, and 'gays' on the other (Alinder, 1970; Gay Liberation Information Service, 1978: 26–7). Such an attack was readily diffused by admitting into the research community a few openly lesbian and gay psychologists and psychiatrists, and today the once clear battle line drawn between 'gays' and 'professionals' has been crossed by too many people claiming expertise on both counts to be fully convincing. It is possible, of course, to redeem the situation by suggesting, as have many radical critics of establishment social science, that those members of the oppressed group who contribute to the development of research on that group have been somehow corrupted, bought off, or persuaded to play the establishment's game in return for positions of power and privilege (e.g. Gorz, 1974). In this analysis, gay affirmative researchers — at least the gay ones amongst them — might be characterized as betrayers of their people, cynical opportunists making a Machiavellian choice in favour of personal professional prestige over radical social change.

A less sinister explanation in the same vein might suggest that the admittance of a few openly gay and lesbian psychologists into the hallowed ranks of social science is permitted only on condition that they reproduce its ideologies, while the systematic exclusion of other lesbians (and radical ideologies) is built in. Moreover, those who *are* admitted are often required to participate in the care and control of excluded members of their own group. This argument has been pursued by a number of researchers (Beit-Hallahmi, 1974; Whiteson, 1983), and is often illustrated with relevance to the police force:

> In reality, in any society, the police are hired to protect the haves from the have-nots. The irony is — as with the British bobby — that the police

are often drawn from the same class they're hired to keep in line. They are have-nots in uniform. They are effective precisely because they know best how to intimidate their own kind. (Whiteson, 1983: 41)

A parallel argument would depict gay and lesbian social scientists as manufacturing precisely those concepts and models of homosexuality that they know, from their own 'insider' experience, to be most effective in prohibiting the development of a radical political analysis of lesbianism. However, this argument is not very useful — in the sense of being likely to change the situation — because it fails to conform to the experience of the overwhelming majority of gay affirmative researchers.

Most gay and lesbian academics carrying out research on homosexuality, myself included, are fully conscious of the risks we run and the compromises we make in pursuing our careers. While accusations of collusion with the forces of oppression may succeed in eliciting a guilty sense of our own privileged position as academics, many of us are also aware of how much more privileged that position could be had we not chosen lesbianism as our research topic, or had we not made our lesbianism obvious to our 'superiors' in the academic hierarchy.

In the assessment of two male academics, 'whether one is a new PhD or a full professor, the mere word 'homosexual'' on a curriculum vitae is a stigma that few careers can stand' (Crew and Norton, 1974), and lesbian academics have described being fired, not rehired, and failing to gain tenure because of their insistence on putting lesbianism into the university curriculum (McDaniel, 1982). Faced with a choice between carrying out research on a 'safe', 'respectable' topic (or opting out of research altogether), leaving the field of homosexuality open for the unchallenged offerings of the 'pathological' school, gay affirmative researchers have taken the more difficult route, and have sometimes paid heavily for it. In this context, accusations of collusion with the oppressor seem naive and simplistic. As Adrienne Rich (1983) points out, while 'Everything we write/will be used against us/or against those we love,' we are also accused (and accuse ourselves) if we remain silent.

I consider the relevance of these arguments because they are commonly invoked by 'grass-roots' participators across a variety of liberation movements, to discredit those of their own members who carry out research on the movement or its members. I want to distinguish them from my own critique of gay affirmative research, which — in conformity with the approach throughout this book — does not rely on ad hominem (or ad feminam) attempts to discredit ideological positions with which I disagree (ascribing such arguments to the dubious motives and Machiavellian motivations of their proponents), but rather analyses them *as accounts*, in terms of their utility or otherwise in achieving particular moral and political goals. My criticism of gay affirmative research, then, is not rooted in any attempt to discredit gay affirmative researchers as people, as gay men or lesbians, or as researchers. Rather I am arguing that replacing heterosexual with homosexual social scientists will not ameliorate the situation for gay people as long as the homosexual social scientists continue to engage in the same kind of science as their displaced predecessors.

Irrespective of their motives, gay affirmative researchers can be shown to have incorporated into their work a host of taken-for-granted 'scientific' assumptions which undermine even their best intentioned efforts to 'liberate' the lesbian. At the root of these assumptions is the widespread acceptance of the positivist empiricist scientific paradigm. It is not 'bad' science, or 'bad' scientists, but this form of science itself which is the appropriate target for critiques of research on homosexuality today.

The positivist empiricist model in gay affirmative research

Positivism still represents the dominant model for social scientific research and contemporary research on homosexuality generally unquestioningly accepts and is formulated within this dominant positivist paradigm — an observation that applies to much of the research that labels itself 'anti-positivistic' or 'humanistic' in orientation, as well as to the explicitly positivist research in this area.

I use the term 'positivist' here in its philosophical sense to refer to the system of belief that bases knowledge on perception. Philosophers (e.g. Kolakowski, 1972) have defined positivism as meaning the belief, based on the liberal commitment to rationality, that human beings can rationally understand phenomena through experiment and observation. The dominant philosophical position, 'widely held among psychologists and other social scientists', is described by Manicas and Secord (1983) as based on a foundationist epistemology which sees scientific propositions as founded on 'data': the test of the truth of propositions is correspondence between theory and data — hypotheses are to be tested against the 'facts'. Positivism, in this sense, is fundamental to all of the social sciences. Tracing the development of sociology as a discipline, Rossides defines positivism as 'the broad modern emphasis on the need to derive knowledge and theory from empirical analysis' and comments that:

> Sociologists tend to take stands for or against positivism (or neopositivism), a fact that obscures the fundamental acceptance of empiricism within sociology. (Rossides, 1978: 9)

Psychologists have recently made the same point about research within their discipline:

> The positivist empiricist model has been an important model for psychology and, despite occasional allusions to post-positivist science, it still guides much of the work in this field. (Unger, 1983: 10)

Similarly, Kenneth Gergen (1985), who also uses the term 'positivist empiricist' to refer to the 'normal' science of psychology, describes the social sciences generally as being 'enchanted by the myth that the assiduous application of sound method will yield sound fact — as if empirical methodology were some variety of meat grinder from which truth could be turned out like so many sausages.'

As illustrated in Chapter 1, the vast majority of 'gay affirmative' research is formulated and implemented within this dominant positivist empiricist model, and implicitly accepts and reinforces the assumptions on which it is based. With specific reference to research on homosexuality, Plummer (1981: 212) characterizes the bulk of research in this area as positivistic, displaying, he says, 'a curious naivety' about even the existence of debates within the sociology of knowledge, and 'producing its "findings" as if all were unproblematic — knowledge is knowledge and that's that.' 'Gay affirmative' and 'pathological' social scientists differ from each other in that they give their allegiance to different theoretical positions on the topic of homosexuality, but resemble each other in their uniform acceptance of the philosophical tenets on which these different theoretical positions are based. Their research is 'conducted within an agreed-upon set of conventions about what counts as a relevant contribution, what counts as answering a question, what counts as having a good argument for that answer or a good criticism of it' (Rorty, 1980: 320), and as such conforms with Rorty's definition of 'normal' science. It is this apparently unquestioning acceptance of certain underlying principles of normal scientific inquiry that locates the overwhelming bulk of research on homosexuality within the positivist empiricist paradigm.

Accepting as given the paradigmatic position of positivism, the emphasis in research on homosexuality is on extending the scope and improving the quality of research within the accepted rules of science. In Cochran's (1984) words, 'research on homosexuality has long been troubled by a lack of scientific discipline and an overabundance of unsupported opinions.' The plea is for more and better data. *More* data is needed, it is claimed, about lesbian mothers (Levine, 1980; Pagelow, 1980; Anthony, 1982), employment and housing discrimination (Levine, 1980), the problems of gay children and adolescents (Morin, 1977; Anthony, 1982), ageing in the gay and lesbian communities (Morin, 1977), the dynamics of gay and lesbian relationships (Morin, 1977; Morris, 1982), as well as on more idiosyncratic topics such as the organization of bike clubs (Freedman, 1978: 321) and families with several homosexual siblings (Dank, 1971). *Better* data is needed which includes longitudinal studies, more replication and better subject selection (Bell, 1975; Sang, 1978; Suppe, 1981; Browning, 1984). Arguing the need for 'rigorous experimental research', Bentler and Abramson (1981) offer the would-be researcher a checklist of questions concerned with research design, subject selection, measurement and data analysis designed to improve the quality of data on homosexuality, adding that 'there will be a direct correspondence between improvement in research methodology and the progress of our science.'

This formulation of gay affirmative research within the dominant positivist empiricist model of 'normal' science, contrasts markedly with a great deal of contemporary feminist social scientific research. While gay affirmative research assumes, for example, that science is the legitimate arbiter of 'facts' about the world, much feminist research argues that all science is necessarily based on the assumptions and ideologies of those who author it, and is used to sustain and legitimate their interests. As a recent review and summary of developments in feminist psychology points out:

> Many feminist researchers argue that because knowledge is socially constructed, and thus dependent on a given social, cultural and historical context, the exploration of women's knowledge must be grounded in the specific contexts in which such knowledge is generated; the existence of multiple — and often inconsistent or contradictory — perspectives is also acknowledged. . . . Many feminist researchers include, as central, an analysis of the role of power in determining the form and representation of social knowledge, either in relation to women's position in society, or in considering the role of the researcher in her/his research. (Wilkinson, 1986: 2).

As such, feminist research requires a total reconceptualization of the notion of 'science', and 'scientific standards' and goes far beyond merely 'adding women in' to existing social scientific theories:

> It is not enough to supplement an established sociology by addressing ourselves to what has been left out, overlooked, or by making sociological issues of relevance of the world of women. That merely

> extends the authority of existing sociological procedures and makes of a
> women's sociology an addendum. (Smith, 1974)

In rejecting social science's traditional claim to uncover facts about the world, in representing knowledge as historically and culturally situated, institutionally useful and normatively sustained, feminist social science derives its intellectual heritage from, and contributes to the development of, the social constructionist movement in social science.

By contrast, research on homosexuality (male and female) is, by and large, *nothing but* an extended 'addendum' or 'erratum' to be tacked on and assimilated into existing positivist theories. Although this is implicit in most of the research on homosexuality, several authors spell it out explicitly, saying that work in the area should draw on and be integrated into 'the theoretical literature on identity and self-concept' (Cass, 1984) or that it should 'add to our knowledge of the psychology of prejudice' (Henley and Pincus, 1978). 'While much of the work in relational communication stems from marriage research,' say Day and Morse (1981), introducing their research on lesbian communication, 'it is useful to consider relational control messages in non-traditional pairs.' The following extracts provide two further illustrations of this perceived need to 'add homosexuals in' to existing theories:

> Studies of homosexual couples also provide an opportunity to test the generality of social science theories of 'human behavior' which have been derived almost exclusively from heterosexual models and tested on heterosexual samples. In this way, research on lesbian and gay male couples contribute not only to our knowledge about homosexuality, but also to our more general knowledge about close human relationships. (Peplau, 1983)

> Homosexuals are people and, as such, they provide a wonderful test case for general theories of ethnic identity, personal identity, gender development, hormonal influence, self-labelling, informal communication networks, folklore, political mobilization and so forth. As sex researchers integrate their inquiries with the rest of the human sciences, questions aimed at defining types of homosexuality may seem less pressing. (Koertge, 1984)

These authors want research on homosexuality to become part of the mainstream of their disciplines, testing its theories, adding to its knowledge, and improving its scope and general applicability. The problem with 'adding lesbians in' to existing theories is that these theories represent, as I argued in Chapters 2–6, manifestations of liberal humanistic ideology fundamentally incompatible with political approaches to lesbianism.

Psychological theories of human relationships, personal identities, gender development and the rest have not just left lesbians out: they have been constructed, in accordance with liberal humanistic ideology, in such a way that it is impossible to put lesbians back in except in individualistic terms as persons making private sexual choices, enjoying particular kinds of personal relationships, and pursuing private goals of self-actualization and personal development. Such theories are formulated within a conceptual framework which is fundamentally individualistic and cannot contain lesbianism as a political reality. And the liberal humanistic notions incorporated into theories of maturity and adjustment, or implicit in definitions of prejudice, are shaped by and serve to maintain precisely those institutionally protected power differences through which the continuing oppression of lesbians is ensured. In so far as gay affirmative research aims to add lesbians in to existing positivist theories, it is complicit in the silencing of lesbianism as a political reality.

The social constructionist alternative
Discussions about the relevance of social constructionist theory (or the author's interpretation of that theory) do crop up occasionally in the 'gay affirmative' literature. One author identifies several researchers (including some criticized in earlier chapters as operating within a positivist-empiricist model) as working within the social constructionist perspective, and criticizes them for having adopted 'unarticulated and undefended positions on what is scientific' and for tapping (at best) only the dimension of the 'self-concept', ignoring other supposed components of sexual identity such as 'biological sex . . . behavioral, fantasy, and affectational dimensions of sexual orientation, as well as psychobiologically mediated arousal cue-response patterns' (Suppe, 1984a). As the concepts of science, biological sex, sexual orientation and psychobiologically mediated anythings are amongst some of the more important social constructions against which social constructionists have directed their deconstructive energies, this criticism would seem to be based on a misunderstanding of social constructionist theory.

Similarly, in another recent article, the authors call for a study of reactions to homosexuality 'within a model of the "social construction of reality" in order to place such studies within the mainstream of sociology and social psychology.' Their recommendations for future research, however, include the need for refining and improving 'homophobia' scales by incorporating more affective items, checking on their validity, carrying out test-retest studies of attitudes, and, they say, 'researchers should make use of experimental methods, especially the behavioral laboratory, by involving *groups* of subjects in the study of the *social* process of reactions to homosexuality' (Plasek and Allard, 1985; their emphases). It is not clear in what way the authors imagine that these recommendations would serve to place future research on homosexuality within a social constructionist framework. Thus, despite the accurate recognition, by some 'gay affirmative' researchers, of social constructionism as an important theoretical development for the social sciences, there seems to be considerable confusion about how research on homosexuality might proceed within this framework.

Social constructionist theory means more than (although it includes) the concept of a homosexual or lesbian 'identity' as being socially constituted and historically determined. The argument that the terms 'homosexual' and 'lesbian' (as nouns) are of relatively recent origin; that, historically, same-gender sexual activity had no particular implications for identity; and that there are a variety of contemporary socially sanctioned mechanisms for evading self-identification as 'gay' even when such acts have taken place, is part of what could be included under the umbrella of social constructionism — which is, in many ways, related to, and incorporates versions of labelling theory, phenomenology, ethnomethodology and symbolic interactionism. It is this argument that homosexuality is socially and historically constructed that seems to have been identified as 'social constructionism' by some authors (e.g. Suppe, 1984a). But the social constructionist movement has questioned not only the taken-for-granted category 'homosexual', but other taken-for-granted categories which necessarily impinge on research in this area, including the notion of 'sexual orientation' and even the notion of gender itself (Kessler and McKenna, 1978), the concepts of the 'individual', the 'self' and the 'mind' (Coulter, 1979; Sampson, 1983; Shweder and Miller, 1985; Verhave and van Hoorne, 1984), the constructed nature of emotions, including anger, sincerity, and romantic love (Averill, 1982 and 1985), and, of course, the categories of 'mental health' and 'mental disorder' (Szasz, 1971). For each, as Gergen (1985) points out, 'the objective criteria for identifying such "behaviors", "events", or "entities" are shown to be either highly circumscribed by culture, history, or social context or altogether nonexistent.'

If these social constructionist challenges to taken-for-granted categories are to be taken seriously by the 'gay affirmative' social scientist, then the research enterprise takes on a very different appearance. The 'individual', or the individual's 'self' or 'identity' can no longer be seen as unproblematic units of study, nor can they, or supposedly associated 'emotional states' or 'affective reactions', be rated according to 'mental health' criteria. Most basic of all, social constructionism represents the taken-for-granted category of 'science' itself as socially constituted and historically determined, arguing that our notions about what it is to 'do' science, what 'count' as facts, and what constitutes 'good' scientific practice are the products of the particular place, time and culture in which they are embedded. Not only the familiar categories which make up the *content* of science, but the very nature of science itself is thrown into question by the social constructionist movement.

Social constructionism, as Semin (1986) points out, does not assert any unitary doctrine or 'theory' about people, or love, or sexuality, or any of the other traditional concerns of research in the field of homosexuality. Rather it 'proposes a general research policy which aims to treat "mental" or "psychological processes" or "constructs" as generated from situated and constitutive social practices.'

A social constructionist approach to research on lesbianism (or male homosexuality) will involve, I suggest, five tasks, the first of which is the deconstruction of the ideological content of research in this area — a process initiated in Chapters 2–6. The second is the deconstruction of the mystique surrounding social science itself and the dismantling, brick-by-brick, of the wall of linguistic terminology, scientific methodology and rhetorical strategy which social scientists have constructed to contrast their own knowledge with that of ordinary folk (see Chapter 1). Only by undermining the means whereby social science constructs the conditions for its own legitimacy can the ideologies produced and promoted by science be finally denied the privileged position they now command as mirrors of reality.

A critique of ideological content alone is insufficient because it would be, as Harvey (1972: 111) points out, an endlessly recurring task. Social science could continue indefinitely swapping one discredited ideology for another — just as the critique of the 'lesbianism-as-personal pathology' position led to its substitution with an alternative ideology ('lesbianism-as-personal-lifestyle') serving the same oppressive and depoliticizing function. Similarly, I have no doubt that if my critique of liberal humanistic scientific ideology were to become widely known and accepted, then social science would succeed in finding yet another ideological position with which to defuse the threat of lesbianism and preserve its own status. As long as we critique only the ideological content of social science we are faced with a multiheaded hydra: as soon as we expose one ideology, another will spring up in its place. What is needed is not the continual deconstruction of the content of scientific ideologies, but the deconstruction of the privileged epistemological status of social science itself.

Thirdly, a social constructionist approach will recognize and appreciate the reflexivity of its own theory. That is, social constructionists' deconstructive endeavours, as much as the normal science they replace, do not have the status of objective facts and cannot be warranted empirically. Sometimes described as 'the Cretan dictum' (in memory of Epimenides, a Cretan philosopher who declared that 'all Cretans are liars', cf. Park, 1967), this has often been seen as a problem for social constructionism. Lacking criteria of truth and falsehood, and deprived of a priori reliance on empiricist methodologies, how can we judge the adequacy of our social constructionist methods and theories? As Gergen argues, the success of the social constructionist account depends primarily on the analyst's capacity to invite, compel, stimulate or delight the audience, and not on criteria of veracity. In this sense, it is to the extent that the arguments of Chapters 4, 5 and 6 are compelling, vivid or convincing, that Q (and interviewing) can be seen as useful methodologies.

> Virtually any methodology can be employed so long as it enables the analyst to develop a more compelling case. Although some methods may hold the allure of large samples, others can attract because of their purity, their sensitivity to nuance, or their ability to probe in depth. Such assets do not thereby increase the 'objective validity' of the resulting constructions. However, like vivid photographs or startling vignettes drawn from daily life, when well wrought they may add vital power to the pen. (Gergen, 1985)

The attempt to induce in the reader a willing suspension of disbelief, while simultaneously acknowledging that one's argument is an 'account', a 'construction' or 'version' rather than objective truth, can take social constructionist writing into the realm of the arts. Recent writing in the sociology of science has appeared in the form of parables or fables (Latour, 1980), one-act plays (Mulkay, 1984) and poems (Anon, 1984), and modern dance was used as a medium of communication at a recent academic conference on self and identity (Cohen, 1984). As Mulkay (1984) says in the 'Programme notes' that accompany his play:

> Sociologists, in general, have aped the natural sciences in adopting a strongly empiricist format for their research reports. As a result, much of their interpretative work is hidden from view and empirical material is often treated as if it speaks for itself. In this text I have used my material to construct an imaginary dramatic confrontation. In this way I have sought to emphasize the interpretative, creative character of my own as well as of participants' discourse.

In emphasizing the interpretative and creative character of the social constructionist text, multiple deconstruction of the same material by those of different ideological persuasions is welcomed — an approach which accords well with Feyerabend's 'principle of proliferation' ('invent and elaborate theories which are inconsistent with the accepted point of view, even if the latter should happen to be highly confirmed and generally accepted' [1970: 26]). In this book I have deconstructed research on lesbianism from 'within' a radical feminist ideology; a Marxist or anarchist analysis, for example, would approach and deconstruct liberal humanism and the construction of lesbianism from a different (perhaps incompatible) perspective (cf. Arblaster's [1977] Marxist deconstruction of research on terrorism and Tifft's [1979] anarchist deconstruction of crime). What is important is, as Star (1978) says, to build into our ideologies a non-reification clause.

Fourthly, social constructionists will offer radically different definitions of the world, which startle, shock, anger or surprise the reader in a way that focuses awareness on the taken-for-granted nature of the normative definition. This was one of the early achievements of radical feminism in redefining the word 'lesbian' (which was, and is, defined by social science in terms of 'sexual/ emotional preference') in terms of 'a blow against the patriarchy'. Although now part of the repertoire of feminist slogans, this definition initially gained its power through its conceit — the violent yoking together of two apparently incongruous ideas. Regardless of the acceptability or otherwise of this new definition, its existence serves to render problematic the taken-for-granted definition, at least to the extent that, having acquired a competitor, it now requires a defence. Similarly, while the reader might choose not to forswear liberal humanism as a result of my arguments (and there are good reasons why white, middle-class heterosexual men might well make that choice), my argument, if successful, will at least have forced some recognition of liberal humanism *as* ideological and unsettled the customary acceptance of liberalism as a set of self-evident truths.

Finally, social constructionists will engage in overt and explicit moral and political evaluation of the alternative constructions they present, and will not pass them off as 'value free'.

> It is not enough as a social constructionist to point out that there are any number of lenses to use for looking at what is going on around us and that different lenses will provide different views. We believe it is a social scientist's obligation to enumerate the features of their own lens and tell why it is a better lens through which to view the world than the others currently available. (McKenna and Kessler, 1985: 244)

At the same time it is necessary to evaluate and perhaps to reassess our own lens or ideological perspective, as I have asked liberal humanistic 'gay affirmative' researchers to do, and as I have done myself throughout my writing here. As Gouldner says, in a criticism of Becker and his school of deviance theory for its 'unexamined, comfortable commitment to political liberalism':

> A bland confession of partisanship merely betrays smugness and naïveté. It is smug because it assumes that the values we have are good enough: it is naïve because it assumes that we know the values we have. (Gouldner, 1968)

Liberals, as I have shown, typically do not know the values they have until they are challenged. When they are challenged, liberals must do more than retreat into declarations of their own 'objectivity' and lack of ideological bias, but must be prepared critically to evaluate and then to reject or defend their ideological position in terms of its political, social and moral context.

As is perhaps indicated by the preceding description of what social constructionist research involves, research within this paradigm is in many ways far more demanding than is positivist empiricist research. For many Western intellectuals, the deconstruction of liberal humanism is an extremely challenging task. In the next section I explore what such deconstruction involves, why it is so difficult, and why it is so important for gay affirmative researchers to address this task.

Deconstructing liberal humanism

Liberalism is 'an intellectual compromise so extensive that it includes most of the guiding beliefs of modern Western opinion', says Minogue (1963: vii) and he adds that 'it has even, in the form of Humanism, begun to work out an appropriate set of religious beliefs.' The liberal values of the dignity of the individual and his or her inalienable rights to justice, liberty, privacy, freedom of thought, and the pursuit of happiness irrespective of colour, class, creed, or gender, are often accepted as literally 'self-evident' moral truths, and to reject or even seriously to question them can feel like a violation of our fundamental moral beings.

Humanism elevates the values of liberalism to the supreme good: it represents a refusal to sacrifice values like justice, freedom and personal dignity for any supposed 'higher good' and makes a claim that 'all social principles and doctrines must be justified by their fruits in enriching the quality of *personal* experience here and now' (Hook, 1948: 1059), considering 'the complete realisation of human personality to be the end of man's [sic] life, and seeking its development and fulfilment in the here and now' (Lamont, 1965). For many middle-class Western intellectuals, liberal humanism is a fundamental faith — rarely recognized as such, and rarely questioned. To imagine alternative values can seem, as Brittan says, 'impossible':

> In a society in which the individual is made the focus of ideological and political commitment, it seems impossible to envisage other cultural forms in which privacy and the self are not taken for granted. The belief in the interiorisation of a world of meaning and uniqueness of experience is embodied in the language and literature of Western society, particularly the language and literature of bourgeois society. Privacy is not only taken for granted, it is elevated to a moral category. The violation of an individual's privacy is viewed in the same way as the desecration of the sacred by the unfaithful. (Brittan, 1977: 49)

The acceptance by most middle-class Western academics of liberal values like that of privacy can make it very difficult seriously to entertain the idea that such values might, as I have argued in this book, serve the interests of the patriarchy in ensuring the continuing oppression of women.

Even those very political radicals who spend much of their time and energy attacking liberalism and exposing it as an ideology of social control, have nonetheless confessed to the peculiar pull that liberal humanistic ideology has for them, and to the difficulty they have in discarding liberal assumptions and the liberal world view (cf. Arblaster, 1972). As one socialist writer says:

> As I drove home from my interview with the leader, I had to realise that a liberal, incurably, was what I was. . . . The revolutionary idea had impressed me and struck me as more *immediately* relevant for most of humanity than were the liberal concepts. But it was the liberal concepts and their long-term importance — though not the name of liberal — that held my allegiance. . . . Liberal values, tarnished by the spurious tributes of the rich world's media, today make the rich world yawn and the poor world sick. For my part I had had so little enthusiasm for them in theory that I was surprised and disconcerted at the depth of commitment to them experienced when, in practice, I met challenges to them. (O'Brien, 1965: xiii)

My own experience is similar in that I too find it difficult to exorcise the spirit of liberal humanism from my thinking. Brought up in a white, middle-class, academic family, with a mother who was an outspoken defender of the values of liberal humanism against the forces of oppression, and a father whose experience as a refugee from Nazi Germany provided a vivid illustration of the dangers of fanaticism and the evils of overriding the rights of individuals with a political program; reaching my teenage years in the late 1960s and early 1970s in the wake of the 'sexual revolution' and in time to receive support and validation as a woman and a lesbian not only from my family but also from the Gay and Women's Liberation Movements, I have always enjoyed the benefits liberal humanistic ideology has to offer, and my thinking is steeped in its values, my ideas moulded in its context. And perhaps for that very reason I can say more readily that it is not enough.

It is precisely those values that are most deeply embedded in our culture, and which exert the most hold on our thinking, that are most in need of deconstruction — meaning the capacity to see and believe that things might be otherwise, and that it might even be beneficial that they should be so. Challenges to liberal values are frequently greeted with incredulity and characterized as the demented outpourings of the crazed and depraved, the morally perverse and the socially disruptive. While deconstruction does not necessarily entail the rejection of liberalism, it does mean the recognition that liberal values are not always and everywhere 'true', that they are ideologically produced and maintained and that they serve specific political functions. Most importantly, deconstruction means recognizing that liberal humanism *is* an ideology and not, as it presents itself, the voice of reason and moderation occupying some supposed 'middle ground' between the warring ideologists of Left and Right. It is easier to de-reify our thinking about liberal humanism, and to be clear about our opposition to it, if we are also able to acknowledge and explore its seductive power over us.

Part of liberalism's power lies in its claim to be on the side of the oppressed, the dispossessed and the humble masses yearning to be free. Liberalism has traditionally opposed discrimination against individuals because of race, sex, colour or creed, and has defended the right of the individual to private activities and attitudes independent of state intervention. The arguments of liberalism have been used to gain rights for women in general and for lesbians in particular, based, as Koerner (1985: 327) points out, on claims for the individual's right to 'freedom, authenticity and self-expression'. The hard won freedoms of liberal humanism are now challenged by the rise of the new right, the antifeminist backlash and the rampant heterosexism that has emerged with the AIDS epidemic.

Whatever the appeal of liberal humanism to the middle-class intellectual, its grass-roots support is less and diminishing: most Americans, for example, do not even recognize the Declaration of Independence or the Bill of Rights when presented to them minus the heading, and when asked to sign these statements, supposedly the most fundamental documents of the American political system, about 90 percent refuse, calling them 'radical', 'subversive' or 'communist' (Holt, 1972: 126). Support for human rights (as defined by Western liberal ideology) is quite weak among the population as a whole and is generally found to be strongest — as with most positively valued attitudes and characteristics — amongst people most similar to the middle-class liberal social scientist (i.e. college-educated, high socioeconomic class, urban residence etc.) (cf. the review in Stainton Rogers and Kitzinger, 1985).

Recent surveys have shown a shift in public opinion in Britain against homosexuality (from 62 percent who thought homosexuality was mostly or always wrong in 1983, to 69 percent in 1985), and in the United States 75 percent of the population consider homosexual relationships mostly or always wrong (Jowell et al., 1986: 152). In a review of the research literature on attitudes, Meredith and Riester (1980) conclude that there is a discrepancy between the opinions of professionals and those of the general public, with professionals tending towards liberalism while public attitudes generally tend to be punitive or curative. In this context the 'tolerance' and 'acceptance' of liberalism become very appealing, compared with the intolerance and explicit rejection of the reactionaries. As Koerner (1985: 329) reminds the opponents of liberalism, 'from John Milton to John Stuart Mill to Sir Isaiah Berlin, the most powerful pleas for tolerance of diversity have come from within the liberal tradition.' It is this that makes the ideological framework of liberal humanism so attractive to gay affirmative (and other) researchers whose stated aim is rather to liberate than to subjugate and whose identification is with (rather than against) the oppressed.

The values of liberal humanism also appeal strongly to many people's moral sensibilities. The priceless value of the individual person, the reliance on concepts of justice, human rights and human needs as criteria for social action, and the emphasis on co-operation rather than conflict, reason rather than rhetoric, respect for persons rather than anger against abstract groups — all are endowed with an aura of moral superiority over the alternatives offered by lesbian separatist and homophobe, by black power radical and racist, by Jewish nationalist and anti-Semite. The liberal emphases on the need for the lamb to lie down with the lion, on the need to build bridges of shared communication, to generate light not heat, and for the family of humankind — black and white, gay and straight, male and female — to join hands in a circle of universal love combine in a moral message that is hard to ignore. The political opposition to liberalism's message is, as Halmos points out — using the word 'personalist' to refer to what I have here described as liberal humanist — often 'burdened by moral ambiguity':

On the one hand it deplores the clinical-psychotherapeutic absorption in insular and personal renewal and in the personalist privacies of intimacy and mutuality. On the other hand, it never fails to use rhetoric about the fraternal [*sic*] social order for which it is fighting. This order will richly extend the opportunities for forming and sustaining the very relationships which personalists cultivate in the here and now. (Halmos, 1978: 68)

The reification of liberal ideology as the apex of moral development in psychological models, such as Kohlberg's (1969), is simultaneously an accurate portrayal of existing social values as perceived by the Western social scientist, and an ideological lever in support of those values. Such models elevate into universal values the codes which prevail among a particular social and historical class, and reify them as constituting some kind of psychological essence.

Psychological reifications clothe existing social arrangements in terms of basic and inevitable characteristics of individual psychological functioning; this inadvertently [*sic*] authenticates the status quo, but now in a disguised psychological costume. What has been mediated by a socio-historical process — the forms and contents of human consciousness — is treated as though it were an 'in itself', a reality independent of these very origins. (Sampson, 1981)

The attempt to justify radical action in terms of liberal moral values (as discussed by Halmos above) is itself indicative of the extent to which these values are morally compelling over even those who, it would seem, have the most to gain by their rejection. Attempts to construct alternative radical moralities have met with mixed degrees of success. The feminist challenge to patriarchal morality can be traced back at least to the turn of the century (e.g. Pankhurst, 1914, quoted in Partnow, 1978), but quickly degenerated into rather unconvincing assertions about the moral superiority of the oppressed.

Recently there has been a more sustained effort to replace the male-defined morality of justice and rights, and its 'feminine' version of love and caring, with something more powerful and relevant to radical lesbian feminist ideology: the publication of the journal *Lesbian Ethics*, in the United States, and *Gossip: A Journal of Lesbian Feminist Ethics*, in Britain, represent moves towards the de-reification of liberal humanistic morality and the development of a radical alternative. (The issues involved in the construction of radical feminist morality are explored in detail in Kitzinger, forthcoming.)

The ideals of liberal humanism, its moral aspirations and its concern for the oppressed, all of which make it so attractive to many radicals, conceal its failure to deal with the issue of power. Its theory of society as an aggregate of individuals ignores or glosses over the differential power possessed by those individuals by virtue of their group membership; its faith in reason, rationality, the inevitability of progress, and the importance of communication between individuals cannot contend with the realities of socio-political conflict arising out of institutionalized power differences. As C. Wright Mills (1952) argues, 'if the moral force of liberalism is stimulating, its sociological content is weak; it has no theory of society adequate to its moral aims'. Radical feminists have argued the same point:

> Abstract talk of individuals and their rights is nothing but a red herring. What is really at stake is the collective power of opposing social groups: in this case, men and women. (Cameron and Fraser, 1984: 26)

Ignoring the issue of power, liberalism dissolves entire areas of sociopolitical conflict into interpersonal problems which can be resolved through the learning of good communication skills. Liberalism, as I have shown in the preceding chapters, leaves the structure of patriarchy and the institution of heterosexuality un-examined in favour of the belief that lesbianism is a personal choice or preference and that lesbians will achieve 'equality' with hetero-sexual women, or women with men, through shared communication and understanding, through education and the application of reason.

Radicals from a variety of movements have criticized the liberal approach for its failure to deal with institutionalized power and its insistence on appeals to the reason and good will of individuals. Discussing the liberal attitude to rape, one radical feminist writes:

> The assumption behind the liberal approach is that the powers-that-be allow us to be victimized because they don't know how bad it hurts. So what we have to do is unite under the mass slogan 'ouch!' Once they understand the enormity of our pain, they will forsake their opposition to us, and moral decency will triumph. It is a communication problem. (Connell, 1974)

Writing about the oppression of American blacks, Kozol similarly characterizes the liberal approach as ignoring the realities of political power:

> Anger between two parties, conflict starting up between two sides is not accepted as the honest manifestation of irreconcilable interests (power and its victim, exploitation and the cause, victimization and the one who has the spoils), but solely as a consequence of poor communication, bad static on the interurban network, poor telephone connections between Roxbury and Evanston, or Harlem and Seattle. Nobody *really* disagrees with someone else once he [sic] explains himself with proper care. (Kozol, 1975: 116–17)

And the same point is made in a sociological analysis of oppression in which the author condemns the liberal approach in these terms:

> The palliative to the Jewish or Negro or homosexual problem is presented as 'education'. 'Good will' and tolerance are liberal prescriptions to smooth away discomfiting disorder. An ideological fog shrouds the fundamental distribution of power and privilege. Bernstein remarks, 'the liberal will not be overly inclined to make a close investigation of enmity relations, as he is a priori convinced that they ought to fade away before his ethical postulates.' (Adam, 1978: 120)

As Mills (1952) argues, then, the ideals of liberalism have been divorced from any theoretical conceptualization of modern social structure that might serve as the means of their realization. More than this, liberalism's failure to examine the structure of institutionalized power not only leaves such power unacknowledged but, through distracting attention away from structural oppression in favour of a focus on individual relationships, actually serves to reinforce that power. It is for this reason that critics have argued that the drift into 'friendly fascism' (Gross, 1980) is not an aberration or departure from liberalism, but rather marks its fulfilment.

Within the feminist movement, liberal humanism has functioned to siphon off women's commitment to radical ideologies. While overtly sexist and explicitly antilesbian psychology was unlikely to detain, for long, a radical en route to the revolution — and might even spur her on — liberal humanism, by contrast, has offered her a beguiling cul de sac. Much of feminism has succumbed to the kind of liberal humanistic identities and ideologies discussed in Chapters 4 and 5; and, as other feminists have argued, contemporary feminism has become more of a 'lifestyle' than a political movement (Ehrenreich, 1977), marked by a glorification of individualism and the other paraphernalia of liberal humanism (Eisenstein, 1981); and the encroachment of psychology and psychiatry has succeeded in swallowing up much of the politics of the 'personal' into the language of therapy and self-fulfilment resulting in 'the humanist dilution of radical feminism' (Cardea, 1985). For feminist researchers of lesbianism, then, an awareness of and willingness to challenge liberalism is especially important. As Eisenstein says:

> Until liberalism is viewed as a political ideology by (liberal) feminists, they will be unable to identify the contradiction inherent in liberal feminism. As long as the liberalism in feminism parades invisibly, it cannot be assessed as contradictory with feminism, nor can dimensions of it be self-consciously reworked. (Eisenstein, 1981: 5)

'Invisible' liberalism is the hallmark not only of much contemporary feminism, but also of the social sciences generally, including developmental psychology (Walkerdine, 1984), occupational psychology (Hollway, 1984), cognitive psychology (Sampson, 1981) and the psychological testing of intelligence (Emler and Heather, 1980). Recent developments in social constructionist theory mean that, whatever the investments in and sense of security engendered by positivism, social scientists today can no longer evade the implication of the social constructionist movement. The accumulation of yet more 'facts' is a pointless exercise in an intellectual climate in which the concept of the 'fact' is becoming increasingly problematic. At best, continuing positivist empiricist research is merely futile; at worst, it is a window-dressing for oppression. For those of us who oppose existing oppressions, and who want our work to contribute to their alleviation, the deconstruction of liberal humanism is an urgent and challenging task.

References

Abraham, K. (1907) 'The Female Castration Complex', in *Selected Papers of Karl Abraham MD*. London: Hogarth Press.

Acosta, F.X. (1975) 'Etiology and Treatment of Homosexuality: A Review', *Archives of Sexual Behaviour* 4(1): 9–29.

Adam, B.D. (1978) *The Survival of Domination: Inferiorization and Everyday Life*. New York: Elsevier.

Adams, R.M. (1980) 'Authenticity-Codes and Sincerity-Formulas' in L. Michaels and C. Ricks (eds) *The State of the Language*. Berkeley: University of California Press.

Adelman, M.R. (1977) 'A Comparison of Professionally Employed Lesbians and Heterosexual Women on the MMPI', *Archives of Sexual Behavior* 6(3): 193–201.

Adorno, T.W., E. Frenkel-Brunswik, D.J. Levinson and R.N. Sanford (1950) *The Authoritarian Personality*. New York: Harper & Row.

Aguero, J.E., L. Bloch and D. Byrne (1984) 'The Relationship among Sexual Beliefs, Attitudes, Experiences and Homophobia', *Journal of Homosexuality* 10: 95–107.

Alderson, L. (1981) Untitled passage, in Onlywomen Press (eds) *Love Your Enemy? The Debate between Heterosexual Feminism and Political Lesbianism*. London: Onlywomen Press.

Alinder, G. (1970) 'Gay Liberation Meets the Shrinks', *Berkeley Tribe* (May). Reprinted in K. Jay and A. Young (eds) (1978) *Out of the Closets: Voices of Gay Liberation*. New York: Harcourt Brace Jovanovich.

Al-Issa, I. (1980) *The Psychopathology of Women*. Englewood Cliffs, NJ: Prentice-Hall.

Allen, H. (1986) 'Psychiatry and the Construction of the Feminine', in P. Miller and N. Rose (eds) *The Power of Psychiatry*. Cambridge: Polity Press.

Allport, G.W. (1961) *Personality and Social Encounter*. Boston: Beacon.

Almvig, C. (1982) 'The Invisible Minority: Aging and Lesbianism'. PhD dissertation. Syracuse: Utica College of Syracuse University.

Alyson Publications (1980) *Young, Gay and Proud*. Boston: Alyson Publications.

Anon (1984) 'On Behalf of the Personae', *Social Studies of Science* 14: 283.

Antaki, C. and G. Fielding (1981) 'Research on Ordinary Explanations', in C. Antaki (ed.) *The Psychology of Ordinary Explanations of Social Behaviour*. London: Academic Press.

Anthony, B.D. (1982) 'Lesbian Client — Lesbian Therapist: Opportunities and Challenges in Working Together', *Journal of Homosexuality* 7: 45–57.

Arblaster, A. (1972) 'Liberal Values and Socialist Values', *Socialist Register* 9: 83–104.

Arblaster, A. (1977) 'Terrorism: Myths, Meaning and Morals', *Political Studies* 25: 413–24.

Armon, V. (1986) 'Some Personality Variables in Overt Female Homosexuality', *Journal of Projective Techniques* 24: 292–309.

Atkinson, T.G. (1974) 'Radical Feminism and Love', in T.G. Atkinson, *Amazon Odyssey*. New York: Link Books.

Averill, J. (1982) *Anger and Aggression*. New York: Springer-Verlag.

Averill, J. (1985) 'The Social Construction of Emotion: With Special Reference to Love', in K.J. Gergen and K.E. Davis (eds) *The Social Construction of the Person*. New York: Springer-Verlag.

Babad, E.Y., M. Birnbaum and K.D. Benne (1983) *The Social Self: Group Influences on Personal Identity*. London: Sage Publications.

Baddeley, A. (1979) 'The Limitations of Human Memory: Implications for the Design of Retrospective Surveys', in L. Moss and H. Goldstein (eds) *The Recall Method in Social Surveys*. London: University of London Institute of Education.

Baetz, R. (1980) 'I See My First Lesbian', in M. Cruickshank (ed.) *The Lesbian Path*. Monterey, CA: Angel Press.

Bancroft, J. and P. Myerscough (1983) *Human Sexuality and Its Problems*. London: Churchill-Livingstone.

Barber, B. and R.C. Fox (1958) 'The Case of the Floppy-Eared Rabbits: An Instance of Serendipity Gained and Serendipity Lost', *American Journal of Sociology* 64: 128–36.

Barnes, B. and D. Edge (1982) *Science in Context: Readings in the Sociology of Science*. Milton Keynes: Open University Press.

Barnes, J.A. (1979) *Who Should Know What? Social Science, Privacy and Ethics*. Harmondsworth: Penguin.

Batya (1978) 'Age', in G. Vida (ed.) *Our Right To Love: A Lesbian Resource Book*. Englewood Cliffs, NJ: Prentice-Hall.

Bazerman, C. (1981) 'What Written Knowledge Does: Three Examples of Academic Discourse', *Philosophy of the Social Sciences* 11: 361–87.

Beck, E.T. (1982a) *Nice Jewish Girls: A Lesbian Anthology*. Watertown, MA: Persephone Press.

Beck, E.T. (1982b) 'Teaching about Jewish Lesbians in Literature: From "Zeitl and Rickel" to "The Tree of Begats" ', in M. Cruickshank (ed.) *Lesbian Studies: Present and Future*. New York: Feminist Press.

Becker, H.S. (1971) 'Whose Side Are We On?', in W. Filstead (ed.) *Qualitative Methodology: Firsthand Involvement with the Social World*. Chicago: Markham Publishing Co.

Becker, H.S. (1986) *Writing for Social Scientists: How To Start and Finish Your Thesis, Book or Article*. Chicago: University of Chicago Press.

Becker, H.S. and I.L. Horowitz (1972) 'Racial Politics and Sociological Research: Observations on Methodology and Ideology', *American Journal of Sociology* 78: 48–66.

Beckford, J.A. (1983) 'Talking of Apostasy: or Telling Tales and "Telling" Tales', in G.N. Gilbert and P. Abell (eds) *Accounts and Action: Surrey Conferences on Sociological Theory and Method*. Aldershot: Gower Press.

Beit-Hallahmi, B. (1974) 'Salvation and Its Vicissitudes: Clinical Psychology and Political Values', *American Psychologist* 29: 124–9.

Bell, A.P. (1975) 'Research in Homosexuality: Back to the Drawing Board', *Archives of Sexual Behavior* 4: 421–31.

Bell, A.P. and M.S. Weinberg (1978) *Homosexualities: A Study of Diversity Among Men and Women*. London: Mitchell Beazley.

Bell, A.P., M.S. Weinberg and S.K. Hammersmith (1981) *Sexual Preference: Its Development in Men and Women*. Bloomington: Indiana University Press.

Bellah, R.N. (1983) 'Social Science as Practical Reason', in D. Callahan and B. Jennings (eds) *Ethics, the Social Sciences and Policy Analysis*. London: Plenum Press.

Benny, M. and E.C. Hughs (1956) 'Of Sociology and the Interview', *American Journal of Sociology* 62: 137–42.

Bentler, P.M. and P.R. Abramson (1981) 'The Science of Sex Research: Some Methodological Considerations', *Archives of Sexual Behavior* 10: 225–51.

Berg, C. (1958) *Homosexuality: A Subjective and Objective Investigation*. London: Allen & Unwin.

Berger, P.L. (1965) 'Towards a Sociological Understanding of Psychoanalysis', *Social Research* 32: 26–41.

Berger, P.L., B. Berger and H. Kellner (1973) *The Homeless Mind: Modernization and Consciousness*. Harmondsworth: Penguin.

Berger, P. and H. Kellner (1964) 'Marriage and the Construction of Reality: An Exercise in the Microsociology of Knowledge', *Diogenes* 4: 1–24.

Berger, P.L. and T. Luckmann (1967) *The Social Construction of Reality*. Harmondsworth: Penguin.

Berger, R.M. (1984) 'Realities of Gay and Lesbian Aging', *Social Work* 29: 57–62.

Bergler, E. (1954) 'Spurious Homosexuality', *Psychiatric Quarterly Supplement* 28: 68–77.

Bergler, E. (1956) *Homosexuality: Disease or Way of Life?* New York: Collier Books.

Berry, R.J. (1980) 'Is Homosexuality a Cause for Concern?' Unpublished paper presented at the London Medical Group Symposium (November).

Bieber, I. (1969) 'Homosexuality', *American Journal of Nursing* 69: 2637–41.

Bieber, I. (1971) 'Speaking Frankly on a Once Taboo Subject', in R.V. Guthrie (ed.) *Psychology in the World Today: An Interdisciplinary Approach*. 2nd edn. Reading, MA: Addison-Wesley.

Bieritz, L. (1976) 'I Came Out in Class', in *Growing Up Gay: A Youth Liberation Pamphlet*. Ann Arbor, MI: Youth Liberation Press, Inc.

Billig, M. (1976) *Social Psychology and Intergroup Relations*. London: Academic Press.

Birke, L. (1980) 'From Zero to Infinity: Scientific Views of Lesbians', in Brighton Women and Science Group (ed.) *Alice Through the Microscope: The Power of Science over Women's Lives*. London: Virago.

Birke, L. (1981) 'Is Homosexuality Hormonally Determined?' *Journal of Homosexuality* 6: 35–49.

Blachford, G. (1981) 'Male Dominance and the Gay World', in K. Plummer (ed.) *The Making of the Modern Homosexual*. London: Hutchinson.

Black, K.N. and M.R. Stevenson (1984) 'The Relationship of Self-Reported Sex Role Characteristics and Attitudes toward Homosexuality', *Journal of Homosexuality* 10: 83–93.

Blackdykewomon, L. (1981) 'By the Grace of God (the Goddess Isis)', *Common Lives/Lesbian Lives: A Lesbian Feminist Quarterly* 1: 37–41.

Bloch, I. (1909) *The Sexual Life of Our Time*. London: Heinemann.

Block, J. (1956) 'A Comparison of Forced and Unforced Sorting Procedures', *Educational and Psychological Measurement* 16: 481–93.

Blum, A.F. and P. McHugh (1971) 'The Social Ascription of Motives', *American Sociological Review* 36: 98–109.

Bogardus, E.S. (1925) 'Measuring Social Distance', *Journal of Applied Sociology* 9: 299–308.

Bowman, C.C. (1949) 'Cultural Ideology and Heterosexual Reality: A Preface to Sociological Research', *American Sociological Review* 14: 624–33.

Brake, M. (1982) 'Sexuality as Praxis — a Consideration of the Contribution of Sexual Theory to the Process of Sexual Being', in M. Brake (ed.) *Human Sexual Relations*. Harmondsworth: Penguin.

Brant, B. (1981) 'Seeking My Own Vision', *Common Lives/Lesbian Lives: A Lesbian Feminist Quarterly* 2: 5–8.

Breinberg, P. (1977) 'Review of "A Woman's Right to Cruise"', *Sappho* 5(9): 24–5.

Brittan, A. (1977) *The Privatised World*. London: Routledge & Kegan Paul.

Broad, W. and N. Wade (1983) *The Betrayers of Truth*. London: Century.

Brown, R.M. (1972) 'Take a Lesbian to Lunch', in K. Jay and A. Young (eds) *Out of the Closets: Voices of Gay Liberation*. New York: Harcourt Brace Jovanovich.

Brown, R.M. (1975) 'We'd Better All Hang Together or Surely We'll All Hang Separately', in K. Jay and A. Young (eds) *After You're Out*. New York: Links.

Brown, R.M. (1976) *A Brown Paper Rapper*. Oakland, CA: Diana Press.

Brown, S.R. (1968) 'Bibliography on Q Technique and Its Methodology', *Perceptual and Motor Skills* 26: 587–613.

Brown, S.R. (1979) 'Forward', *Operant Subjectivity* 2(2): 37–9.

Brown, S.R. (1980) *Political Subjectivity: Applications of Q Methodology in Political Science*. New Haven: Yale University Press.

Browning, C. (1984) 'Changing Theories of Lesbianism: Challenging the Stereotypes', in T. Darty and S. Potter (eds) *Women-Identified Women*. Palo Alto, CA: Mayfield Publications.

Broyard, A. (1950) Portrait of the Inauthentic Negro', *Commentary* 10: 56–64.

Brummett, B. (1981) 'Ideologies in Two Gay Rights Controversies', in J.W. Chesebro (ed.) *GaySpeak*. New York: Pilgrim Press.

Bühler, C. (1971) *The Way to Fulfillment: Psychological Techniques*. New York: Hawthorne Books.

Bunch, C. (1978) 'Lesbians in Revolt', in A.M. Jaggar and P. Seruhl (eds) *Feminist Frameworks*. New York: McGraw-Hill.

Burt, C. (1937) 'Correlations between Persons', *British Journal of Psychology* 28: 59–96.

Burt, C. (1940) *The Factors of the Mind*. London: University of London Press.

Burt, C. (1972) 'The Reciprocity Principle', in S.R. Brown and D.J. Brenner (eds) *Science, Psychology and Communication: Essays Honoring William Stephenson*. New York: Teachers College Press.

Buss, A.R. (1975) 'The Emerging Field of the Sociology of Psychological Knowledge', *American Psychologist* 30: 988–1002.

Butler, E.W. (1979) *Traditional Marriage and Emerging Alternatives*. London: Harper & Row.

Butler, R. and T. Haigh (1954) 'Changes in the Relation between Self-Concepts and Ideal Concepts Consequent upon Client-Centered Counseling', in C.R. Rogers and R.F. Dymond (eds) *Psychotherapy and Personality Change*. Chicago: University of Chicago Press.

Byrne, D. (1977) 'Social Psychology and the Study of Sexual Behaviour', *Personality and Social Psychology Bulletin* 3: 3–30.

Calderone, M.S. (1976) 'Book Review', *Archives of Sexual Behavior* 5(4): 341–5.

Cameron, D. and L. Fraser (1984) 'The Liberal Organ: Porn in the Guardian', *Trouble and Strife* 4: 22–6.

Campbell, B. (1986) 'Family Matters', *Marxism Today* (18–21 December).

Campbell, P.N. (1975) 'The Personae of Scientific Discourse', *Quarterly Journal of Speech* 61: 392–405.

Canter, D. and G. Breakwell (1986) 'Psychologists and "the Media"', *Bulletin of the British Psychological Society* 39 (August): 281–6.

Caplan, N. and S.D. Nelson (1973) 'On Being Useful: The Nature and Consequences of Psychological Research on Social Problems', *American Psychologist* 28: 199–211.

Cappon, D. (1965) *Toward an Understanding of Homosexuality*. Englewood Cliffs, NJ: Prentice-Hall.

Cardea, C. (1985) 'The Lesbian Revolution and the 50-Minute Hour: A Working-Class Look at Therapy and the Movement', *Lesbian Ethics* 1(3): 46–68.

Cartledge, S. and S. Hemmings (1982) 'How Did We Get This Way?' in M. Rowe (ed.) *Spare Rib Reader*. Harmondsworth: Penguin.

Cartwright, S.A. (1981) 'Report on the Diseases and Physical Peculiarities of the Negro Race', in A.L. Caplan, H.T. Engelhardt and J.J. McCartney (eds) *Concepts of Health and Disease: Interdisciplinary Perspectives*. Reading, MA: Addison-Wesley.

Cass, V. (1979) 'Homosexual Identity Formation: A Theoretical Model', *Journal of Homosexuality* 4: 219–21.

Cass, V. (1984) 'Homosexual Identity: A Concept in Need of Definition', *Journal of Homosexuality* 9: 105–26.

Cattell, R.B. (1944) 'Psychological Measurement: Normative, Ipsative, Interactive', *Psychological Review* 51: 293–303.

Cattell, R.B. (1946) *The Description and Measurement of Personality*. New York: World Book Company.

Cattell, R.B. (1951) 'On the Disuse and Misuse of P, Q, Qs and O Techniques in Clinical Psychology', *Journal of Clinical Psychology* 7: 203–14.

Chapman, D. (1965) 'What Is a Lesbian?' *Family Doctor* (August) 474–5.

Chassegut-Smirgel, J. (1964) *Female Sexuality*. London: Virago.

Cheong, L.K. (1978) *Syntax of Scientific English*. Singapore: Singapore University Press.

Cherry, N. and B. Rodgers (1979) 'Using a Longitudinal Study To Assess the Quality of Retrospective Data', in L. Moss and H. Goldstein (eds) *The Recall Method in Social Surveys*. London: University of London Institute of Education.

Chesebro, J.W. (1981) 'Introduction', in J.W. Chesebro (ed.) *GaySpeak*. New York: Pilgrim Press.

Chesler, P. (1972) *Women and Madness*. New York: Avon Books.

Chesser, E. (1958) *Live and Let Live: The Moral of the Wolfenden Report*. London: Heinemann.

Chodorkoff, B. (1954) 'Self-Perception, Perceptual Defence and Adjustment', *Journal of Abnormal Social Psychology* 49: 508–12.

Chrystos (1982) 'Nidishenok (Sisters)', *Maenad: A Women's Literary Journal* 2(2): 23–32.

Churchill, W. (1967) *Homosexual Behavior among Males*. Englewood Cliffs, NJ: Prentice-Hall.

Clarke, C. (1983) 'The Failure to Transform: Homophobia in the Black Community', in B. Smith (ed.) *Home Girls: A Black Feminist Anthology*. New York: Kitchen Table/Women of Color Press.

Clifford, J. (1983) 'On Anthropological Authority', *Representations* 1: 118–46.

Cloutte, P. (1981) Letter in *Love Your Enemy? The Debate between Heterosexual Feminism and Political Lesbianism*. London: Onlywomen Press.

Cochran, S. (1984) 'Book Review', *Journal of Homosexuality* 10: 159–63.

Cochrane, R. (1977) 'Mental Illness in Immigrants to England and Wales: An Analysis of Mental Hospital Admissions', *Social Psychiatry* 12: 22–35.

Cohen, D. and R. Dyer (1980) 'The Politics of Gay Culture', in Gay Left Collective (ed.) *Homosexuality: Power and Politics*. London: Allison & Busby.

Cohen, J. (1984) Dance presented at International Conference on Self and Identity. (July) Cardiff, Wales.

Cohen, S. and L. Taylor (1976) *Escape Attempts: The Theory and Practice of Resistance to Everyday Life*. Harmondsworth: Penguin.

Cole, J.K. (1973) 'Homosexuality and Homosexual Love', in M.E. Curtin (ed.) *Symposium on Love*. New York: Behavioral Publications.

Coleman, E. (1982) 'Developmental Stages of the Coming-Out Process', *American Behavioral Scientist* 25(4): 426–82.

Collins, H.M. (1982) 'The Replication of Experiments in Physics', in B. Barnes and D. Edge (eds) *Science in Context: Readings in the Sociology of Science*. Milton Keynes: Open University Press.

Collins, H.M. (1983a) 'An Empirical Relativist Programme in the Sociology of Scientific Knowledge', in K.D. Knorr-Cetina and M. Mulkay (eds) *Science Observed*. London: Sage Publications.

Collins, H.M. (1983b) 'The Meaning of Lies: Accounts of Action and Participatory Research', in G.N. Gilbert and P. Abell (eds) *Accounts and Action: Surrey Conferences on Sociological Theory and Method*. Aldershot: Gower Press.

Collins, R. (1968) 'Competition and Social Control in Science: An Essay in Theory Construction', *Sociology of Education* 41: 123–40.

Connell, N. (1974) 'Introduction', in N. Connell and C. Wilson (eds) *Rape: The First Sourcebook for Women*. New York: Plume Books.

Conrad, P. (1975) 'The Discovery of Hyperkinesis: Notes on the Medicalization of Deviant Behavior', *Social Problems* 23: 12–21.

Cook, B.W. (1979) 'The Historical Denial of Lesbianism', *Radical History Review*, 20: 60–5.

Cooper, A.M. (1980) 'Review of *Homosexuality in Perspective* by W.H. Masters and V.E. Johnson, Boston: Little, Brown and Co.', in C.R. Stimpson and E.S. Person (eds) *Women: Sex and Sexuality*. Chicago: University of Chicago Press.

Cooper, J.B. (1959) 'Emotion in Prejudice', *Science* 130: 314–18.

Coulter, J. (1979) *The Social Construction of the Mind*. New York: Macmillan.

Coward, D. (1977) 'The Sociology of Literary Response', in I. Roath and J. Wolff (eds) *The Sociology of Literature: Theoretical Approaches*. British Sociological Association Monograph Number 25.

Cowley, M. (1956) 'Sociological Habit Patterns in Linguistic Transmogrification', *The Reporter* 20 (20 September): 41–3.

Crew, L. and R. Norton (1974) 'The Homophobic Imagination: An Editorial', *College English* 36(3): 272–90.

Cronbach, L.J. (1956) 'Assessment of Individual Differences', *Annual Review of Psychology* 7: 173–96.

Cruickshank, M. (1980) (ed.) *The Lesbian Path*. New York: Caroline House.

Cuenot, R.G. and S.S. Fugita (1982) 'Perceived Homosexuality: Measuring Heterosexual Attitudinal and Nonverbal Reactions', *Personality and Social Psychology Bulletin* 8: 100–6.

Cuff, E.C. (1980) 'Some Issues in Studying the Problem of Versions in Everyday

Situations', Occasional Paper No. 3, Department of Sociology, University of Manchester.

Daly, M. (1979) *Gyn/Ecology: The Metaethics of Radical Feminism*. London: Women's Press.

Daniel, S. (1954) 'The Homosexual Woman in Present Day Society', *International Journal of Sexology* (May): 223–4.

Dank, B.M. (1971) 'Six Homosexual Siblings', *Archives of Sexual Behavior* 1: 193–204.

Dannecker, M. (1981) *Theories of Homosexuality*. London: Gay Men's Press.

Davenport, D. (1982) 'Black Lesbians in Academia: Visible Invisibility', in M. Cruickshank (ed.) *Lesbian Studies: Present and Future*. New York: Feminist Press.

Davidson, D. (1973) 'The Furious Passage of the Black Graduate Student', in J.A. Ladner (ed.) *The Death of White Sociology*. New York: Random House.

Davis, M. (1971) "That's Interesting!" Towards a Phenomenology of Sociology and a Sociology of Phenomenology', *Philosophy of the Social Sciences* 1: 309–44.

Davison, G.C. (1976) 'Homosexuality: The Ethical Challenge', *Journal of Consulting and Clinical Psychology* 44: 157–62.

Day, C.L. and B.W. Morse (1981) 'Communication Patterns in Established Lesbian Relationships', in J.W. Chesebro (ed.) *GaySpeak*. New York: Pilgrim Press.

De Cecco, J.P. (1981) 'Definition and Meaning of Sexual Orientation', *Journal of Homosexuality* 6: 51–67.

De Cecco, J.P. and M.G. Shively (1984) 'From Sexual Identity to Sexual Relationships: A Context Shift', *Journal of Homosexuality* 9: 1–26.

Decker, B. (1983) 'Counseling Gay and Lesbian Couples', *Journal of Social Work and Human Sexuality* 2: 39–52.

Defries, Z. (1976) 'Pseudohomosexuality in Feminist Students', *American Journal of Psychiatry* 133: 400–4.

DeMonteflores, C. and S.J. Schultz (1978) 'Coming Out: Similarities and Differences for Lesbians and Gay Men', *Journal of Social Issues* 34: 59–72.

De Ruggiero, G. (1959) *The History of European Liberalism*. Trans. R.G. Collingwood. Boston: Beacon Press.

Deutscher, I. (1968) 'On Social Science and the Sociology of Knowledge', *American Sociologist* 3: 291–2.

Dexter, L.A. (1970) *Elite and Specialized Interviewing*. Evanston, IL: Northwestern University Press.

Donna (1978) 'Age', in G. Vida (ed.) *Our Right to Love: A Lesbian Resource Book*. Englewood Cliffs, NJ: Prentice-Hall.

Douglas, J.D. (1971) 'The Rhetoric of Science and the Origins of Statistical Social Thought: The Case of Durkheim's "Suicide"', in E.A. Tiryakian (ed.) *The Phenomenon of Sociology*. New York: Appleton-Century-Crofts.

Duijker, H.C.J. (1979) 'Mind and Meaning', *Operant Subjectivity* 3: 15–31.

Dumont, M. (1969) 'Social Science and the Survival of Cities', *Psychiatry and Social Science Review* 3: 161–9.

Dunbar, J., M. Brown and D.M. Amoroso (1973) 'Some Correlates of Attitudes toward Homosexuality', *Journal of Social Psychology* 89: 271–9.

Duncan, D.C. (1986) 'Achievements of Psychology', *Bulletin of the British Psychological Society* 39 (October): 378–9.

Dworkin, A. (1981) *Pornography: Men Possessing Women*. London: Women's Press.

Dymond, R.F. (1954) 'Adjustment Changes over Therapy from Self-Sorts', in

C.R. Rogers and R.F. Dymond (eds) *Psychotherapy and Personality Change.* Chicago: University of Chicago Press.

Eagly, A.H. and L.L. Carli (1981) 'Sex of Researchers and Sex-typed Communications as Determinants of Sex Differences in Influenceability: A Meta-Analysis of Social Influence Studies', *Psychological Bulletin* 90: 1–20.

Eaves, L. and H.J. Eysenck (1974) 'Genetics and the Development of Social Attitudes', *Nature* 249: 288–9.

Ehrenreich, B. (1977) 'Toward a Political Morality', *Liberation* (July/August): 21–3.

Ehrlich, L.G. (1981) 'The Pathogenic Secret', in J.W. Chesebro (ed.) *GaySpeak.* New York: Pilgrim Press.

Eisenstein, Z.R. (1981) *The Radical Future of Liberal Feminism.* New York and London: Longman.

Eisenthal, S. (1973) 'Evaluation of a Community Mental Health Role Using a Structured Q Sort', *Community Mental Health Journal* 9: 25–33.

Elliott, M.A. (1953/4) 'Pressures Upon Research and Publication in Sociology', *Social Problems* 1: 94–7.

Ellis, A. (1969) 'The Use of Sex in Human Life', *Journal of Sex Research* 5: 41–9.

Ellis, A. (1971) 'Interview with Albert Ellis', in A. Karlen, *Sexuality and Homosexuality: A New View.* New York: W.W. Norton.

Ellis, H. (1934) *Psychology of Sex.* London: Heinemann.

Emler, N.P. and N. Heather (1980) 'Intelligence: An Ideological Bias of Conventional Psychology', in P. Salmon (ed.) *Coming To Know.* London: Routledge & Kegan Paul.

Escamilla-Mondanaro, J. (1977) 'Lesbians and Therapy', in E.I. Rawlings and D.K. Carter (eds) *Psychotherapy for Women.* Springfield, IL: Charles C. Thomas.

Ettinger, S. (1976) 'The Bottom Rung', in *Growing Up Gay: A Youth Liberation Pamphlet.* Ann Arbor, MI: Youth Liberation Press.

Ettorre, E. (1980) *Lesbians, Women and Society.* London: Routledge & Kegan Paul.

Evans, P. (1977) Letter, in *Sappho* 5(12): 11–12.

Evans-Pritchard, E.E. (1950) *Witchcraft, Oracles and Magic among the Azandi.* Oxford: Oxford University Press.

Eysenck, H.J. (1953) *Uses and Abuses of Psychology.* Harmondsworth: Penguin.

Eysenck, H.J. and G.D. Wilson (eds) (1978) *The Psychological Basis of Ideology.* Lancaster, Lancs: MTP Press Ltd.

Faderman, L. (1980) *Surpassing the Love of Men: Romantic Friendship and Love between Women from the Renaissance to the Present.* London: Junction Books.

Faderman, L. (1985) 'The "New Gay" Lesbians', *Journal of Homosexuality* 10: 65–75.

Faraday, A. (1981) 'Liberating Lesbian Research', in K. Plummer (ed.) *The Making of the Modern Homosexual.* London: Hutchinson.

Faye, C. (1980) 'Come Again', in S.J. Wolfe and J.P. Stanley (eds) *The Coming Out Stories.* Watertown, MA: Persephone Press.

Feuer, L.S. (1975) *Ideology and the Ideologists.* Oxford: Basil Blackwell.

Feyerabend, P.K. (1970) 'Against Method: Outline of an Anarchistic Theory of Knowledge', in M. Radner and S. Winokur (eds) *Minnesota Studies in the Philosophy of Science: Vol. IV.* Minneapolis: University of Minnesota Press.

Firestone, S. (1971) *The Dialectic of Sex: The Case for Feminist Revolution.* Reprinted, 1979. London: Women's Press.

Fisher, S. and R. Fisher (1955) 'Relationship between Personal Insecurity and Attitude toward Psychological Methodology', *American Psychologist*, 10: 538–40.

Fluckiger, F. (1966) '"Through a Glass Darkly": An Evaluation of the Bieber Study on Homosexuality', *The Ladder* 10: 10–12.

Forel, A. (1908) *The Sexual Question: A Scientific, Psychological, Hygienic and Sociological Study*. Trans. C.F. Marshall. New York: Physicians & Surgeons Book Co.

Foucault, M. (1979) *The History of Sexuality: Volume I*. Harmondsworth: Penguin.

FPS (1975) 'Curing Hyperactivity', *FPS: A Magazine of Young People's Liberation* (March): 9.

Franklin, S. and J. Stacey (1986) 'Lesbian Perspectives on Women's Studies', University of Kent Women's Studies Occasional Papers, No. 11.

Freedman, M. (1971) *Homosexuality and Psychological Functioning*. Belmont, CA: Brook/Cole.

Freedman, M. (1975) 'Homosexuals May Be Healthier than Straights', *Psychology Today* 8: 28–32.

Freedman, M. (1978) 'Towards a Gay Psychology', in L. Crew (ed.) *The Gay Academic*. Palm Springs, CA: ETC Publications.

Freud, S. (1977) *On Sexuality*. Penguin Freud Library, Vol. 7. Harmondsworth: Penguin.

Friedrichs, R.W. (1970) *A Sociology of Sociology*. New York: The Free Press.

Frye, M. (1983) *The Politics of Reality: Essays in Feminist Theory*. New York: Crossing Press.

Furfey, P.H. (1971) 'The Sociologist and Scientific Objectivity', in E.A. Tiryakian (ed.) *The Phenomenon of Sociology*. New York: Appleton-Century-Crofts.

Gagnon, J.H. (1977) *Human Sexualities*. Glenview, IL: Scott, Foresman & Co.

Gagnon, J.H. and W. Simon (1973) *Sexual Conduct*. New York: Aldine.

Gaito, J. (1962) 'Forced and Free Q Sorts', *Psychological Reports* 10: 251–4.

Garfinkle, A. (1981) *Forms of Explanation: Rethinking the Questions in Social Theory*. New Haven and London: Yale University Press.

Garfinkle, H., M. Lynch and E. Livingstone (1982) 'The Work of a Discovering Science Construed with Materials from the Optically Discovered Pulsar', *Philosophy of the Social Sciences* 11: 131–58.

Gartrell, N. (1984) 'Combating Homophobia in the Psychotherapy of Lesbians', *Women and Therapy* 3: 13–29.

Gauger, S.E. and J.B. Wyckoff (1973) 'Aesthetic Preference for Water Resource Projects: An Application of Q Methodology', *Water Resources Bulletin* 9: 522–8.

Gay Christian Movement (1978) *The Bible and Homosexuality*. 2nd edn. Gay Christian Movement Pamphlets No. 3. London: Gay Christian Movement.

Gay Liberation Information Service (1978) *Psychiatry and the Homosexual: A Brief Analysis of Oppression*. Gay Liberation Pamphlet No. 1. London: Gay Liberation Information Service.

Gellner, E. (1985) *Relativism and the Social Sciences*. Cambridge: Cambridge University Press.

Gergen, K.J. (1973) 'Social Psychology as History', *Journal of Personality and Social Psychology* 26: 309–20.

Gergen, K.J. (1982) *Toward Transformation in Social Knowledge*. New York: Springer-Verlag.

Gergen, K.J. (1985) 'The Social Constructionist Movement in Modern Psychology', *American Psychologist* 40: 266–75.

Gerlach, L.P. and V.H. Hine (1970) *People, Power, Change: Movements of Social Transformation*. Indianapolis, IN: Bobbs-Merrill.

Gilbert, G.N. (1977) 'Referencing as Persuasion', *Social Studies of Science* 7: 113–22.

Gilbert, G.N. (1983) 'Accounts and Those Accounts Called Actions', in G.N. Gilbert and P. Abell (eds) *Accounts and Action: Surrey Conferences on Sociological Theory and Method*. Aldershot: Gower Press.

Gilbert, G.N. and M. Mulkay (1980) 'Contexts of Scientific Discourse: Social Accounting in Experimental Papers', in K.D. Knorr, R. Krohn and R. Whitley (eds) *The Social Process of Scientific Investigation*. Dordrach: Reidel.

Gilbert, G.N. and M. Mulkay (1982) 'Warranting Scientific Belief', *Social Studies of Science* 12: 383–408.

Gilbert, G.N. and M. Mulkay (1984) *Opening Pandora's Box: A Sociological Analysis of Scientists' Discourse*. Cambridge: Cambridge University Press.

Glassner, B. and C. Owen (1976) 'Variations in Attitude toward Homosexuality', *Cornell Journal of Social Relations* 11: 161–76.

Glickman, K. (1980) 'Book Review of *The Lesbian Community* by D.G. Wolf, University of California Press', *Journal of Homosexuality* 5: 237–9.

Goffman, E. (1963) *Stigma: Notes on the Management of Spoiled Identity*. Harmondsworth: Penguin.

Gonsiorek, J.C. (1981) 'Book Review of *Homosexuality in Perspective* by Masters and Johnson', *Journal of Homosexuality* 6: 81–8.

Gonsiorek, J.C. (1982a) 'The Use of Diagnostic Concepts in Working with Gay and Lesbian Populations', *Journal of Homosexuality* 7: 9–20.

Gonsiorek, J.C. (1982b) 'Introduction: Present and Future Directions in Gay/ Lesbian Mental Health', *Journal of Homosexuality* 7: 5–7.

Gonsiorek, J.C. (1982c) 'An Introduction to Mental Health Issues and Homosexuality', *American Behavioral Scientist* 23: 367–84.

Goode, E. (1969) 'Marijuana and the Politics of Reality', *Journal of Health and Social Behavior* 10: 83–94.

Goode, E. and L. Haber (1977) 'Sexual Correlates of Homosexual Experience: An Exploratory Study of College Women', *Journal of Sex Research* 13: 12–21.

Goodison, L. (1983) 'Really Being in Love Means Wanting To Live in a Different World', in S. Cartledge and J. Ryan (eds) *Sex and Love: New Thoughts on Old Contradictions*. London: Women's Press.

Goodman, G., G. Lakey, J. Lashof and E. Thorne (1983) *No Turning Back: Lesbian and Gay Liberation for the '80s*. Philadelphia: New Society Publishers.

Gorer, G. (1971) *Sex and Marriage in England Today: A Study of the Views and Experiences of the Under-45s*. London: Nelson.

Gorz, A. (1974) 'The Scientist as Worker: Speed-Up at the Think-Tank', *Liberation* 118: 12–18.

Gouldner, A.W. (1968) 'The Sociologist as Partisan', *American Sociologist* 3: 103–16.

Gouldner, A.W. (1970) *The Coming Crisis in Western Sociology*. London: Heinemann.

Gouldner, A.W. (1976) *The Dialectic of Ideology and Technology: The Origins, Grammar and Future of Ideology*. London: Macmillan.

Greenberg, C. (1950) 'Self-Hatred and Jewish Chauvinism', *Commentary* 10: 426–33.

Gross, B. (1980) *Friendly Fascism: The New Face of Power in America*. Boston: South End Press.

Grygier, T.G. (1957) 'Homosexuality', *Journal of Mental Science* 103: 514–22.

Gundlach, R.H. and B.F. Riess (1968) 'Self and Sexual Identity in the Female: A Study of Female Homosexuals', in B.F. Riess (ed.) *New Directions in Mental Health*. New York: Grune & Stratton.

Gundlach, R.H. and B.F. Riess (1973) 'The Range of Problems in the Treatment of Lesbians', in D.S. Milman and G.D. Goldman (eds) *The Neurosis of Our Time: Acting Out*. Springfield, IL: Charles C. Thomas.

Gusfield, J.R. (1967) 'Moral Passage: The Symbolic Process in Public Designations of Deviance', *Social Problems* 15: 175–88.

Gusfield, J. (1976) 'The Literary Rhetoric of Science: Comedy and Pathos in Drinking Driver Research', *American Sociological Review* 41: 16–34.

Guth, J.T. (1978) 'Invisible Women: Lesbians in America', *Journal of Sex Education and Therapy* 4: 3–6.

Hall, C.S. and G. Lindzey (1978) *Theories of Personality*. 3rd edn. London: Wiley.

Hall, M. (1985) *The Lavender Couch*. Boston: Alyson.

Hall, R. (1928) *The Well of Loneliness*. Reprinted 1981. New York: Bard Avon Books.

Hall, W.S., W.E. Cross and R. Freedle (1975) 'Stages in the Development of Black Awareness', in E. Krupat (ed.) *Psychology is Social: Readings and Conversation in Social Psychology*. Glenview, IL: Scott Foresman & Co.

Halmos, P. (1978) *The Personal and the Political: Social Work and Political Action*. London: Hutchinson.

Hanisch, C. (1975) 'Men's Liberation', in Redstockings (ed.) *Feminist Revolution*. New York: Random House.

Hansen, G.L. (1982) 'Measuring Prejudice against Homosexuality (Homosexism) among College Students: A New Scale', *Journal of Social Psychology* 117: 233–6.

Hardley, E. (1984) 'Fraud in Science and its Implications for the Science of Psychology', paper presented at the British Psychological Society London Conference, December.

Hare, E.H. (1962) 'Masturbatory Insanity: The History of an Idea', *Journal of Mental Science* 108: 1–25.

Harris, H. (1976) 'I was a Teenage Lesbian', in *Growing Up Gay: A Youth Liberation Pamphlet*. Ann Arbor, MI: Youth Liberation Press Inc.

Harry, J. (1984) 'Sexual Orientation as Destiny', *Journal of Homosexuality* 10: 111–24.

Hart, J. (1981) 'Theoretical Explanations in Practice', in J. Hart and D. Richardson (eds) *The Theory and Practice of Homosexuality*. London: Routledge & Kegan Paul.

Hart, J. and D. Richardson (1980) 'The Differences between Homosexual Men and Women', *Bulletin of the British Psychological Society* 33: 451–4.

Hart, J. and D. Richardson (1981) *The Theory and Practice of Homosexuality*. London: Routledge & Kegan Paul.

Hauser, R. (1962) *The Homosexual Society*. London: Mayflower Books Ltd.

Hautzig, G. (1978) *Hey Dollface*. New York: Bantam.

Hayes, G. (1986) 'Marketing Psychology', *Bulletin of the British Psychological Society* 39 (October): 376.

Hayes, J.J. (1976) 'GaySpeak', *Quarterly Journal of Speech* 62: 256–66.

Hedblom, J.H. (1972) 'The Female Homosexual: Social and Attitudinal Dimensions', in J.A. McCaffrey (ed.) *The Homosexual Dialectic*. Englewood Cliffs, NJ: Prentice-Hall.

Hedblom, J.H. (1973) 'Dimensions of Lesbian Sexual Experience', *Archives of Sexual Behavior* 2: 329–41.

Hencken, J.D. (1982) 'Homosexuality and Psychoanalysis: Toward a Mutual Understanding', *American Behavioral Scientist* 25: 435–68.

Henderson, D. and I. Batchelor (1962) *Textbook of Psychiatry*. 9th edn. Oxford: Oxford University Press.

Hendin, H. (1978) 'Homosexuality: The Psychosocial Dimension', *Journal of the American Academy of Psychoanalysis* 6: 476–96.

Henley, N.M. and F. Pincus (1978) 'Interrelationship of Sexist, Racist and Antihomosexual Attitudes', *Psychological Reports* 42: 83–90.

Henriques, J., W. Hollway, C. Urwin, C. Venn and V. Walkerdine (1984) *Changing the Subject: Psychology, Social Regulation and Subjectivity*. London: Methuen.

Henry, S. (1976) 'Fencing with Accounts: The Language of Moral Bridging', *British Journal of Law and Society* 3: 91–100.

Herek, G.M. (1984) 'Attitudes toward Lesbians and Gay Men: A Factor-Analytic Study', *Journal of Homosexuality* 10: 39–51.

Heritage, J. (1983) 'Accounts in Action', in G.N. Gilbert and P. Abell (eds) *Accounts and Action: Surrey Conferences on Sociological Theory and Method*. Aldershot: Gower Press.

Hess, E.P. (1983) 'Feminist and Lesbian Development: Parallels and Divergences', *Journal of Humanistic Psychology* 23: 67–78.

Hidalgo, H. (1984) 'The Puerto Rican Lesbian in the United States', in T. Darty and S. Potter (eds) *Women-Identified Women*. Palo Alto, CA: Mayfield Publishing Co.

Hindley, C.B. (1979) 'Problems of Interviewing in Obtaining Retrospective Information', in L. Moss and H. Goldstein (eds) *The Recall Method in Social Surveys*. London: University of London Institute of Education.

Hodges, A. and D. Hutter (1977) *With Downcast Gays: Aspects of Homosexual Self-Oppression*. Toronto: Pink Triangle Press.

Hoffman, M. (1976) 'Book Review of *The Homosexual Matrix* by C.A. Tripp, *Archives of Sexual Behavior* 5: 345–7.

Hollway, W. (1984) 'Fitting Work: Psychological Assessment in Organizations', in J. Henriques, W. Hollway, C. Urwin, C. Venn and V. Walkerdine, *Changing the Subject: Psychology, Social Regulation and Subjectivity*. London: Methuen.

Holt, J. (1972) *Escape from Childhood: The Needs and Rights of Children*. Harmondsworth: Penguin.

Holzinger, K.J. (1946) 'A Comparison of the Principal-Axis and Centroid Factors', *Journal of Educational Psychology* 37: 449–72.

Hood, R.W. (1973) 'Dogmatism and Opinions about Mental Illness', *Psychological Reports* 32: 1283–90.

Hook, S. (1948) 'Humanism and the Labour Movement' in F. Gross (ed.) *European Ideologies: A Survey of Twentieth-Century Political Ideas*. New York: Philosophical Library.

Hopkins, J. (1969) 'The Lesbian Personality', *British Journal of Psychiatry* 115: 1433–6.

Horowitz, I.L. and M. Liebowitz (1968) 'Social Deviance and Political Marginality: Toward a Redefinition of the Relation between Sociology and Politics', *Social Problems* 15: 280–96.

Horton, J. (1964) 'The Dehumanization of Anomie and Alienation', *British Journal of Sociology* 15: 283–300.

Hudson, L. (1972) *The Cult of the Fact*. London: Jonathan Cape.

Hudson, L. (1980) 'Language, Truth and Psychology', in L. Michaels and C. Ricks (eds) *The State of the Language*. Berkeley: University of California Press.

Hudson, W.W. and W.A. Ricketts (1980) 'A Strategy for the Measurement of Homophobia', *Journal of Homosexuality* 5: 357–72.

Hughes, E. (1945) 'Dilemmas and Contradictions of Status', *American Journal of Sociology* 50: 253–9.

Ingleby, D. (1974) 'The Job Psychologists Do', in N. Armistead (ed.) *Reconstructing Social Psychology*. Harmondsworth: Penguin.

Jackson, M. (1981) 'The Male Sexual Revolution', unpublished paper presented at the Women's Research and Resources Centre Conference on Feminism and Sexuality, London.

Jacoby, R. (1975) *Social Amnesia: A Critique of Conformist Psychology from Adler to Laing*. Hassocks, East Sussex: Harvester Press.

Jahoda, M. (1958) *Current Conceptions of Positive Mental Health*. New York: Basic Books.

James, M. and D. Jongeward (1971) *Born To Win: Transactional Analysis with Gestalt Experiments*. Reading, MA: Addison-Wesley.

Jefferson, W. (1976) 'Combatting Homophobia', *Alternatives to Alienation* 7: 7–19.

Jeffreys, S. (1982) '"Free from All Uninvited Touch of Man": Women's Campaigns around Sexuality, 1880–1914', *Women's Studies International Forum* 5: 629–45.

Jeffreys, S. (1985) *The Spinster and Her Enemies: Feminism and Sexuality, 1880–1930*. London: Pandora.

Jem (1975) 'A Bi-Sexual Offers Some Thoughts on Fences', in K. Jay and A. Young (eds) *After You're Out: Personal Experiences of Gay Men and Lesbian Women*. New York: Links.

Jenkins, M.M. (1984) 'Review of *GaySpeak: Gay Male and Lesbian Communication* by J.W. Chesebro (ed.) New York: Pilgrim Press', *Signs* 9: 720–1.

Jennings, B. (1983) 'Interpretative Social Science and Policy Analysis', in D. Callahan and B. Jennings (eds) *Ethics, the Social Sciences and Policy Analysis*. New York: Plenum Press.

Johnston, J. (1973) *Lesbian Nation: The Feminist Solution*. New York: Simon & Schuster.

Jones, A. (1956) 'Distribution of Traits in Current Q Sort Methodology', *Journal of Abnormal and Social Psychology* 52: 90–5.

Jones, B. (1970) 'The Dynamics of Marriage and Motherhood', in *The Florida Papers of Women's Liberation*. Florida.

Jones, J.M. (1972) *Prejudice and Racism*. Reading, MA: Addison-Wesley.

Josephson, E. (1970) 'Resistance to Community Surveys', *Social Problems* 18: 117–29.

Jowell, R., S. Witherspoon and L. Brook (eds) (1986) *British Social Attitudes Interim Reports*. Aldershot, Hants: Gower Press.

Justice, J. (1977) 'Vision', *Sinister Wisdom* 4: 46–52.

Kameny, F.E. (1971a) 'Gay Liberation and Psychiatry', *Psychiatric Opinion* 8: 18–27.

Kameny, F.E. (1971b) 'Homosexuals as a Minority Group', in E. Sagarin (ed.) *The Other Minorities: Non Ethnic Collectivities Conceptualized as Minority Groups*. Waltham, MA: Ginn and Co.

Kanin, E.J., K.R. Davidson and S.R. Schneck (1972) 'A Research Note on Male-Female Differentials in the Experience of Heterosexual Love', in J.S. DeLora and J.R. DeLora (eds) *Intimate Lifestyles*. Pacific Palisades, CA: Goodyear.

Karlen, A. (1971) *Sexuality and Homosexuality: A New View*. New York: W.W. Norton.

Karlen, A. (1972) 'A Discussion of "Homosexuality as a Mental Illness"', *International Journal of Psychiatry* 10: 108–13.

Katz, J. (1976) *Gay American History: Lesbians and Gay Men in the USA*. New York: Thomas Crowell.

Kayal, P.M. (1978) 'Researching Behavior: Sociological Objectivity and Homosexual Analysis', *Corrective and Social Psychology and Journal of Behavioral Technology, Methods and Therapy* 22: 25–31.

Kaye, H.E. (1967) 'Homosexuality in Women', *Archives of General Psychiatry* 17: 626–32.

Kaye, L.W. (1947) 'Frames of Reference in "Pro" and "Anti" Evaluations of Test Items', *Journal of Social Psychology* 25: 63–8.

Kaye, M. (1982) 'Some Notes on Jewish Lesbian Identity', in E.T. Beck (ed.) *Nice Jewish Girls: A Lesbian Anthology*. Watertown, MA: Persephone Press.

Kelly, J. (1972) 'Sister Love: An Exploration of the Need for Homosexual Experience', *Family Coordinator* (October): 473–5.

Kelly, J. (1977) 'The Ageing Male Homosexual: Myth and Reality', *Gerontologist* 17(4): 328–32.

Kemeny, J.G. (1959) *A Philosopher Looks at Science*. Princeton, NJ: Van Nostrand Reinhold.

Kenyon, F.E. (1968) 'Studies in Female Homosexuality — Psychological Test Results', *Journal of Consulting and Clinical Psychology* 32: 510–13.

Kenyon, F.E. (1978) *Overcoming Common Problems: Sex*. London: Sheldon Press.

Kerlinger, F.N. (1958) *Q-Methodology and the Testing of Theory*. New York University Press.

Kerlinger, F.N. (1973) *Foundations of Behavioral Research*. 2nd edn. New York: Holt, Rinehart and Winston.

Kessler, D.R. (1981) 'Review of C.W. Socarides, *Homosexuality*', *Journal of Homosexuality* 6: 89–95.

Kessler, S. and W. McKenna (1978) *Gender: An Ethnomethodological Approach*. New York: Wiley.

Kinsey, A.C., W.B. Pomeroy and C.E. Martin (1948) *Sexual Behavior in the Human Male*. Philadelphia: W.B. Saunders Co.

Kinsey, A.C., W.B. Pomeroy, C.E. Martin and P.H. Gebhard (1953) *Sexual Behavior in the Human Female*. Philadelphia: W.B. Saunders Co.

Kirk, R. (1961) 'Is Social Science Scientific?' *New York Times Magazine* Section 6 (25 June): 15–16.

Kite, M.E. (1984) 'Sex Differences in Attitudes toward Homosexuals: A Meta-Analytic Review', *Journal of Homosexuality* 10: 69–81.

Kitzinger, C. (forthcoming) *Feminist Morality*. Milton Keynes: Open University Press.

Kitzinger, C. and R. Stainton Rogers (1985) 'A Q Methodological Study of Lesbian Identities', *European Journal of Social Psychology* 15: 167–87.

Klaich, D. (1974) *Woman + Woman: Attitudes toward Lesbianism*. New York: Morrow and Co.

Kleinberg, S. (1977) *The Other Persuasion*. London: Picador.

Klepfisz, I. (1982) 'Anti-Semitism in the Lesbian/Feminist Movement', in E.T. Beck (ed.) *Nice Jewish Girls: A Lesbian Anthology*. Watertown, MA: Persephone Press.

Knorr-Cetina, K. (1983) 'The Ethnographic Study of Scientific Work: Towards a Constructivist Interpretation of Science', in K. Knorr-Cetina and M. Mulkay (eds) *Science Observed*. London: Sage Publications.

Koerner, K.F. (1985) 'Introduction: Liberalism and the End of Ideology', in K.F. Koerner (ed.) *Liberalism and Its Critics*. London: Croom Helm.

Koertge, N. (1984) 'The Fallacy of Misplaced Precision', *Journal of Homosexuality* 10: 15–21.

Kohlberg, L. (1969) 'Stage and Sequence: The Cognitive-Developmental Approach to Socialization', in D.A. Goslin (ed.) *Handbook of Socialization Theory and Research*. Chicago: Rand-McNally.

Kohn, A. (1986) *False Prophets*. Oxford: Basil Blackwell.

Kolakowski, L. (1972) *Positivist Philosophy: From Hume to the Vienna Circle*. Trans. N. Guterman. Harmondsworth: Penguin.

Kozol, J. (1975) *The Night is Dark and I am Far from Home*. Boston: Houghton Mifflin.

Krafft-Ebing, R. (1882) *Psychopathia Sexualis*. Reprinted 1965. Trans. M.E. Wedneck. New York: Putnams.

Krausz, E. (1969) 'Psychology and Race', *Race* 10: 361–8.

Krema, M. and A. Rifkin (1969) 'The Early Development of Homosexuality: A Study of Adolescent Lesbians', *American Journal of Psychiatry* 126: 129–34.

Krieger, S. (1982) 'Lesbian Identity and Community: Recent Social Science Literature', *Signs* 8(1): 91–108.

Kriegman, G. (1969) 'Homosexuality and the Educator', *Journal of School Health* (May): 305–11.

Kronemeyer, R. (1980) *Overcoming Homosexuality*. New York: Macmillan.

Kuhn, T.S. (1962) *The Structure of Scientific Revolutions*. Chicago: University of Chicago Press.

Kupferberg, T. (1978) 'An Insulting Look at Lawyers through the Ages', *Juris Doctor* (October/November): 62.

Kurtz, R.A. and J.R. Maiolo (1968) 'Surgery for Sociology: The Need for Introductory Text Opening Chapterectomy', *American Sociologist* 3: 39–41.

Lakoff, R.T. (1980) 'When Talk Is Not Cheap: Psychotherapy as Conversation', in L. Michaels and C. Ricks (eds) *The State of the Language*. Berkeley: University of California Press.

Lamont, C. (1965) *The Philosophy of Humanism*, 5th edn. London: Barrie and Rockliff.

Laner, M.R. and R.H. Laner (1980) 'Sexual Preference or Personal Style? Why Lesbians Are Disliked', *Journal of Homosexuality* 5: 339–56.

LaPiere, R.T. (1934) 'Attitudes vs. Actions', *Social Forces* 13: 230–7.

Larsen, K., M. Reed and S. Hoffman (1980) 'Attitude of Heterosexuals toward Homosexuality: A Likert-type Scale and Construct Validity', *Journal of Sex Research* 16: 245–57.

Latour, B. (1980) 'The Three Little Dinosaurs: or a Sociologist's Nightmare', *Fundamenta Scientiae* 1: 79–85.

Laurie, A.J. (1978) 'Between the Ears: A Lesbian Play in One Act', *Sappho* 6(11): 14–20.

Lauritsen, J. and D. Thorstad (1974) *The Early Homosexual Rights Movement (1864–1935)*. New York: Times Change Press.

Law, J. and R.J. Williams (1982) 'Putting Facts Together: A Study of Scientific Persuasion', *Social Studies of Science* 12: 535–8.

Laws, S. (1981) Letter in Onlywomen Press (eds) *Love Your Enemy? The Debate between Heterosexual Feminism and Political Lesbianism*. London: Onlywomen Press.

Lee, J.A. (1977) 'Going Public: A Study in the Sociology of Homosexual

Liberation', *Journal of Homosexuality* 3: 49–78.

Leeds Revolutionary Feminists (1981) 'Political Lesbianism: The Case against Heterosexuality', in Onlywomen Press (eds) *Love Your Enemy? The Debate between Heterosexual Feminism and Political Lesbianism*. London: Onlywomen Press.

Lepine, L.T. and B. Chodorkoff (1955) 'A Q Sort Study', *Journal of Clinical Psychology* 11: 395–7.

Lessard, S. (1972) 'Gay Is Good for Us All', in J.A. McCaffrey (ed.) *The Homosexual Dialectic*. Englewood Cliffs, NJ: Prentice-Hall.

Levine, M. (1974) 'Scientific Method and the Adversary Model', *American Psychologist* 29: 661–77.

Levine, M. (1980) 'The Sociology of Male Homosexuality and Lesbianism: An Introductory Bibliography', *Journal of Homosexuality* 5: 249–75.

Levitin, T. (1975) 'Deviants as Active Participants in the Labeling Process: The Visibly Handicapped', *Social Problems* 22: 548–57.

Levitt, E.E. and A.D. Klassen (1974) 'Public Attitudes toward Homosexuality', *Journal of Homosexuality* 1: 29–43.

Lewin, K. (1948) *Resolving Social Conflicts*. New York: Harper.

Lewis, L.S. (1975) *Scaling the Ivory Tower: Merit and Its Limits in Academic Careers*. Baltimore and London: Johns Hopkins University Press.

Lewis, S.G. (1979) *Sunday's Women: A Report on Lesbian Life Today*. Boston: Beacon Press.

Leznoff, M. (1956) 'Interviewing Homosexuals', *American Journal of Sociology* 62: 202–4.

Linn, L.S. (1965) 'Verbal Attitudes and Overt Behavior: A Study of Racial Discrimination', *Social Forces* 44: 353–64.

Littlewood, R. and M. Lipsedge (1982) *Aliens and Alienists: Ethnic Minorities and Psychiatry*. Harmondsworth: Penguin.

Loewen, J.W. (1970) 'Action and Sociology', *Sociological Inquiry* 40: 105–9.

London Lesbian Offensive Group (1983) 'By "Parties Not Connected with the Case": A Commentary by LLOG on the Sackings of Two Lesbian Childcare Workers by Anti-Sexist Heterosexuals'. Unpublished paper.

Lumby, M.E. (1976) 'Homophobia: The Quest for a Valid Scale', *Journal of Homosexuality* 2: 39–47.

Lyon, P. and D. Martin (1972) *Lesbian/Woman*. New York: Bantam.

Lyons, J.O. (1978) *The Invention of the Self: The Hinge of Consciousness in the Eighteenth Century*. Carbondale and Edwardsville, IL: Southern Illinois University Press.

MacCulloch, M.J., J.L. Waddington and J.E. Sambrooks (1978) 'Avoidance Latencies Reliably Reflect Sexual Attitude Change during Aversion Therapy for Homosexuality', *Behavior Therapy* 9: 562–77.

MacDonald, A.P. (1976) 'Homophobia: Its Roots and Meanings', *Homosexual Counseling Journal* 3: 23–33.

MacDonald, A.P. and R.G. Games (1974) 'Some Characteristics of Those Who Hold Positive and Negative Attitudes toward Homosexuals', *Journal of Homosexuality* 1: 9–27.

MacDonald, A.P., J. Huggins, S. Young and R.A. Swanson (1972) 'Attitudes toward Homosexuality: Preservation of Sex Morality or the Double Standard?' *Journal of Consulting and Clinical Psychology* 40: 61–8.

MacDonald, B. and C. Rich (1983) *Look Me in the Eye: Old Women, Aging and Ageism*. San Francisco: Spinsters Ink.

MacDonald, G. (1981) 'Misrepresentation, Liberalism and Heterosexual Bias in Introductory Psychology Textbooks', *Journal of Homosexuality* 6: 45–60.

MacDonald, G. and R.J. Moore (1978) 'Sex-Role Self-Concept of Homosexual Men and Their Attitudes toward Both Women and Male Homosexuality', *Journal of Homosexuality* 4: 3–14.

Mainardi, P. (1975) 'The Marriage Question', in Redstockings (ed.) *Feminist Revolution*. New York: Random House.

Manicas, P.T. and P.F. Secord (1983) 'Implications for Psychology of the New Philosophy of Science', *American Psychologist,* 38: 399–413.

Manning, P.K. (1967) 'Problems in Interpreting Interview Data', *Sociology and Social Research* 51: 302–16.

Marano, H. (1979) 'New Light on Homosexuality', *Medical World News* 20: 8–19.

Marcuse, H. (1955) *Eros and Civilization*. Boston: Beacon Press.

Marmor, J. (ed.) (1965) *Sexual Inversion: The Multiple Roots of Homosexuality*. New York: Basic Books.

Marmor, J. (1972) 'Homosexuality — Mental Illness or Moral Dilemma?' *International Journal of Psychiatry* 10: 114–17.

Marmor, J. (1980) *Homosexual Behavior*. New York: Basic Books.

Marshall, J. (1981) 'Pansies, Perverts and Macho Men: Changing Conceptions of Male Homosexuality' in K. Plummer (ed.) *The Making of the Modern Homosexual*. London: Hutchinson.

Marson, S.M. (1982) 'Review of *Gay is Not Good* by Frank M. du Mas, Nashville Thomas Nelson, 1979', *Journal of Homosexuality* 8: 79–80.

Martin, D. and P. Lyon (1976) 'The Realities of Lesbianism', in G. Johnson and C. Gordon (eds) *Readings in Human Sexuality: Contemporary Perspectives*. New York: Harper & Row.

Martin, D. and P. Mariah (1972) 'Homosexual Love — Woman to Woman, Man to Man', in H.A. Otto (ed.) *Love Today: A New Exploration*. New York: Delta.

Mary (1970) *A Letter from Mary*. (Pamphlet) Somerville, MA: New England Free Press. Reprinted in K. Jay and A. Young (eds) *Out of the Closets: Voices of Gay Liberation*. New York: Harcourt Brace Jovanovich.

Maslow, A. (1962) *Toward a Psychology of Being*. Princeton, NJ: Van Nostrand.

Masters, W.H. and V.E. Johnson (1974) 'Counseling with Sexually Incompatible Partners', in R.S. Rogers (ed.) *Sex Education: Rationale and Reaction*. Cambridge University Press.

Masters, W.H. and V.E. Johnson (1979) *Homosexuality in Perspective*. Boston: Little, Brown and Co.

Masterton, J. (1983) 'Lesbian Consciousness-Raising Discussion Groups', *Journal for Specialists in Group Work* 8: 24–30.

May, E. P. (1974) 'Counselors', Psychologists' and Homosexuals' Philosophies of Human Nature and Attitudes toward Homosexual Behavior', *Homosexual Counseling* 1: 3–25.

McCaffrey, J.A. (1972a) 'Introduction' in J.A. McCaffrey (ed.) *The Homosexual Dialectic*. Englewood Cliffs, NJ: Prentice-Hall.

McCaffrey, J.A. (1972b) 'Homosexuality: The Stereotype and the Real', in J.A. McCaffrey (ed.) *The Homosexual Dialectic*. Englewood Cliffs, NJ: Prentice-Hall.

McCaghy, C.H. (1968) 'Drinking and Deviance Disavowal: The Case of Child Molesters', *Social Problems* 16: 43–9.

McCandlish, B.M. (1982) 'Therapeutic Issues with Lesbian Couples', *Journal of Homosexuality* 7: 71–8.

McCormack, T.H. (1950) 'The Motivation of Radicals', *American Journal of Sociology* 56: 17–24.

McCrea, F.B. (1983) 'The Politics of Menopause: The Discovery of a Deficiency Disease', *Social Problems* 31: 111–23.

McDaniel, J. (1982) 'We Were Fired: Lesbian Experiences in Academe', *Sinister Wisdom* 20: 30–43.

McKee, J.B. (1970) 'Some Observations on the Self-Consciousness of Sociologists', in J.E. Curtis and J.W. Petras (eds) *The Sociology of Knowledge: A Reader*. London: Duckworth.

McKenna, W. and S. Kessler (1985) 'Asking Taboo Questions and Doing Taboo Deeds', in K.J. Gergen and K.E. Davis (eds) *The Social Construction of the Person*. New York: Springer-Verlag.

Medawar, P.B. (1963) 'Is the Scientific Paper a Fraud?' *The Listener* 70 (12 September): 377–8.

Meerloo, J.A.M. (1967) 'Contributions of Psychiatry to the Study of Human Communication', in F.X. Dance (ed.) *Human Communication Theory*. New York: Holt, Rinehart and Winston.

Mendola, M. (1980) *The Mendola Report: A New Look at Gay Couples*. New York: Crown Publishers Inc.

Menneer, P. (1979) 'Retrospective Data in Survey Research Problems', in L. Moss and H. Goldstein (eds) *The Recall Method in Social Surveys*. University of London Institute of Education.

Mercer, K. (1986) 'Racism and Transcultural Psychiatry', in P. Miller and N. Rose (eds) *The Power of Psychiatry*. Cambridge: Polity Press.

Meredith, R.L. and R.W. Riester (1980) 'Psychotherapy, Responsibility and Homosexuality', *Professional Psychology* 11: 174–93.

Merton, R.K. (1957) *Social Theory and Social Structure*. Glencoe, IL: Free Press.

Merton, R.K. (1971) 'The Precarious Foundations of Detachment in Sociology', in E.A. Tiryakian (ed.) *The Phenomenon of Sociology*. New York: Appleton-Century-Crofts.

Meyer, R.G. and W.M. Freeman (1977) 'A Social Episode Model of Human Sexual Behavior', *Journal of Homosexuality* 2: 123–31.

Millham, J., C.L.S. Miguel and R. Kellogg (1976) 'A Factor Analytic Conceptualization of Attitudes toward Male and Female Homosexuals', *Journal of Homosexuality* 2: 3–10.

Mills, C.W. (1940) 'Situated Actions and Vocabularies of Motive', *American Sociological Review* 5: 904–13.

Mills, C.W. (1943) 'The Professional Ideology of the Social Pathologists', *American Journal of Sociology* 49: 165–80.

Mills, C.W. (1952) 'Liberal Values in the Modern World'. Reprinted in I.L. Horowitz (ed.) (1963) *Power, Politics and People*. Oxford: Oxford University Press.

Minnigerode, F.A. (1976) 'Attitudes toward Homosexuality: Feminist Attitudes and Sexual Conservatism', *Sex Roles* 2: 347–52.

Minogue, K. (1963) *The Liberal Mind*. London: Methuen.

Minton, H.L. and G.J. McDonald (1984) 'Homosexual Identity Formation as a Developmental Process', *Journal of Homosexuality* 9: 91–104.

Mitroff, I.I. (1974) *The Subjective Side of Science*. Amsterdam: Elsevier.

Moberly, E.R. (1983) *Psychogenesis: The Early Development of Gender Identity*. London: Routledge & Kegan Paul.

Money, J. (1979) Interview with John Money in Marano, H. 'New Light on Homosexuality', *Medical World News* 20: 8–19.

Monique (1980) 'Against Heteroppression' Leaflet reprinted in *Trouble and Strife* 2 (Spring, 1984): 27–8.

Moraga, C. and B. Smith (1982) 'Lesbian Literature: A Third World Perspective', in M. Cruickshank (ed.) *Lesbian Studies: Present and Future*. New York: Feminist Press.

Morgan, R. (1978) *Going Too Far: The Personal Chronicle of a Feminist*. New York: Random House.

Morin, S.F. (1974) 'Educational Programs as a Means of Changing Attitudes toward Gay People', *Homosexual Counseling Journal* 1: 160–5.

Morin, S.F. (1977) 'Heterosexual Bias in Psychological Research on Lesbianism and Male Homosexuality', *American Psychologist* 19: 629–37.

Morin, S.F. and E.M. Garfinkel (1981) 'Male Homophobia', in J.W. Chesebro (ed.) *GaySpeak*. New York: Pilgrim Press.

Morris, D. (1967) *The Naked Ape*. London: Corgi.

Morris, V. (1982) 'Helping Lesbian Couples Cope with Jealousy', *Women and Therapy* 1: 27–34.

Moses, A.E. (1978) *Identity Management in Lesbian Women*. New York: Praeger.

Mosher, D.L. and K.E. O'Grady (1979) 'Homosexual Threat, Negative Attitudes towards Masturbation, Sex Guilt and Males' Sexual and Affective Reactions to Explicit Sex Films', *Journal of Consulting and Clinical Psychology* 47: 860–73.

Mukerji, C. (1977) 'Bullshitting: Road Lore among Hitchhikers', *Social Problems* 24: 241–52.

Mulkay, M. (1984) 'The Scientist Talks Back: A One-Act Play, with a Moral, about Replication in Science and Reflexivity in Sociology', *Social Studies of Science* 14: 265–82.

Mulkay, M. and G.N. Gilbert (1982) 'Accounting for Error: How Scientists Construct Their Social Worlds when They Account for Correct and Incorrect Belief', *Sociology* 16: 165–83.

Mulkay, M., J. Potter and S. Yearley (1983) 'Why an Analysis of Scientific Discourse Is Needed', in K.D. Knorr-Cetina and M. Mulkay (eds) *Science Observed*. London: Sage Publications.

Nahinsky, E.D. (1958) 'The Relationship between Self-Concept and the Ideal-Self Concept as a Measure of Adjustment', *Journal of Clinical Psychology* 14: 360–4.

Nestle, J. (1981) 'A Place for All of Us', *Sinister Wisdom* 18: 97–107.

Nobles, W.W. (1973) 'Psychological Research and the Black Self-Concept: A Critical Review', *Journal of Social Issues* 29: 11–31.

Nuehring, E.M., S.B. Fein and M. Tyler (1975) 'The Gay College Student: Perspectives for Mental Health Professionals', *Counseling Psychologist* 4: 64–72.

Oakley, A. (1981) 'Interviewing Women: A Contradiction in Terms', in H. Roberts (ed.) *Doing Feminist Research*. London: Routledge & Kegan Paul.

O'Brien, C.C. (1965) *Writers and Politics*. London: Chatto & Windus.

Onlywomen Press (1981) *Love Your Enemy? The Debate between Heterosexual Feminism and Political Lesbianism*. London: Onlywomen Press.

Overington, M.A. (1977) 'The Scientific Community as Audience: Toward a Rhetorical Analysis of Science', *Philosophy and Rhetoric* 10: 143–64.

Pagelow, M.D. (1980) 'Heterosexual and Lesbian Single Mothers: A Comparison of Problems, Coping and Solutions', *Journal of Homosexuality* 5: 189–204.

Park, P. (1967) 'The Cretan Dictum', *American Sociologist* 2: 155–7.

Partnow, E. (1978) *The Quotable Woman*. New York: Anchor Press/Doubleday.

Pattison, E.M. (1974) 'Confusing Concepts about the Concept of Homosexuality', *Psychiatry* 37: 340–9.

Pearson, G. (1975) *The Deviant Imagination: Psychiatry, Social Work and Social Change.* London: Macmillan.

Penelope, J. (1986) 'The Mystery of Lesbians', *Gossip: A Journal of Lesbian Feminist Ethics* 2: 16–68.

Pepitone, A. (1981) 'Lessons from the History of Social Psychology', *American Psychologist* 36: 972–85.

Peplau, L.A. (1983) 'Research on Homosexual Couples: An Overview', *Journal of Homosexuality* 8: 3–8.

Peplau, L.A., S. Cochran, K. Rook and C. Padesky (1978) 'Loving Women: Attachment and Autonomy in Lesbian Relationships', *Journal of Social Issues* 34: 7–27.

Peplau, L.A. and S.L. Gordon (1983) 'The Intimate Relationships of Lesbians and Gay Men', in E.R. Allgeier and N.B. McCormick (eds) *Changing Boundaries: Gender Roles and Sexual Behavior.* Palo Alto, CA: Mayfield Publications.

Perrin, E. (1980) *So Long as There Are Women.* (Trans. H.J. Salemson) New York: Morrow and Co.

Peterson, N. (1980) 'Is Lesbianism Feminism?' *bitches, witches and dykes* (August): 6.

Pettitt, A. (1981) Letter in Onlywomen Press (eds) *Love Your Enemy? The Debate between Heterosexual Feminism and Political Lesbianism.* London: Onlywomen Press.

Phillips, D., S.C. Fisher, G.A. Groves and R. Singh (1976) 'Alternative Behavioral Approaches to the Treatment of Homosexuality', *Archives of Sexual Behavior* 5: 223–8.

Pickvance, S. (1976) '"Life" in a Biology Lab', *Radical Science Journal*, 4: 11–28.

Pillard, R.C. (1982) 'Psychotherapeutic Treatment for the Invisible Minority', *American Behavioral Scientist* 25: 407–22.

Plasek, J.W. and J. Allard (1985) 'Misconceptions of Homophobia', in J.P. De Cecco (ed.) *Bashers, Baiters and Bigots: Homophobia in American Society.* New York: Harrington Park Press.

Plummer, D. (1963) *Queer People: The Truth about Homosexuals.* London: W.H. Allen.

Plummer, K. (1981) 'Homosexual Categories: Some Research Problems in the Labelling Perspective of Homosexuality', in K. Plummer (ed.) *The Making of the Modern Homosexual.* London: Hutchinson.

Pollner, M. (1975) '"The Very Coinage of Your Brain": The Anatomy of Reality Disjunctures', *Philosophy of the Social Sciences* 5: 411–30.

Ponse, B. (1978) *Identities in the Lesbian World: The Social Construction of Self.* Contributions in Sociology No. 28. Westport, CT: Greenwood Press.

Poole, K. (1972) 'The Etiology of Gender Identity and the Lesbian', *Journal of Social Psychology* 87: 51–7.

Poor, M. (1982) 'Older Lesbians', in M. Cruikshank (ed.) *Lesbian Studies: Present and Future.* New York: Feminist Press.

Porter, D. (1984) 'Gays and the Script Vacuum', *Self and Society* 12: 80–5.

Potter, J. (1983) 'A Stiff Approach to Soft Data: or What Should Be Done with Participants' Accounts?' Unpublished paper presented at the British Psychological Society, Social Psychology Division, Annual Conference, September 1983, University of Sheffield.

Potter, J. and M. Mulkay (1982) 'Making Theory Useful: Utility Accounting in Social Psychologists' Discourse', *Fundamenta Scientiae* 3: 259–78.

Potter, S. and T. Darty (1981) 'Social Work and the Invisible Minority', *Social Work* 26: 187–92.

Poussaint, A.F. (1973) 'Black Alienation and Black Consciousness', in F. Johnson (ed.) *Alienation: Concept, Term and Meanings*. New York: Seminar Press.

Price, J.H. (1972) *Psychiatric Investigations*. London: Butterworth.

Price, J.H. (1982) 'High School Students' Attitudes toward Homosexuality', *Journal of School Health* 52: 469–74.

Radicalesbians (1969) *Woman-Identified Woman*. Somerville, MA: New England Free Press.

Rand, C., D.L.R. Graham and E.I. Rawlings (1982) 'Psychological Health and Factors the Court Seeks To Control in Lesbian Mother Custody Trials', *Journal of Homosexuality* 8: 27–39.

Raphael, S. and M. Robinson (1984) 'The Older Lesbian: Love, Relationships and Friendship Patterns' in T. Darty and S. Potter (eds) *Women-Identified Women*. Palo Alto, CA: Mayfield Publications.

Rathje, N. and T. Hughes (1975) 'A Garbage Project as a Non-Reactive Approach: Garbage In . . . Garbage Out?' in H.W. Sinaiko and L.A. Broedling (eds) *Perspectives on Attitude Assessment: Surveys and Their Alternatives*. Manpower and Advisory Services, Technical Report No. 2. Washington, DC: Smithsonian Institution.

Ravetz, J.R. (1973) 'Tragedy in the History of Science', in M. Teich and R. Young (eds) *Changing Perspectives in the History of Science*. Dordrech: Reidel.

Reinharz, S. (1979) *On Becoming a Social Scientist*. San Francisco: Jossey-Bass.

Rich, A. (1978) 'Disloyal to Civilization: Feminism, Racism and Gynephobia', *Chrysalis: A Magazine of Women's Culture* 7: 29–38. Reprinted in A. Rich (1980) *On Lies, Secrets and Silence*. London: Virago.

Rich, A. (1980) 'Compulsory Heterosexuality and Lesbian Existence', *Signs: A Journal of Women in Culture and Society* (Summer): 631–57.

Rich, A. (1983) 'North American Time', reprinted in A. Rich (1984) *The Fact of a Doorframe: Poems Selected and New: 1950–1984*. New York and London: W.W. Norton.

Richardson, D. (1978) 'Do Lesbians Make Good Parents?' *Community Care* 224: 16–17.

Richardson, D. and J. Hart (1980) 'Gays in Therapy: Getting It Right', *New Forum: The Journal of the Psychology and Psychotherapy Association* 6: 58–60.

Richter, M.N. (1972) *Science as a Cultural Process*. Cambridge, MA: Schenkman.

Rickford, F. (1981) Letter in Onlywomen Press (eds) *Love Your Enemy? The Debate between Heterosexual Feminism and Political Lesbianism*. London: Onlywomen Press.

Riebel, L. (1982) 'Theory as Self-Portrait and the Ideal of Objectivity', *Journal of Humanistic Psychology* 22: 91–110.

Riess, B.F. and J. Safer (1979) 'Homosexuality in Females and Males', in E.S. Gomberg (ed.) *Gender and Disordered Behavior: Sex Differences in Psychopathology*. New York: Brunner/Mazel.

Robb, J. (1954) *Working Class Anti-Semite: A Psychological Study*. London: Tavistock.

Robinson, J.A. (1963) *Honest to God*. Philadelphia: Westminster Press.

Rochlin, M. (1979) 'Becoming a Gay Professional', in B. Berzon and R. Leighton (eds) *Positively Gay*. Millbrae, CA: Celestial Arts.

Roden, R.G. (1983) 'Threatening Homosexuality: A Case Treated by Hypnosis', *Medical Hypnoanalysis* 4: 166–9.

Rogers, C.R. (1959) 'A Theory of Therapy, Personality and Interpersonal Relationships, as Developed in the Client-Context Framework', in S. Koch (ed.)

Psychology: A Study of a Science: Vol. 3. New York: McGraw-Hill.

Rogers, J.W. and M.P. Buffalo (1974) 'Fighting Back: Nine Modes of Adaptation to a Deviant Label', *Social Problems* 22: 101–18.

Roiser, M. (1974) 'Asking Silly Questions', in N. Armistead (ed.) *Reconstructing Social Psychology.* Harmondsworth: Penguin.

Rokeach, M. (1960) *The Open and Closed Mind: Investigations into the Nature of Belief Systems and Personality Systems.* New York: Basic Books.

Romanowski, S. (1973) 'Descartes: From Science to Discourse', *Yale French Studies* 49: 96–109.

Romm, M.E. (1965) 'Sexuality and Homosexuality in Women', in J. Marmor (ed.) *Sexual Inversion: The Multiple Roots of Homosexuality.* New York: Basic Books.

Rorhbaugh, J.B. (1981) *Women: Psychology's Puzzle.* London: Abacus.

Rorty, R. (1980) *Philosophy and the Mirror of Nature.* Oxford: Basil Blackwell.

Rose, N. (1986) 'Psychiatry: The Discipline of Mental Health', in P. Miller and N. Rose (eds) *The Power of Psychiatry.* Cambridge: Polity Press.

Rosenfels, P. (1971) *Homosexuality: The Psychology of the Creative Process.* New York: Libra Publishers Inc.

Ross, E. and R. Rapp (1983) 'Sex and Society: A Research Note from Social History and Anthropology' in A. Snitow, C. Stansell and S. Thompson (eds) *The Politics of Sexuality.* London: Virago.

Rossides, D.W. (1978) *The History and Nature of Sociological Theory.* Boston: Houghton Mifflin.

Routsong, A. (1978) 'Love and Courtship', in G. Vida (ed.) *Our Right To Love: A Lesbian Resource Book.* Englewood Cliffs, NJ: Prentice-Hall.

Rudin, J. (1969) *Fanaticism: A Psychological Analysis.* Notre Dame, IN: University of Notre Dame Press.

Ruitenbeck, H.M. (ed.) (1973) *Homosexuality: A Changing Picture.* London: Souvenir Press.

Rule, J. (1975) *Lesbian Images.* London: Peter Davis.

Ruse, M. (1981) 'Are Homosexuals Sick?', in A. Caplan and H.T. Engelhardt (eds) *Current Concepts of Health and Disease.* Boston: Addison-Wesley.

Ruse, M. (1984) 'Nature/Nurture: Reflections on Approaches to the Study of Homosexuality', *Journal of Homosexuality* 10: 141–51.

Saghir, M.T. (1979) Interview with Marcel Saghir in Marano, H. 'New Light on Homosexuality', *Medical World News* 20: 8–19.

Saghir, M.T. and E. Robins (1969) 'Female Homosexuality', *Archives of General Psychiatry* 20: 192–9.

Saghir, M.T., E. Robins, B. Warran and K.A. Gentry (1970) 'Homosexuality IV: Psychiatric Disorders and Disability in the Female Homosexual', *American Journal of Psychiatry* 127: 147–54.

Samelson, F. (1978) 'From "Race Psychology" to "Studies in Prejudice": Some Observations of the Thematic Reversals in Social Psychology', *Journal of the History of the Behavioral Sciences* 14: 265–78.

Sampson, E.E. (1978) 'Scientific Paradigms and Social Values: Wanted — A Scientific Revolution', *Journal of Personality and Social Psychology* 36: 1332–43.

Sampson, E.E. (1981) 'Cognitive Psychology as Ideology', *American Psychologist* 36: 730–43.

Sampson, E.E. (1983) 'Deconstructing Psychology's Subject', *Journal of Mind and Behavior* 4: 135–64.

Sand, C.T. (1982) 'Lesbian Writing: Adventure into Autonomy', *Fireweed: A Feminist Quarterly* 13: 24–38.

Sanford, N. (1973) 'The Roots of Prejudice: Emotional Dynamics', in P. Watson (ed.) *Psychology and Race*. Harmondsworth: Penguin.

Sang, B. (1977) 'Psychotherapy with Lesbians: Some Observations and Tentative Generalizations', in E.I. Rawlings and D.K. Carter (eds) *Psychotherapy for Women*. Springfield, IL: Charles C. Thomas.

Sang, B. (1978) 'Lesbian Research: A Critical Evaluation', in G. Vida (ed.) *Our Right to Love: A Lesbian Resource Book*. Englewood Cliffs, NJ: Prentice-Hall.

Sappenfield, B. (1965) 'Stereotypical Perception of Masculinity-Femininity', *Journal of Psychology* 61: 177–82.

Sarachild, K. (1975) 'Psychological Terrorism', in Redstockings (ed.) *Feminist Revolution*. New York: Random House.

Sarnoff, I. (1951) 'Identification with the Aggressor', *Journal of Personality* 20: 199–218.

Sartre, J.P. (1948) 'The Situation of the Jew', *Commentary* 5: 306–16.

Scharfetter, C. (1980) (trans. H. Marshall) *General Psychopathology: An Introduction*. Cambridge University Press.

Schmidt, G. and E. Schorsch (1981) 'Psychosurgery of Sexually Deviant Patients', *Archives of Sexual Behavior* 10: 301–21.

Schultz, H.J. (ed.) (1972) *English Liberalism and the State*. London: D.C. Heath and Co.

Schuman, H. and J. Harding (1964) 'Prejudice and the Norm of Rationality', *Sociometry* 27: 353–71.

Schur, E. (1976) *The Awareness Trap: Self-Absorption instead of Social Change*. New York: Quadrangle.

Schwartz, J. (1978) Untitled short story, *Sinister Wisdom* 7: 15–17.

Scott, M.B. and S.M. Lyman (1968) 'Accounts', *American Sociological Review* 33: 46–62.

Scott, R. (1969) *The Making of Blind Men: A Study of Adult Socialization*. New York: Russell Sage Foundation.

Scully, D. and J. Marolla (1984) 'Convicted Rapists' Vocabulary of Motive', *Social Problems* 31: 530–44.

Seeman, M. (1958) 'The Intellectual and the Language of Minorities', *American Journal of Sociology* 64: 25–35.

Seidenberg, R. (1973) 'The Accursed Race', in H.M. Ruitenbeck (ed.) *Homosexuality: A Changing Picture*. London: Souvenir Press.

Semin, G.R. (1986) 'Book Review of K.J. Gergen and K.E. Davis (eds) *The Social Construction of the Person*', *British Journal of Social Psychology* 25: 354–5.

Serdahely, W.J. and G.J. Ziemba (1985) 'Changing Homophobic Attitudes through College Sexuality Education', in J.P. De Cecco (ed.) *Bashers, Baiters and Bigots: Homophobia in American Society*. New York: Harrington Park Press.

Shavelson, E., M.K. Biaggio, H.H. Cross and R.E. Lehman (1980) 'Lesbian Women's Perceptions of the Parent-Child Relationship', *Journal of Homosexuality* 5: 205–15.

Shea, P. (1979) 'Bloodroot: Four Views of One Woman's Business', *Heresies* 7(2): 23–5.

Shelley, M. (1972) 'I Am a Lesbian — I Am Beautiful', in J.S. DeLora and J.R. DeLora (eds) *Intimate Lifestyles: Marriage and Its Alternatives*. California: Goodyear.

Shepherd, E. (1984) 'Blinding Illusions: Reflections upon Fundamental Assumptions in Scientific Psychology'. Unpublished paper presented at the Annual London Conference of the British Psychological Society, December.

Shively, M.G., C. Jones and J.P. De Cecco (1984) 'Research on Sexual Orientations: Definitions and Methods', *Journal of Homosexuality* 9: 127–36.

Shoham, S. (1966) *Crime and Social Deviance*. Chicago: Henry Regner.

Shotter, J. (1984) 'The Social Construction of "You" '. Unpublished paper presented at the International Conference on Self and Identity, British Psychological Society (Welsh Branch), 9–13 July, University College, Cardiff.

Schweder, R.A. and J. Miller (1985) 'The Social Construction of the Person: How Is It Possible?' in K.J. Gergen and K.E. Davis (eds) *The Social Construction of the Person*. New York: Springer-Verlag.

Siegelman, M. (1972) 'Adjustment of Homosexual and Heterosexual Women', *British Journal of Psychiatry* 120: 477–81.

Silverstein, C. (1984) 'The Ethical and Moral Implications of Sexual Classification: A Commentary', *Journal of Homosexuality* 9: 29–38.

Simon, W. (1973) 'The Social, the Erotic and the Sensual: The Complexities of Sexual Scripts', in J.K. Cole and R. Dienstier (eds) *Nebraska Symposium on Motivation*. Lincoln: University of Nebraska Press.

Simon, W. and J.H. Gagnon (1967) 'Femininity in the Lesbian Community', *Social Problems* 15: 212–21.

Simon, W. and Gagnon, J.H. (1969) 'On Psychosexual Development', in D.A. Goslin (ed.) *Handbook of Socialization: Theory and Research*. Chicago: Rand-McNally.

Simons, H.W. (1980) 'Are Scientists Rhetors in Disguise? An Analysis of Discursive Processes within Scientific Communities', in E.E. White (ed.) *Rhetoric in Transition: Studies in the Nature and Uses of Rhetoric*. University Park, PA: Pennsylvania State University Press.

Simpson, K. (1979) *Forensic Medicine*. London: Edward Arnold.

Sindermann, C.J. (1982) *Winning the Games Scientists Play*. New York: Plenum Press.

Smith, D. (1974) 'Women's Perspective as a Radical Critique of Sociology', *Sociological Inquiry* 44: 7–13.

Smith, J.L. (1984) 'Accounting for Taste in Music and Song: A Case Study of Sunderland Glebe Folk and Blues Club'. Unpublished paper presented at the Annual London Conference of the British Psychological Society, December.

Smith, K.T. (1971) 'Homophobia: A Tentative Personality Profile', *Psychological Reports* 29: 1091–4.

Smith, M.B. (1978) 'Psychology and Values', *Journal of Social Issues* 34: 181–99.

Smithers, A.G. and D.M. Lobley (1978) 'The Relationship between Dogmatism and Radicalism/Conservatism', in H.J. Eysenck and G.D. Wilson (eds) *The Psychological Basis of Ideology*. Lancaster, Lancs: MTP Press.

Snyder, M. and S.W. Uranowitz (1978) 'Reconstructing the Past: Some Cognitive Consequences of Person Perception', *Journal of Personality and Social Psychology* 36: 941–50.

Sobel, H.J. (1976) 'Adolescent Attitudes toward Homosexuality in Relation to Self Concept and Body Satisfaction', *Adolescence* 11: 443–53.

Socarides, C.W. (1965) 'Female Homosexuality', in R. Slovenko (ed.) *Sexual Behavior and the Law*. Springfield, IL: Charles C. Thomas.

Socarides, C.W. (1972) 'Homosexuality — Basic Concepts and Psychodynamics', *International Journal of Psychiatry* 10: 118–25.

Solomon, R.C. (1981) *Love: Emotion, Myth and Metaphor*. New York: Anchor Press/Doubleday.

Sorenson, R.C. (1973) *Adolescent Sexuality in Contemporary America*. New York: World Publications.

SPSS Inc. (1986) *SPSS Users Guide*. 3rd edn. New York: McGraw-Hill.

Spanier, G.B. (1976) 'Use of Recall Data in Survey Research on Human Sexual Behavior', *Social Biology* 23: 244–53.

Spearman, C. (1927) *The Abilities of Man*. New York: Macmillan.

Sprey, J. (1972) 'On the Institutionalization of Sexuality', in J.S. DeLora and J.R. DeLora (eds) *Intimate Lifestyles: Marriage and Its Alternatives*. Pacific Palisades, CA: Goodyear.

Stainton Rogers, R. and C. Kitzinger (1985) *Understandings of Human Rights*. Report to the Council of Europe. Summary published in *Operant Subjectivity* 9(4): 123–30.

Stanley, E. (1982) '"Male Needs": The Problems and Problems of Working with Gay Men', in S. Friedman and E. Sarah (eds) *On the Problem of Men*. London: Women's Press.

Stanley, J.P. and S.J. Wolfe (1980) *The Coming Out Stories*. Watertown, MA: Persephone Press.

Star, S.L. (1978) 'Lesbian Feminism as an Altered State of Consciousness', *Sinister Wisdom* 5: 83–102.

Steinhorn, A. (1982) 'Lesbian Mothers — The Invisible Minority: Role of the Mental Health Worker', *Women and Therapy* 1: 35–42.

Stephenson, W. (1935) 'Techniques of Factor Analysis', *Nature*, 136: 297.

Stephenson, W. (1936a) 'A New Application of Correlations to Averages', *British Journal of Educational Psychology* 6: 43–57.

Stephenson, W. (1936b) 'The Inverted Factor Technique', *British Journal of Psychology* 22: 344–61.

Stephenson, W. (1939) 'Two Contributions to the Theory of Mental Testing: I. A New Performance Test for Measuring Abilities as Correlation Coefficients', *British Journal of Psychology* 30: 19–35.

Stephenson, W. (1961) 'Scientific Creed — 1961: Abductory Principles', *Psychological Record* 11: 9–17.

Stephenson, W. (1964) 'Operational Study of an Occasional Paper on the Kennedy-Nixon Television Debates', *Psychological Record* 14: 475–88.

Stephenson, W. (1983) 'Against Interpretation', *Operant Subjectivity* 6: 73–103.

Stone, G.P. and H.A. Faberman (1981) *Social Psychology through Symbolic Interaction*, 2nd edn. Chichester, Sussex: Wiley.

Strega, L. (1985) 'The Big Sell-Out: Lesbian Femininity', *Lesbian Ethics* 1(3): 73–84.

Stricker, G. and M. Merbaum (1973) *Growth of Personal Awareness: A Reader in Psychology*. New York: Holt Rinehart and Winston.

Suppe, F. (1981) 'The Bell and Weinberg Study: Future Priorities for Research on Homosexuality', *Journal of Homosexuality* 6: 69–97.

Suppe, F. (1984a) 'In Defense of a Multidimensional Approach to Sexual Identity', *Journal of Homosexuality* 10: 7–14.

Suppe, F. (1984b) 'Classifying Sexual Disorders: The Diagnostic and Statistical Manual of the American Psychiatric Association', *Journal of Homosexuality* 9: 9–28.

Svartvik, J. (1966) *On Voice in the English Verb*. The Hague: Mouton & Co.

Szasz, T. (1962) 'Bootlegging Humanistic Values through Psychiatry', *Antioch Review* 22: 341–9.

Szasz, T. (1966) 'The Mental Health Ethic', in R.T. De George (ed.) *Ethics and*

Society: Original Essays on Contemporary Moral Problems. New York: Doubleday & Co.

Szasz, T. (1971) *The Manufacture of Madness*. London: Routledge & Kegan Paul.

Szasz, T. (1980) *Sex: Facts, Frauds and Follies*. Oxford: Basil Blackwell.

Tannenbaum, P.H. (1953) 'The Effect of Headlines on the Interpretation of News Stories', *Journalism Quarterly* 30: 189–97.

Taylor, L. (1972) 'The Significance and Interpretation of Replies to Motivational Questions: The Case of Sex Offenders', *Sociology* 6: 23–39.

Tedeschi, J.T. and M. Reiss (1981) 'Verbal Strategies in Impression Management', in C. Antaki (ed.) *The Psychology of Ordinary Explanations of Social Behaviour*. London: Academic Press.

Thomas, C.W. (1971) *Boys No More*. Beverly Hills, CA: Glencoe Press.

Thomas, C.W. (1973) 'The Systems-Maintenance Role of the White Psychologist', *Journal of Social Issues* 29: 57–65.

Thomas, K.C. (1978) *Attitude Assessment*. Rediguides 7: Guides in Educational Research, University of Nottingham School of Education.

Thompson, G.H. and W.R. Fishburn (1977) 'Attitudes toward Homosexuality among Graduate Counseling Students', *Counselor Education and Supervision* (December): 121–30.

Thompson, N. (1983) Unpublished paper. Presented at *The Monday Club*, London (14 March).

Tifft, L.L. (1979) 'The Coming Redefinitions of Crime: An Anarchist Perspective', *Social Problems* 26: 392–402.

Toder, N. (1978) 'Couples: The Hidden Segment of the Gay World', *Journal of Homosexuality* 3: 331–43.

Toll, B.J. (1980) 'Strong and Free: The Awakening', in S.J. Wolfe and J.P. Stanley (eds) *The Coming Out Stories*. Watertown, MA: Persephone Press.

Trilling, L. (1972) *Sincerity and Authenticity*. Cambridge, MA: Harvard University Press.

Tripp, C.A. (1975) *The Homosexual Matrix*. New York: McGraw-Hill.

Troiden, R.R. (1979) 'Becoming Homosexual: A Model of Gay Identity Acquisition', *Psychiatry* 42: 362–73.

Troiden, R.R. (1984) 'Self, Self-Concept, Identity and Homosexual Identity: Constructs in Need of Definition and Differentiation', *Journal of Homosexuality* 10: 97–109.

Tubergen, G. and R.A. Olins (1979) 'Mail vs. Personal Interview Administration for Q Sorts: A Comparitive Study', *Operant Subjectivity* 2(2): 51–9.

Tyler, L.E. (1973) 'Design for a Hopeful Psychology', *American Psychologist* 28: 1021—9.

Unger, R.K. (1983) 'Through the Looking Glass: No Wonderland Yet! (The Reciprocal Relationship between Methodology and Models of Reality)', *Psychology of Women Quarterly* 8: 9–32.

Valeska, L. (1981) 'The Future of Female Separatism', in The Quest Staff (eds) *Building Feminist Theory: Essays from Quest, A Feminist Quarterly*. New York and London: Longman.

Verhave, R. and W. van Hoorne (1984) 'The Temporalization of the Self', in K. Gergen and M.M. Gergen (eds) *Historical Social Psychology*. Hillsdale, NJ: Erlbaum.

Vetere, V.A. (1972) 'The Role of Friendship in the Development and Maintenance of Lesbian Love Relationships', *Journal of Homosexuality* 8: 51–67.

Walkerdine, V. (1984) 'Developmental Psychology and the Child-centred Pedagogy: The Insertion of Piaget into Early Education', in J. Henriques, W. Hollway, C. Urwin, C. Venn and V. Walkerdine, *Changing the Subject: Psychology, Social Regulation and Subjectivity*. London: Methuen.

Ward, D.A. and G.C. Kassebaum (1964) 'Homosexuality: A Mode of Adaptation in a Prison for Women', *Social Problems* 12: 179–87.

Warren, C. and B. Ponse (1977), 'The Existential Self in the Gay World', in J. Douglas and J. Johnson (eds) *Existential Sociology*. New York: Cambridge University Press.

Watney, S. (1980) 'The Ideology of GLF', in Gay Left Collective (ed.) *Homosexuality: Power and Politics*. London: Allison & Busby.

Weeks, J. (1980) 'Capitalism and the Organisation of Sex', in Gay Left Collective (ed.) *Homosexuality: Power and Politics*. London: Allison & Busby.

Weeks, J. (1981) *Sex, Politics and Society: The Regulation of Sexuality since 1800*. London: Longman.

Weigert, A.J. (1970) 'The Immoral Rhetoric of Scientific Sociology', *American Sociologist* 5: 111–19.

Weinberg, G. (1973) *Society and the Healthy Homosexual*. New York: Anchor.

Weinberg, M.S. (1970) 'Homosexual Samples: Differences and Similarities', *Journal of Sex Research* 6: 312–25.

Weinberg, T.S. (1983) *Gay Men, Gay Selves: The Social Construction of Homosexual Identities*. New York: Irvington Publishers Inc.

Weinberg, T.S. (1984) 'Biology, Ideology and the Reification of Developmental Stages in the Study of Homosexual Identities', *Journal of Homosexuality* 10: 77–84.

Weis, C.B. and R.N. Dain (1979) 'Ego Development and Sex Attitudes in Heterosexual and Homosexual Men and Women', *Archives of Sexual Behavior*, 8: 341–56.

Weissbach, T.A. and G. Zagon (1975) 'The Effects of Deviant Group Membership upon Impressions of Personality', *Journal of Social Psychology* 95: 263–6.

West, D.J. (1968) *Homosexuality*. Harmondsworth: Penguin.

West, D.J. (1977) *Homosexuality Re-examined*. London: Duckworth.

Westall, R. (1978) 'Hetero, Homo, Bi or Nothing', in M. Dickins and R. Sutcliff (eds) *Is Anyone There?* Harmondsworth: Penguin.

Westwood, G. (1960) *A Minority: A Report on the Life of the Male Homosexual in Great Britain*. Westport, CT: Greenwood.

Whiteson, L. (1983) 'The Word as a Blunt Instrument', in Toronto Arts Group for Human Rights (ed.) *The Writer and Human Rights*. Toronto: Lester and Orpen Dennys Ltd.

Wicker, A.W. (1969) 'Attitudes versus Actions: The Relationship of Verbal and Overt Behavioral Responses to Attitude Objects', *Journal of Social Issues* 25: 41–78.

Wilbur, C.B. (1965) 'Clinical Aspects of Female Homosexuality', in J. Marmor (ed.) *Sexual Inversion: The Multiple Roots of Homosexuality*. New York: Basic Books.

Wilkinson, S. (1986) 'Introduction', in S. Wilkinson (ed.) *Feminist Social Psychology: Developing Theory and Practice*. Milton Keynes: Open University Press.

Williams, C.J. (1972) 'Is There a Relationship between Homosexuality and Creativity?' *Sexual Behavior* 32: 54–7.

Williamson, J. (1983) 'Seeing Spots', *City Limits* (25 February–3 March): 14–16.

Wilson, G. and D. Nias (1976) *Love's Mysteries: The Secrets of Sexual Attraction*. London: Fontana/Collins.

Wilson, M. and R. Greene (1971) 'Personality Characteristics of Female Homosexuals', *Psychological Reports* 28: 407–12.

Winant, F. (1971) 'Looking at Women'. Reprinted in K. Jay and A. Young (eds) *After You're Out: Personal Experiences of Gay Men and Lesbian Women*. New York: Links.

Wirt, R.D. (1981) 'Preface', *Journal of Homosexuality* 7: 3–4.

Wittenborn, J.R. (1961) 'Contributions and Current Status of Q Methodology', *Psychological Bulletin* 58: 132–42.

Wolf, D.G. (1979) *The Lesbian Community*. Berkeley, CA: University of California Press.

Wolff, C. (1971) *Love between Women*. London: Duckworth.

Wolins, L. (1962) 'Responsibility for Raw Data', *American Psychologist* 17: 657–8.

Wood, J. (1981) Letter in Onlywomen Press (eds) *Love Your Enemy? The Debate between Heterosexual Feminism and Political Lesbianism*. London: Onlywomen Press.

Woolgar, S.W. (1976) 'Writing an Intellectual History of Scientific Development: The Use of Discovery Accounts', *Social Studies of Science* 6: 395–422.

Woolgar, S.W. (1983) 'Irony in the Social Study of Science', in K. Knorr-Cetina and M. Mulkay (eds) *Science Observed*. London: Sage Publications.

Yarrow, M.R., J.D. Campbell and R.V. Burton (1970) 'Recollections of Childhood: A Study of the Retrospective Method', *Monograph of the Society for Research in Child Development*. 35(5).

Yearley, S. (1981) 'Textual Persuasion: The Role of Social Accounting in the Construction of Scientific Arguments', *Philosophy of Social Science* 11: 409–35.

Young, A. (1975) 'On Human Identity and Gay Identity: A Liberationist Dilemma', in K. Jay and A. Young (eds) *Out of the Closets: Personal Experiences of Gay Men and Lesbian Women*. New York: Links.

Young, R.M. (1971) 'Scientific Medicine and the Social Order', *Science or Society* 4: 7–12.

Zavalloni, M. and S.W. Cook (1965) 'Influence of Judge's Attitudes on Ratings of Favorableness of Statements about a Social Group', *Journal of Personality and Social Psychology* 1: 43–54.

Zigrany, T.A. (1982) 'Who Should Be Doing What about the Gay Alcoholic?' *Journal of Homosexuality* 7: 27–36.

Zuckerman, H. (1972) 'Interviewing an Ultra-Elite', *Public Opinion Quarterly* 36: 159–75.

Zygmunt, J.F. (1972) 'Movements and Motives: Some Unresolved Issues in the Psychology of Social Movements', *Human Relations* 25: 449–67.

Index

Only those authors are included whose work
is discussed at length, or extensively quoted.